Lady Jane Grey
and the
House of Suffolk

Lady Jane Grey
and the
House of Suffolk

ALISON PLOWDEN

SIDGWICK & JACKSON
LONDON

First published in Great Britain in 1985 by Sidgwick & Jackson Limited

Copyright © 1985 Alison Plowden

ISBN 0-283-99055-4

Photoset by Rapidset and Design Limited, London WC1
Printed in Great Britain by
The Garden City Press Limited, Letchworth, Hertfordshire
for Sidgwick & Jackson Limited
1 Tavistock Chambers, Bloomsbury Way
London WC1A 2SG

Contents

1 Cloth of Frieze   1

2 The Rose of Christendom   20

3 The Noble Race of Suffolk   38

4 So Divine a Maid   57

5 The King's Device   77

6 Jane the Quene   94

7 The Ende of the Lady Jane Duddeley   114

8 The Knot of Secret Might   134

9 A Sorrowful Woman for the Queen's
    Displeasure   152

10 There is No More Left of Them   172

A Note on Sources 188

Genealogical Trees 193

Index 196

Today I saw Lady Jane Grey walking in a grand procession to the Tower. She is now called Queen, but is not popular, for the hearts of the people are with Mary, the Spanish Queen's daughter. This Jane is very short and thin, but prettily shaped and graceful. She has small features and a well-made nose, the mouth flexible and the lips red. The eyebrows are arched and darker than her hair, which is nearly red. Her eyes are sparkling and reddish brown in colour. I stood so near her grace that I noticed her colour was good but freckled. When she smiled she showed her teeth, which are white and sharp. In all a gracious and animated figure. She wore a dress of green velvet stamped with gold, with large sleeves. Her headdress was a white coif with many jewels. She walked under a canopy, her mother carrying her long train, and her husband Guildford walking by her, dressed all in white and gold, a very tall strong boy with light hair, who paid her much attention. The new Queen was mounted on very high chopines to make her look much taller, which were concealed by her robes, as she is very small and short. Many ladies followed, with noblemen, but this lady is very heretical and has never heard Mass, and some great people did not come into the procession for that reason.

Baptisa Spinola, 10 July 1553

1

Cloth of Frieze

Cloth of gold do not despise,
Though thou be match'd with cloth of frieze;
Cloth of frieze, be not too bold,
Though thou be match'd with cloth of gold.

The most important fact of William Brandon's life – from the point of view of his posterity, that is – was his death: when he got himself killed by King Richard Crookback in person at Bosworth Field in August 1485 he was unknowingly laying the foundations of his family's spectacular rise to fame and fortune in the succeeding generation.

Until that moment there had been little or nothing to distinguish the Brandons from the rest of the emergent rural middle class to which they belonged. They claimed to be descended from a Norman knight who had 'come over with the Conqueror', but then so did every family with any aspirations to gentility. More credibly they could claim to come of solid East Anglian farming stock, taking their surname from the ancient flint-mining town on the Norfolk–Suffolk border where it is marked by the Little Ouse river and where, like their contemporaries the Pastons, they got their living by cultivating a modest few score acres of land. Like the Pastons, the Brandons were good plain husbandmen, riding bareback to the mill sitting astride their sacks of corn, fetching the meal in similar homely fashion and selling their surplus grain at the local market as good husbandmen should. Also like the Pastons, by the early years of the fifteenth century the Brandons were beginning to prosper; borrowing money, buying – or marrying – more land, putting their sons to school and their own feet on the next rung of the social ladder.

But although the break-up of the feudal system with its rigid caste structure offered exciting new opportunities for social climbing, it still behoved the prudent social climber to seek the protection of an aristocratic patron, and the first William Brandon to appear in the record attached himself to the Mowbray family, becoming a trusted confidant of the fourth (and last) of the Mowbray Dukes of Norfolk. In the dispute which presently arose between Norfolk and the Pastons over the carving up of Sir John Fastolf's estate, he assisted at the forcible seizure of Caister Castle from John Paston and as a result earned a stinging rebuke from King Edward IV. 'Brandon,' the King is reputed to have said, 'though thou can beguile the Duke of Norfolk, and bring him about the thumb as thou list, I let thee witt thou shalt not do me so.' Edward had evidently recognized William Brandon as a natural ringleader, for he added that if Norfolk ever stepped out of line again he would know where to lay the blame.

William seems to have taken the warning to heart. At any rate this was his only recorded brush with authority and thereafter he concentrated his energies on building up his own empire – becoming a successful businessman, investing in land in Norfolk and Suffolk, and establishing himself as a prominent and 'worshipful' member of county society. He collected a knighthood somewhere along the way and married into the ancient, prolific and well-connected Wingfield clan. The marriage proved highly satisfactory from the dynastic point of view, Elizabeth Wingfield giving her husband five children: three sons, William, Thomas and Robert, and two daughters, Anne and Elizabeth, who married respectively into the Sidney and Cavendish families.

In 1478 the Pastons were reporting rather gleefully that young William Brandon was in trouble for having ravished 'an old gentlewoman' and one of her daughters, and attempting to ravish the other; 'wherefore men say foul of him, and that he would eat the hen and all her chickens'. However, in spite of these shocking goings on, young William made a perfectly respectable marriage to the daughter and co-heir of Sir Henry Bruyn of South Ockendon in Essex (though, again according to the Pastons, he was 'like to be hanged' for marrying a widow without paying the customary fee due to the Crown), and he looked all set to follow uneventfully in his father's footsteps – until, that is, he became involved in politics. With their Mowbray connections the Brandons might have been expected to cleave to the Yorkist faction, but in the uneasy summer of 1483, following the *coup d'état* which had brought Richard of Gloucester to the throne, William the Second and his brother Thomas were caught up in the abortive rebellion master-minded by the Duke of Buckingham and some time that autumn were obliged to leave the country in a hurry, joining the growing band of refugees from Richard III's rule gathering round young Henry Tudor in Brittany.

It was to be nearly two years before the Brandon brothers returned to England, and William, dying at Bosworth on that bloodstained August day, never saw East Anglia again. As Henry Tudor's standard bearer he cut a conspicuous figure – as, of course, he was intended to do – and the red dragon banner of Cadwaladr was torn from his grasp and he himself struck down in the desperate kamikaze attack launched by Richard Plantagenet and his household troops against the position of the 'unknown Welshman'.

Thomas survived to go home to his father's house and make the acquaintance of his infant nephew. There is no record of exactly when William Brandon's son Charles was born. It is only certain that he was conceived before his father fled overseas and the likelihood is that his birthday fell either in 1483 or during the first half of 1484. Old William, his grandfather, died in 1491 and again it seems logical to assume that this was when Charles Brandon was first adopted into the royal household by Henry VII. There would have been nothing surprising or unusual about such an arrangement. The orphan had an undoubted claim on Tudor gratitude; as a sturdy seven- or eight-year-old he was just the right age to be a companion and playmate for Arthur Prince of Wales, born in 1486, and would have been able to earn his keep by helping to initiate the younger child into the mysteries of some of those complicated physical pastimes at which every well-bred youth was expected to show proficiency.

There is nothing to indicate that any specially close bond ever existed between the two of them, but if it did, it was cut brutally short by Arthur's death from tuberculosis in the spring of 1502. In fact, although still only fifteen, the Prince was married by this time and established with his wife, the Spanish Princess Catherine of Aragon, and miniature court at Ludlow Castle on the Welsh Marches to start learning the business of government; so it seems possible that Charles Brandon's allegiance had already been transferred to the King's second son. Henry, Duke of York, was some seven years his junior but was, like Brandon, a big strong boy, a natural athlete and promising all-round sportsman. There was never any question about the camaraderie between these two and the foundations of a lifelong friendship were laid during those adolescent years, when they played tennis together, rode out hunting together and competed with one another at all the popular forms of mock combat and trials of strength – wrestling and shooting at the butts, running at the ring and casting of the bar, throwing a twelve-foot spear and wielding a heavy, two-handed sword and, of course, tilting or jousting, that spectacular neo-mediaeval war-game so beloved by the Tudor court.

Not being of noble blood, Charles Brandon was acceptable only as a sparring partner and unofficial companion of the Prince's leisure hours; he would not have been admitted to the royal schoolroom, except perhaps on an occasional basis, but he would have encountered no lack of opportunity for acquiring a veneer of culture, as well as an intimate knowledge of the elaborate codes of courtesy and ceremonial which governed every aspect of life at the top. Actually, young Charles was probably no more enthusiastic about book learning than any other boy of his type; but his uncle Thomas Brandon, who had successfully undertaken several high level diplomatic missions for the King and become a respected figure in court circles, would doubtless have kept an eye on him, ensuring that he received the necessary basic grounding in Latin, a smattering of French and that superficial familiarity with the workings of the law essential for every member of the property-owning classes in a vigorously litigious age.

Although already modestly established as a member of the royal entourage – an Esquire of the Body with an annual salary of £33.6.8d plus board and lodging – the year 1509 and the accession of Henry VIII marked the beginning of Charles Brandon's long career in public life. The second Henry Tudor was not quite eighteen when he succeeded to his father's throne, and the property-owning classes, who had been finding the last years of the old King's regime increasingly oppressive and expensive, went wild with delight over their new 'young, lusty and courageous Prince and Sovereign Lord, King Harry the Eighth'. Scholars and intellectuals, too, were in transports over the advent of this charismatic Christian Prince, who spoke with all the engaging idealism of youth about his love of learning, and his respect for justice and virtue; while foreigners almost ran out of adjectives in their efforts to describe his liberality, his magnificence, his astonishing good looks, physical presence and personal charm.

Certainly the new reign seemed to be off to the best possible start. Thanks to old Henry's statesmanship and good housekeeping, young Henry had succeeded unopposed to a secure and solvent throne – an advantage not enjoyed by an English monarch for very nearly a century – and for the rest of that first carefree summer the court was given over to a season of 'continual festival', with revels, tilts and tournaments, pageants, banquets, balls, picnics, masques, 'disguisings' and other, more impromptu frolics crowding together in an endless, glittering extravagant stream. The King was always to be found in the thick of the fun, and prominent among the crowd of light-hearted, boisterous young people eagerly helping him to enjoy himself was, of course, his childhood friend Charles Brandon.

The immediate perquisites of that friendship proved to be well worth having. Before the end of 1509 Brandon had been given the office of Chamberlain of the Principality of North Wales and appointed Marshal of the King's Bench – a post formerly held by his uncle Thomas, who died in January 1510. By 1511 he had joined Sir John Carew as Marshal of the royal household and in 1512 became Keeper of the important royal estate of Wanstead in Essex and Ranger of the New Forest. He was promoted to be a Knight of the body and showered with stewardships, receiverships, wardships and valuable licences to export wool, leather, lead and tin – and it was pretty clear that this was only a beginning.

By the winter of 1512 the King was busy getting ready for his first military adventure overseas. England had recently joined an offensive league of European powers aimed at containing French expansionism in northern Italy, and Henry – as yet unaware that his allies were planning to use him to divert the enemy's attention while quietly pursuing certain territorial objectives of their own – was impatient to prove his manhood on the field of battle where, naturally, his best friend would fill a major supporting role. Everyone, therefore, expected the King to confer a title on Charles Brandon before they crossed the Channel, but as it happened his first step in rank came indirectly, almost accidentally, through his eight-year-old ward and affianced wife Elizabeth Grey, daughter and heiress of the late Lord Lisle of Sparsholt in Berkshire.

By now in his late twenties, Brandon already had a colourful matrimonial career behind him. Back in 1505 or thereabouts he had become engaged to Anne Browne, daughter of Anthony Browne, Governor of Calais, and Lucy Neville, niece of the celebrated Warwick the Kingmaker. The couple were betrothed *per verba de praesenti*, thus entering into a contract theoretically regarded as binding in canon law even if, as not infrequently happened, there were no witnesses and no church ceremony followed the exchange of vows. In practice, in such cases, it was not uncommon for an unprincipled man to repudiate his fiancée, which is what appears to have happened here. Certainly Charles Brandon and Anne Browne slept together without benefit of clergy, for she bore him a daughter, some time in 1506. At about the same time, however, Charles married Margaret Mortimer, born Margaret Neville, a wealthy widow of approximately twice his age and aunt of the deserted Anne, thus leading a Venetian observer of the English social scene to comment caustically on the mercenary habits of young men who were willing to marry for money ladies old enough to be their mothers. The Brandon–Mortimer union, though, was short-lived and, probably as a result of action taken by the Browne family, was annulled on the grounds of the groom's pre-contract and cohabitation with his previous partner. Charles and Anne now went through a public marriage ceremony and another daughter was born *circa* 1510. Anne Browne died in 1512 and that December her widower acquired the wardship of Elizabeth Grey.

Under English law, the wardship of any minor child who inherited landed property passed automatically to the Crown which normally gave or, more usually, sold it back to relatives of the child concerned or some other favoured applicant. The guardian was then free to enjoy the income from the property until the minor came of age – by which time he would either have sold his ward's marriage to the highest bidder or else have arranged a marriage ensuring that control of the inheritance remained within his own family circle. In an acquisitive and intensely status-conscious society marriages were most definitely not made in heaven when the transfer of property was involved and no one was surprised when, in the spring of 1513, Charles Brandon announced his engagement to Elizabeth Grey. On 15 May, Letters Patent were issued creating him Viscount Lisle in right of his 'wife' and a few weeks later the new Lord Lisle accompanied the King to France, being 'marshal of the host and captain of the fore-ward' with three thousand men under his command.

The rest of the summer was spent playing soldiers in Picardy and both Henry and Viscount Lisle duly established their reputations as fighting men. It was bad luck that the King should have missed the best bit of action – a scrambling cavalry skirmish near Guinegate, later dignified by the name of the Battle of the Spurs – but on the whole it was a very jolly little war and Henry enjoyed himself so much that he quite failed to notice that the two fortified frontier towns of Thérouanne and Tournai, captured by the English army, were of strategic value only to his ally, the Hapsburg Emperor Maximilian.

Relations between the Tudor and Hapsburg families were especially cordial just then, and Henry and Charles Brandon spent most of October, after the campaigning season had ended, entertaining and being entertained by the Emperor and his daughter Margaret, Regent of the Netherlands. Henry was bubbling over with plans for next year's conquests and arrangements were discussed for a renewal of hostilities against France in the spring; also a date for the long-projected marriage between the King's sister Mary and the Emperor's grandson. The English princess and young Charles of Castile, heir not only to all the far-flung Flemish and Germanic Hapsburg dominions but also, through his Spanish mother, to the kingdoms of Aragon and Castile, had been formally contracted since 1508, but the affair had seemed to be languishing rather in recent years. Now, however, it was agreed that the wedding would definitely take place at Calais not later than mid-May 1514, three months after the bridegroom had attained the dignity of his fourteenth birthday.

This union, of course, was a matter of high politics alone, but romance of another sort was in the air of Flanders that autumn for, according to the chronicler Edward Hall, 'the noise went that the Lord Lisle made request of marriage to the Lady Margaret Duchess of Savoy, daughter to the Emperor Maximilian' and that she 'favoured him highly'. The English were in high spirits after the summer's triumphs and at a tournament held at Tournai on 18 October before the Lady Margaret and the Prince of Castile, Henry and Lord Lisle, their horses caparisoned in purple velvet and gold bullion, challenged all comers in the lists. There were, says Hall, 'many spears broken, and many a good buffet given', and that night the King provided a sumptuous banquet for his guests. Afterwards the ladies danced and Henry, who had an insatiable passion for dressing up, staged a masque with eleven other gentlemen 'all richly apparelled in bonnets of gold' which were later distributed as souvenirs among the ladies 'take who could take'.

The party seems to have been an unqualified success. Everyone enjoyed themselves, especially Lord Lisle, who had reason to be feeling more than usually pleased with life and himself that evening. He had done very well at the assault on Tournai, being the first commander to have captured one of the town's gates, and now he was apparently ready to try his luck at storming a different kind of citadel. After the banquet, therefore, he came to kneel at the Lady Margaret's side, to murmur sweet nothings in her ear and playfully slide one of her rings from her finger and show it off on his own large hand, pretending not to follow her laughing protests that the King of England had brought thieves with him out of his country.

Margaret of Austria, now in her early thirties, twice married and nine years widowed, was still a pretty woman, charming, elegant and sophisticated. With her wide experience of men and affairs, she would not have needed more than about ten minutes to take the measure of Charles Brandon, but equally it would not do to risk offending the King of England, who was earnestly pleading his friend's cause, acting as his interpreter and telling the Duchess that she was far too young and beautiful to think of remaining single. In any case, Margaret was quite feminine enough to respond to the flattering attentions of a good-looking Englishman possessing his full share of sexual magnetism, and had no objection to a little civilized love-play as they sat together late in the firelight, exchanging tokens in the shape of small items of jewellery and facetious promises that neither of them would marry anyone else that year. But there is nothing to suggest that she ever seriously considered Lord Lisle as husband material. The Viscount might be an influential figure at the Engish court – he and the King's almoner, a rising churchman named Thomas Wolsey, were reported to govern everything between them – but that still did not make him a fit match for a Hapsburg Princess accustomed to being wooed by reigning monarchs, and she reacted angrily when the story of their 'romance' was leaked in London. Gossip brought over by English traders with contacts in Flanders spread to Holland and Germany, and was soon openly linking Duchess Margaret's name with Charles Brandon and confidently predicting an announcement of their forthcoming marriage.

Talk of this kind, involving the bandying of a lady's name, making her the object of wagers and crude jokes in the taverns where 'merchant strangers' gathered, could, of course, be extremely damaging to international relations. It was also very difficult to stop. Margaret felt that her confidence had been cynically betrayed, that her reputation both personal and professional had been smeared and that she would now be 'holden for a fool and light'. She made her annoyance and distress very plain to the English ambassador, Richard Wingfield, and in an attempt to kill the story, let it be known that she would not receive another planned visit from Lord Lisle on official business – though she kept her promise to take his elder daughter Anne Brandon into her household. She also demanded a public apology from the King of England. This was issued in March 1514, but rumours about an engagement persisted well into the summer and the Venetian Andrea Badoer was reporting from London as late as 29 July that the wedding could still be expected to take place.

By this time the putative bridegroom had been given another and a giant step in rank. On 1 February 1514 Charles Brandon, Viscount Lisle, was created Duke of Suffolk, an honour once held by the great Yorkist de la Pole family, and before the end of the year he had been granted the bulk of the confiscated de la Pole estates to help him support his new dignity. Since there were currently only two other English dukedoms – Norfolk, just restored to Thomas Howard in recognition of his victory over the Scots at Flodden the previous September, and Buckingham, held by Edward Stafford, a four times great-grandson of Edward III – this sudden and startling elevation of the grandson of a Suffolk yeoman had raised eyebrows and hackles in high places, and certainly lent credence to the talk of a marriage with Margaret of Austria. It has been conjectured that Charles Brandon's latest promotion was recommended by Wolsey, who saw him as a counter-balance to the reactionary influence of the Duke of Norfolk at the council table. More probably, though, the explanation lay in the King's genuine regard for his friend, and a desire to reward and encourage him. Like all the Tudors, Henry was a shrewd judge of his fellow men, and while Charles Brandon may have been no high flier, he was considerably more than the amiable nincompoop often depicted.

If the year 1514 marked a crucial stage in the Brandon family saga, it also saw a significant development in the political education of young Henry Tudor. At any rate, it marked his emergence from a fantasy world of knights in shining armour re-fighting the Hundred Years War and brought him face to face with the less agreeable realities of European diplomacy. The King owed this somewhat overdue awakening to Ferdinand, King of Aragon, who had spent the winter methodically preparing to sell the English down the river by making a separate peace with France. The King of France, having, so it was hoped, been sufficiently impressed by the implacable hostility and growing military might of England, was now to be offered a bargain: if he would relinquish his claims to Milan and Genoa, then Ferdinand and his jackal, the Emperor Maximilian, would be only too delighted to live like brothers with him in future and would, naturally, come to his aid should the English attempt another invasion.

But dealing with the guileless Henry seems to have made Ferdinand over-confident and he forgot that the King of France was also a poker player. Louis XII had no intention of submitting to Spanish blackmail. On the other hand, he had never wanted a war with England and was perfectly prepared to pay any reasonable price for English neutrality. He therefore waited quietly until Ferdinand had been drawn into exposing his hand, by no means unhopeful of the outcome. The King of England might still be a trifle inexperienced in the ways of the world, but Louis had the feeling that he would learn fast. Sure enough, on 22 April 1514, Lorenzo Pasqualigo, a merchant of Venice trading in London, wrote home that nothing more was being said about an English invasion of France and that the King was 'much exasperated' against the King of Aragon.

This was an understatement. Henry was seething with resentment over Ferdinand's treacherous behaviour, and when the French offered peace on very gentlemanly terms they found him more than ready to listen. When King Louis himself presently offered marriage to the Princess Mary, he also offered Henry an irresistibly tempting opportunity to get his own back. Since the May deadline set for Mary's wedding to Charles of Castile had come and gone with nothing but excuses from the Hapsburg family, the King considered his sister to be released from her engagement and by mid-summer Anglo-French negotiations were reaching their final stages. At the end of July, down at Wanstead, Mary publicly renounced her compact of marriage with Charles Prince of Spain. A week later the new marriage contract and peace treaty had been signed and the King of France, the King of England and Thomas Wolsey (who was rapidly becoming the King of England's principal man of business) were able to congratulate themselves on the completion of a very satisfactory deal. The Princess Mary was less enthusiastic. Not that she had any reason to regret Charles of Castile, an unappealing pasty-faced adolescent; but Louis, a widower in his fifties ('old, pocky and feeble' said the Dutch nastily) and a martyr to gout, could hardly be described as an especially enticing alternative.

Mary Tudor, born most probably on 18 March 1495, the youngest surviving child of King Henry VII and his wife Elizabeth of York, was the beauty as well as the baby of the English royal family – she was indeed generally conceded to have been one of the loveliest women of her day. High-spirited, wilful and more than a little spoilt, she had been enjoying a most unusual amount of fun and freedom for an unmarried princess in the five years since her father's death; but Henry VIII was very fond of his sister, who shared his exuberant delight in dancing, party-going, amateur theatricals and showing off, he liked having her around and encouraged her to play a full part in the hectic social life of the court. The dangers inherent in this sort of casual permissiveness were obvious enough – it was not for nothing that royal brides were normally shipped off to their husbands the moment they became nubile. Mary was a warm-blooded young woman surrounded by the pick of the eligible men in the kingdom – inevitably she had formed an attachment of her own, the object of her affections being no less a person than the controversial new Duke of Suffolk. She would, of course, have known Charles Brandon all her life, but by 1514 what had perhaps begun as a child's hero-worship for one of her brother's lordly friends was ripening into something altogether more mature.

There was no scandal. Not a whisper of gossip linking this Princess's name with the Duke's had yet reached the outside world, but inside the family circle the affair seems to have been a pretty open secret. In fact Mary herself had confided in her brother, telling him frankly that she loved Charles Brandon and was only willing to marry the old and ailing King of France on condition that, as soon as

she was free again, Henry would allow her to make her own choice as
her own heart and mind should be best pleased. 'And upon that your
good comfort and faithful promise', she wrote later, 'I assented to the
said marriage; else I would never have granted to, as at the same
time I showed unto you more at large.'

Whether this compromise was Mary's own idea, or whether it was
hammered out in a family conference, we have no means of knowing.
Nor do we know how seriously Henry took it. But he was undoubtedly anxious that nothing should interfere with the smooth running
of his new foreign policy, and it would have made things very awkward with the French if Mary had chosen to be difficult. In the circumstances, it looks as though he was ready to promise anything she
asked – anything to avoid tears and scenes and keep her happy until
she was safely across the Channel.

The betrothal was solemnized at Greenwich on 13 August in the
presence of the King and Queen and all the leading members of the
nobility. The Archbishop of Canterbury officiated, and Louis d'Orléans, Duc de Longueville, who had been taken prisoner at the Battle
of the Spurs, acted as the groom's proxy. As soon as the *de praesenti*
vows had been exchanged and the ring placed on the fourth finger of
her right hand, Mary retired to put on an elaborate 'nightgown'. She
and de Longueville then lay down side by side and he touched her
briefly with his naked leg in a gesture intended to symbolise intercourse. The Archbishop pronounced the marriage consummated
and Mary went off to change again, into a gown of chequered purple
satin and cloth of gold worn over a petticoat of ash-coloured satin.
The whole company then went in stately procession to hear mass –
the Duke of Suffolk being among the noble personages leading the
way. This ended the serious part of the proceedings. There was the
usual banquet with the usual display of exotic dishes and 'subtleties',
castles and temples sculpted in marchpane or jelly, and afterwards
the floor was cleared for dancing. According to the Venetian ambassador, who was present by special invitation, the musical accompaniment was provided by a flute, a harp, a violetta and a certain kind of
small fife which produced a particularly harmonious effect. The
King and several other English lords danced in their doublets, and
everyone was so gay and the music so catchy that the ambassador felt
strongly tempted to throw off his own gown and join in. Prudently,
though, he remembered his age and his dignity and abstained.

Wedding presents and letters of congratulations were now flowing
in from all over Europe – King Louis had sent his bride a magnificent
diamond and pearl known as the Mirror of Naples, valued by the
London jewellers at sixty thousand crowns – and Mary was kept so

busy during her last few weeks at home, receiving deputations, attending receptions and entertainments given in her honour and undergoing a crash course in French, that she had very little time for repining. Indeed, she would have been less than human if she had not rather enjoyed being the centre of so much attention and certainly less than female if she had not taken some pleasure in the splendour of her trousseau – originally designed to impress the impoverished Hapsburgs and far grander than anything her elder sister Margaret had had when she married King James IV of Scotland back in 1503. At any rate, Mary was presenting a resolutely cheerful face to the world and one Italian remarked cattily that the Princess did not appear to mind that Louis was a gouty old man and she 'a young and beautiful damsel', so great was her satisfaction at becoming Queen of France.

Meanwhile, from across the Channel, came reports of Louis's eager impatience to see his bride. In spite of his age and his gout (which was more likely to have been arthritis) he was said to 'yearn hourly for her presence' and according to the Earl of Worcester, who had gone over to France to act as Mary's proxy at the betrothal ceremonies there, he had 'a marvellous mind to content and please the queen'. It seemed the King had shown Worcester 'the goodliest and richest sight of jewels' he had ever seen, telling him they were all for the Queen but that she should not have them all at once, 'for he would have at many and divers times kisses and thanks for them'. Worcester, greatly struck by this lover-like attitude, told Thomas Wolsey he had no doubt that, by the grace of God, Mary would have a good life with her husband.

By mid-September everything was ready. There was a final burst of entertaining and Mary herself gave a farewell reception to which all the foreign merchants in London were invited. Wearing a French gown of woven gold with the Mirror of Naples flashing on her bosom, the new Queen of France was very affable and gracious, giving her hand to everyone. She was obviously in her best looks, one of the guests going so far as to describe her as 'a nymph from heaven', but even allowing for some natural exaggeration there's no doubt that Mary Tudor was something quite outstanding. Of slightly above average height, slender and graceful, she had a clear glowing complexion and a glorious mane of reddish gold hair. Most eyewitnesses, too, were dazzled by her bubbling gaiety and outgoing charm of manner.

Mary left London on 19 September, accompanied by the King and Queen and an escort which, according to Lorenzo Pasqualigo, included 'four of the chief lords of England, besides four hundred knights and barons and two hundred gentlemen and other squires'. The court on the move was always an impressive sight and seldom more so than on this occasion when, Pasqualigo told his brother, 'the lords and knights were all accompanied by their wives and there were so many gowns of woven gold and with gold grounds, housings for the horses of the same material, and chains and jewels that they are worth a vast amount of treasure'. Some of the noblemen, he added, had spent as much as 200,000 crowns 'to do themselves honour'.

The cavalcade reached the coast before the end of the month, but late September was not the best time of year to choose for a Channel crossing. The weather was appalling and Henry rapidly grew bored with waiting for it to improve. Dover in a howling gale and pouring rain offered few attractions and he was never a man to put other people's comfort before his own. So, when the wind dropped temporarily on the evening of 1 October, it was decided that the fleet should sail on the early tide, despite a forecast of more storms to come. Mary was woken in the small hours of the second and Henry went with her down to the quayside. As they said their goodbyes in the chill damp of that dismal dawn, Mary, in tears by this time, clung to her brother and rather desperately reminded him about his promises for the future. He kissed her and committed her to God, the fortune of the sea (which, considering the look of the sea at that moment, cannot have been very cheering) and to the governance of her husband. Mary, with all her 'noble company', then went reluctantly on board while the King rode back to Dover Castle and a good breakfast.

The sea fully lived up to its ominous appearance. Of the fourteen ships conveying the Queen of France, her wardrobe and her retinue to Boulogne, only four reached their destination on schedule – the rest fetching up at various points along the coast from Calais to Flanders. The bride's own vessel made Boulogne but ran ingloriously aground just inside the harbour. Mary had to be transferred to an open boat and, soaked to the skin and prostrate with seasickness, was finally carried ashore through waist-high surf by one of her gentlemen, the appropriately named Sir Christopher Garnish.

It was not a very auspicious beginning, but with the resilience of youth and health she recovered quickly and was soon winning golden opinions from the French, who were delighted by their new Queen's beauty, pretty manners and elegant clothes. For the journey from Montreuil to Abbeville she wore cloth of gold on crimson with tight English sleeves and a shaggy hat of crimson silk cocked over one eye. Louis came to meet her by carefully pre-arranged 'accident' on the outskirts of the town, and took her in his arms and 'kissed her as kindly as if he had been five-and-twenty'. In Abbeville itself a royal welcome had been prepared and there on 9 October Mary was finally married to the King of France in person.

Not surprisingly such an ill-assorted couple were made the butt of unkind jokes in certain quarters – in Spain it was being freely predicted that his young wife would soon be the death of a bridegroom in his dotage who constantly licked his lips and gulped his spittle! However, to the outward eye, Louis appeared very jovial, gay and in love. He had temporarily quite thrown off his invalidish habits, boasting that on his wedding night he had 'crossed the river' three times and would have done more had he chosen.

Apart from a brief unpleasantness over the dismissal of some of Mary's English attendants, Louis proved an indulgent and generous husband, and the newly-weds had established quite a cosy relationship by the time Charles Brandon paid a visit to France in November. The Duke of Suffolk had come over with the Marquess of Dorset and a number of other gentlemen, ostensibly to take part in a tournament forming part of the celebrations for Mary's forthcoming coronation, but he also had certain confidential matters to discuss with the French government. Suffolk had an audience with the King and Queen at Beauvais, where he found Louis lying on a couch with Mary sitting beside him, and was able to report to Henry 'that never Queen behaved herself more wisely and honourably, and so say all the noblemen of France'. Charles Brandon was clearly impressed by her dignity and restraint which, he told Henry, 'rejoiced me not a little', adding significantly, 'Your Grace knows why'. It sounds rather as though he had been afraid Mary might embarrass him in public, but he need not have worried. The Queen of France knew what was due to her position, and whatever her inner turmoil on seeing her lover again, her outward self-possession was faultless.

Mary's marriage to King Louis lasted for just eighty-two days – an even shorter period than either she or Henry had envisaged – and of course there were those who did not hesitate to say she had danced the old man into his grave. In fact, after her first few weeks in France, she had spent a good deal of her time sitting at her husband's bedside, helping to keep him amused by singing to him and playing on her lute, and Louis, surprised and grateful, had written to tell Henry that 'the Queen has so conducted herself towards me, and continues so to do daily, that I know not how I can sufficiently praise and express my delight in her'. But when he collapsed and died on New Year's Eve 1514, Mary's position changed abruptly. No longer an old man's darling, cushioned in luxury and protected from every wind that blew, she became a childless dowager alone in a foreign country and heavily dependent on the goodwill of the new King of France. She also had to endure the forty days of strict seclusion imposed by French custom on a newly widowed queen. This period of mourning – or, more accurately, quarantine – was a practical method of ensuring that if a newly widowed queen proved to be pregnant, there should be as little doubt as possible over the paternity of her child, but in Mary's case there was a special reason for interest in her condition. Louis's various marriages had given him only daughters and the prospects of the heir presumptive, François d'Angoulême, might be radically affected if the late King's widow was found to be with child.

François himself did not regard the danger very seriously, but his doting mother and sister were taking no chances and Mary was bundled off to the Hôtel de Cluny to spend the next six weeks behind drawn curtains in a stuffy, black-draped mourning chamber. It was a depressing enough situation for an active, healthy girl, added to which Mary was rather scared of François, and even more so of his formidable mother Louise of Savoy, and immured at Cluny she felt very much in their power. She had been separated from her remaining English ladies and surrounded by a posse of sharp-eyed Frenchwomen, handpicked by François's sister Marguerite. She was suffering acutely from boredom, loneliness and toothache, but far worse than any of these relatively minor discomforts was her consuming anxiety that Henry or François could be bargaining her away to the highest bidder while she was thus cut off from the outside world and helpless to stop them.

Mary had received a letter from Thomas Wolsey, written during Louis's last illness, warning her to be careful to say nothing 'whereby any person . . . may have you at any advantage' and to refuse any offers of marriage which might be made to her. 'And thus doing', Wolsey had continued, a shade patronizingly, 'ye shall not fail to have the King fast and loving to you, to attain your desire and come home again into England with as much honour as Queen ever had.'

This was reassuring, as far as it went, but Mary knew she was once again a first-rate matrimonial prize – and she knew her brother. Terror that he would break his word is apparent in every line of the letter she wrote to him from Cluny early in January 1515, begging him to send for her as soon as possible,

> for as now I am all out of comfort, saving that all my trust is in your grace and so shall be during my life. . . . Sir, I beseech your grace that you will keep all the promises that you promised me when I took my

leave of you by the waterside. Sir, your grace knoweth well that I did marry for your pleasure at this time and now I trust you will suffer me to marry as me liketh for to do . . . wherefore I beseech your grace for to be a good lord and brother unto me.

If Henry did try to dispose of her anywhere 'saving where my mind is', then the next he would hear of her would be that she had gone into a nunnery where 'never no man shall have joy of me'.

Though there can be no doubt that Henry wanted his sister back – neither he nor Wolsey trusted François a yard – just what his long-term plans were regarding her future remains a trifle unclear. Certainly if he did *not* intend to honour those famous promises made 'by the waterside' the previous autumn, it was not very wise to appoint the Duke of Suffolk as head of the mission charged with the task of winding up Mary's affairs in France and bringing her safely home. But the King had complete confidence in his friend. Like Thomas Wolsey, Charles Brandon was his own creation, dependent on royal favour and royal bounty for his very existence. He did, however, take the precaution of asking the Duke for a solemn undertaking that he would keep his relations with Mary on a strictly formal basis while they were abroad. There may well have been a tacit understanding that if he succeeded in extricating her on satisfactory financial terms, Henry would be prepared to agree to their marriage – rumours to this effect were already beginning to circulate – but at this stage Suffolk was probably a good deal less concerned with thoughts of dalliance than with nervousness about the complex diplomatic chore which lay ahead and which was by far the most important yet entrusted to him. He could foresee hours of hard and tedious bargaining over Mary's plate and jewels and dower rights. He did not foresee the other and infinitely more alarming complications lying in wait for him.

Henry and Wolsey had been right in thinking that François would try to persuade Mary into another marriage – he suggested two possible candidates to her, both of them his kinsmen. There were whispers, too, that he was making suggestions to her of an improper nature and Mary later dropped hints that she had been persecuted by his attentions. It's true that the French king paid frequent visits to Cluny and probably did amuse himself with a little amorous by-play – at twenty-one he was already an experienced and cynical philanderer – but his chief interest in his widowed *'belle-mère'* was political rather than personal. The Anglo-French alliance had recently begun to show signs of strain, and François was naturally anxious to frustrate any plans the English might be hatching to use the former Queen of France to help create some new alignment with the perennially hostile Spanish-Hapsburg bloc. He therefore told Mary he had definite information that Henry meant to revive her engagement with Charles of Castile and warned her that, if she was foolish enough to insist on going home, she would quickly find herself being shipped off to Flanders to be married. As this was exactly what Mary was most afraid of, his insinuations did nothing to calm her overwrought nerves. Embarrassed and affronted by François's gallantries (despite her three months at the sophisticated French court she was still almost schoolgirlishly innocent) but not daring to offend him, exhausted by his nagging persistence, deeply suspicious of her brother's intentions, and with no one she could trust to advise her, she was being steadily driven into a course of action which might easily have ruined her.

On the eve of Suffolk's arrival, François decided it was time to stop playing games. Since Mary had stubbornly rejected all his proposals for her future, he wanted to know if this meant that her affections were already engaged. If she would only be frank with him, he told her, he would do his best to help her. This was just the sort of eventuality Wolsey had tried to guard against, but by now Mary was past caring. Forgetting all caution, she proceeded to disclose 'the secret of her heart' and her determination to marry Charles Brandon or no one. To her surprise and relief François proved wonderfully sympathetic. He quite understood how she felt, and now that he knew the truth, of course he wouldn't tease her any further. More than that, he promised he would do everything in his power to promote the match. As well he might. Married to her English duke Mary would present no danger to France and her confession had also provided a valuable bargaining counter in the forthcoming negotiations with her unsuspecting sweetheart.

Suffolk, together with Sir Richard Wingfield and Dr Nicholas West, landed on 27 January and the English delegation had their first audience with François five days later at Senlis. After the formal public exchange of compliments, Suffolk was summoned to a private interview with the King, who wasted no time in coming to the point. He had been informed, he said, that the Duke had come to France to marry the Queen, his master's sister. Horribly taken aback, Suffolk broke into vehement denials that he was contemplating any such thing. He was cut short. 'Not so,' said François, 'for if you will not be plain with me, I will be plain with you.' And he went on to reveal the full extent of Mary's indiscretion, even down to a certain 'ware word' – that is, some secret term of endearment used between the lovers – which the Duke knew 'no man alive but her' could have betrayed.

Having thus reduced him to a state of floundering dismay, François was ready to reassure his victim. He had told Mary that he would help her to attain her heart's desire and Suffolk, too, should find him a kind and loving friend who would never fail 'but to help and advance this matter betwixt her and you with as good will as I would for mine own self'.

When Suffolk began to stammer that he was like to be undone if the matter came to Henry's ears at all, François replied: 'Let me alone for that. I and the Queen shall so instance your master that I trust he will be content.' He would speak to his wife as soon as he got back to Paris, and they would both write personally to Henry 'in the best manner that can be devised'.

Suffolk emerged from this unnerving encounter not knowing whether to be more relieved or alarmed. He took the precaution of sending off his own version of the interview post-haste to Thomas Wolsey, but the acquisition of so powerful a champion as the King of France could surely be counted as a favourable omen. It was not until he saw Mary in private for the first time that the real nature of his predicament was brought home to him.

The moment they were alone together, the distracted widow unloosed all the pent-up emotional strain of the past six weeks. The more she had thought about it, the more convinced Mary had become that François was right and Suffolk's mission was nothing more or less than a trap to entice her back to England to be forced into another political match, and she would rather be torn in pieces, she sobbed. Either that or Suffolk's enemies on the Privy Council would find some way of preventing their marriage. Nothing her harassed lover could say would pacify her and in floods of tears – according to the Duke, he had never seen a woman so weep – she presented him with an ultimatum: either he agreed to marry her there and then, while they had the chance, or he 'might never look to have the same proffer again'. With his promise to Henry weighing heavily on his conscience, Suffolk tried to evade the issue (or so he said later) but his protests were swept imperiously aside. Mary reminded him that she had her brother's promise that this time she could marry as she pleased; François was ready to help them; they might never have such an opportunity again. She almost certainly added that he couldn't really love her if he was not willing to take so small a risk for her sake.

All this put Charles Brandon in a nightmarish quandary. His whole career had been founded on total commitment to the Tudor family, and now he was fairly and squarely caught between the Scylla and Charybdis of Tudor passion and Tudor despotism. He was genuinely devoted to his sovereign lord and stood in very healthy awe of him but, at the same time, it is hard for any man to stand like a stone while the most beautiful princess in Europe is literally begging and praying him to take her to his bed. Besides which, Mary was far too great a material prize to be lightly surrendered.

Although it was not tactful to draw attention to it, the fact remained that after nearly six years, Henry VIII's marriage to his brother's widow had still not produced a living child. It was, therefore, by no means beyond the bounds of possibility that his younger sister and her husband might found a new royal line, and dreams of fathering a future king of England must unquestionably have passed through Suffolk's head – for all his bluff, easy-going exterior, he was an ambitious man. Forced into the unaccustomed exercise of thinking on his feet, Mary's tears and vainglorious intimations of dynastic immortality overcame considerations of trust and honour, self-restraint and even self-preservation; and on an undisclosed date early in February 1515, Charles Brandon and Mary Tudor, Queen of France, were married very quietly indeed in the chapel at Cluny, with only a trusted handful of the bride's personal servants as witnesses.

So, driven by greed for private happiness and worldly gain and by the urgency of physical desire, cloth of gold was matched with cloth of frieze; and so, in a highly charged emotional atmosphere of haste and secrecy and fear, the stage was set for the unfolding tragedy of Jane Grey.

2

The Rose of Christendom

Madame, you are the rose of Christendom. You should have stayed in France. We would have appreciated you.

It was not long before the consequences of their reckless behaviour began to catch up with the Duke of Suffolk and his new wife. The King of France had kept his promise to write to Henry on their behalf – although the lovers do not appear to have taken him fully into their confidence – and now he was raising the question of the restitution of the town of Tournai which, as he pointed out, was no more than an expensive liability to the English. He was ready to pay a fair price for its return and made it clear that he expected Suffolk's help in arranging the deal. There was also the matter of Mary's finances. Her widow's jointure and the plate and jewels she had brought from England were, of course, secured to her; but already a dispute was looming over the jewels showered upon her by King Louis, and the gold plate and other 'furniture' she had used as Queen of France. Henry and Mary claimed that these, too, should be regarded as her personal property, while the French retorted that she would automatically forfeit any rights she might have to keep them by leaving the country.

In a letter to Suffolk, Thomas Wolsey emphasized the importance being attached to this issue in London. 'Inasmuch as the King's grace hath great mind to the French King's plate of gold and jewels', he wrote bluntly,

> I require and advise you substantially to handle that matter and to stick thereunto. For I assure you that the hope the King hath to obtain the said plate and jewels is the thing that most constantly stayeth his grace to assent that you should marry his sister. The lack whereof I fear me might make him cold and remiss.

In present circumstances this did not have a very reassuring sound. But by the beginning of March the story of that furtive wedding at Cluny was circulating freely in Paris, and Mary believed she might be pregnant. Confession could no longer be postponed and on the fifth of the month Charles Brandon sat down to write to his friend and ally Thomas Wolsey, now Archbishop of York and without question the most influential man in English politics. Literary composition and spelling were never the Duke's strong points but the operative paragraph of this particular missive was commendably straightforward:

> My lord, so it was that when I came to Paris I heard many things which put me in great fear, and so did the Queen both. And the Queen would never let me be in rest till I had granted her to be married. And so, to be plain with you, I have married her heartily, and have lyen with her, insomuch that I fear me lest she be with child. My lord, I am not in a little sorrow lest the King should know of it and be displeased with me, for I assure you I had rather have died than he should be miscontent. And therefore, mine own good lord, since you have brought me hither, let me not be undone now, the which I fear me I shall be without the especial help of you.

In view of the talk going on about his ambiguous relationship with the Queen, Suffolk was anxious to arrange another and more public marriage ceremony as soon as possible, for in France 'they marry as well in Lent as out of Lent with licence of any bishop'. He begged for an answer without delay, 'for I ensure you I have as heavy a heart as any man living and shall have till I may hear good tidings from you'.

There followed a fortnight's painful suspense. The Suffolks both knew that their 'privy marriage' could easily be invalidated, as by some counts the duke had two ex-wives in his background. Margaret Mortimer was still very much alive and so was young Elizabeth Grey, although her guardian had ungallantly broken off their engagement some time in 1514, probably during his pursuit of Margaret of Austria. They also feared the machinations of Suffolk's enemies, headed by the Duke of Norfolk, who would certainly not consider him a fit match for the King's sister. The right-wing Howard faction also disapproved of Wolsey's pro-French policies, favouring instead a renewal of England's traditional ties with Spain and Flanders – a renewal in which Mary's remarriage might have played a vital part.

The newly wedded pair, who were beginning rather late in the day to count the possible cost of their impetuosity, knew that everything would depend on how Henry took the news and waited with mounting disquiet for Wolsey's reply. 'My lord, with sorrowful heart I write unto you', it began and went on to inform the Duke that the King's first reaction had been one of utter disbelief that his friend, the man in all the world he had loved and trusted best, could have so wantonly betrayed his confidence. Wolsey had had to show him Suffolk's actual writing before he would give it credence and now he was bitterly hurt and angry; 'for he doth well understand that he is deceived of the assured trust he thought to have found in you. . . . Cursed be the blind affection and counsel that hath brought you hereunto', the Archbishop went on grimly, 'fearing that such sudden and unadvised dealing shall have sudden repentance'. Let Charles Brandon make no mistake, by his acts and doings he had put himself 'in the greatest danger that ever man was in'.

Welsey could suggest only one remedy for 'this great perplexity' and he was far from certain whether it would answer. Suffolk and Mary must beg Henry's forgiveness, that went without saying. More importantly, they must bind themselves to repay Mary's marriage portion in annual instalments of £4,000, leaving her only £6,000 a year to live on and keep up her royal state. She must also give back all the plate and jewels she had taken to France as part of her dowry, and surrender the plate and jewellery King Louis had given her. 'This is the way to make your peace', wrote Wolsey; 'whereat, if ye deeply consider what danger ye be in and shall be in, having the King's displeasure, I doubt not both the Queen and you will not stick.' As far as other matters were concerned, the Duke must put himself unreservedly in Wolsey's hands. For example, he was to take no further part in the talks about Tournai. He would have more than enough to do trying to redress his own causes, and should reflect that 'it will be hard to induce the King to give you a commission of trust, which hath so lightly regarded the same towards his Grace'.

The effect of this archiepiscopal broadside was devastating. Shivering in their shoes, the culprits hastened to follow Wolsey's advice. They were ready to strip themselves of every penny if it would appease the king's wrath, and now Suffolk cast himself at Henry's feet:

> Most dread sovereign lord, with the most sorrowful heart I, your most poor subject, beseech forgiveness of mine offences and for this marriage in which I have done greatly amiss. Sir, for the passion of God, let it not be in your heart against me, and rather than you should hold me in mistrust, strike off my head and let me not live.

For her part, Mary did her best to shield her husband from blame. 'I will not in any wise deny that I have offended Your Highness,' she wrote, 'for the which I do put myself most humbly in your clemency and mercy.' All the same, she had not acted simply out of 'sensual appetite' or because she had no regard for the King's wishes. It was just that she had been thrown into such terrible 'consternation, fear and doubt' that his Council would somehow succeed in preventing her marriage – the one thing she wanted most in all the world. 'Whereupon, sir, I put my lord of Suffolk in choice whether he would accomplish the marriage within four days, or else that he should never have enjoyed me; whereby I know well that I constrained him to break such promises as he made your grace.' She, too, begged for forgiveness 'and that it will please your grace to write to me and to my lord of Suffolk some comfortable words'.

But no words, comfortable or otherwise, were forthcoming and now the atmosphere in Paris had turned decidedly chilly. Knowing her brother, Mary had wasted no time in sending him a tangible token of her repentance, sacrificing the most sumptuous of all King Louis's gifts – the Mirror of Naples itself. But as this particular bauble unquestionably formed part of the French crown jewels, the new King and Queen were justifiably annoyed when they discovered its loss, and acrimonious (and unavailing) demands for its return played a considerable part in delaying and generally snarling up the final settlement of Mary's financial affairs. In the end, François agreed to let her keep a proportion of Louis's plate and jewels on the clear understanding that this was to be recognized as his generosity and not her right, and with this they had to be content for, as Suffolk truly pointed out, they could not compel him to give so much 'without he list'.

It was April before the negotiations were complete and by then Mary and Suffolk were longing to go home – Paris had long since become 'a stinking prison' for them both – but so far all their abject pleas for mercy had been ignored. They set out on their journey to the coast on 16 April and from Calais Mary wrote again, informing her brother that she had put herself within his jurisdiction once more and beseeching him for the last time, 'for the sake of the great and tender love' which had always been between them, to let bygones be bygones and to certify her 'by your most loving letters of the same'. In the meantime, she and her husband would stay where they were. Mary had always felt fairly certain that Henry would come round in the end, but she wasn't taking any unnecessary risks.

In fact, permission to cross the Channel, and with it some hint of a break in the clouds, was not long delayed and the Suffolks sailed for Dover at the beginning of May. Their arrival was unmarked by any special ceremony and their first meeting with Henry took place in private at the manor of Barking on the eastern outskirts of London, but these were the only overt signs that they were still in disgrace and François was informed that King Louis's widow had been very honourably and affectionately welcomed.

All the accounts of Henry's dire displeasure had, of course, been filtered through Thomas Wolsey in his role as mediator and it is more than possible that they were somewhat exaggerated. Wolsey and Charles Brandon were natural allies in the running feud with the Howard faction on the Council and it may well have suited the devious Archbishop to impress his yokefellow with a proper sense of his indebtedness. No doubt Henry had been both hurt and angry – though he cannot surely have been so very surprised – but it is clear enough that it was Suffolk's breach of faith rather than the actual marriage which had so enraged him. It's equally clear that he had never intended to proceed to extremes against his best friend and his favourite sister. This, after all, was the young Henry, before the lion had learnt his own strength, before he had tasted blood.

But although the lovers were forgiven, there was still a reckoning to be paid. Mary handed over all the valuables salvaged from France, which were later assessed to be worth just over sixteen hundred pounds, and as well as the whole of her dowry she signed a deed undertaking to repay in annual instalments the £24,000 which had been spent on her trousseau and the other expenses of her first marriage. This was a formidable total and the debt was to hang round the Suffolks' necks for the rest of their lives, but all things considered it was felt they had got off pretty lightly. The Duke forfeited his wardship of Elizabeth Grey, who was transferred to the custody of the Courtenay family, but he kept all his offices and estates, and he and Mary were soon fully restored to the life-giving sunshine of royal favour.

There had been a second, semi-private wedding in France, probably at the end of March, but now, to put a stop to any further speculation about the exact marital status of the King's sister, 'to guard the King's honour and hers' and, of course, to ensure the legitimacy of her unborn children, the Suffolks were married again in England. This time everything was done as openly as possible, with the banns called and the ceremony, which took place at Greenwich on 13 May, 'performed in due form and manner' down to the last detail. The King and Queen and all the court were present and there was plenty of feasting and dancing, but it remained very much a family affair, with none of the civic celebrations which usually marked such royal occasions. This, according to the Venetian ambassador, was because 'the kingdom did not approve of the marriage' and the ambassador himself, who found the whole situation frankly incredible, hesitated to offer his congratulations until he was quite certain they would be acceptable.

It is true that there was a body of opinion which took exception to the Suffolk match. 'Many men grudged', wrote the chronicler Edward Hall, referring to the pro-Spanish party of older and more conservative peers. 'The wisest sort', however, were content, pointing out that another foreign marriage would have entailed another expensive bridal outfit and wedding journey, while, as matters stood, the Queen–Duchess would actually be bringing money into the country with the rents from her dower lands in France. As for Suffolk himself, his genial good fellowship, his tall, auburn-haired good looks and athletic prowess combined to make him a popular figure and, apart from his political rivals, few people seriously grudged him his good fortune. Few people, after all, could resist a love story, especially one with a happy ending – always a rare enough event in royal circles.

That summer the King went off on a progress through the West Country and the Suffolks retired to East Anglia, partly to rest and recuperate after the stresses of the past few months, and partly as an economy measure. The Duke's prolonged sojourn in Paris had cost him a lot of money and in present circumstances he could hardly apply to Henry for assistance. By the autumn, though, they were back at court, attending the great banquet held at York Place in November to celebrate the arrival from Rome of Thomas Wolsey's cardinal's hat. They were also both very much in evidence at the launching of a new warship, christened the *Virgin Mary* but more often known as the *Princess Mary*. Mary herself was guest of honour at a dinner given on board the flagship the *Great Harry* at which the King presided, dressed in a sailor-suit of cloth of gold, with an enormous bosun's whistle hung round his neck on a gold chain which he blew as loudly as a trumpet at the slightest provocation. Everyone was in high spirits that day. Henry was never happier than when he was with the navy; and the French Queen, as she continued to be called, having got everything she had ever wanted, was radiant.

The Suffolks were expecting their first child in the spring – Mary's supposed pregnancy in Paris the previous March had been a false alarm – and her sister-in-law the Queen was also once again in the family way. With Catherine of Aragon's history of miscarriages, of babies born dead or living only a few weeks, no one felt very hopeful of the outcome, but this time she succeeded in carrying her child to term and on 18 February 1516 was delivered of a daughter who gave every promise of survival. The new Princess was christened at the

Friars' Church adjoining Greenwich Palace and given the name of Mary as a compliment to her aunt. Henry was apparently delighted –his fondness for babies and young children was one of his more attractive characteristics – and when the Venetian ambassador ventured to commiserate with him over the infant's sex, he replied philosophically that he and the Queen were both still young, Catherine was thirty-one, and that 'if it was a daughter this time, by the grace of God the sons will follow'.

Mary Brandon was to be more fortunate than her sister-in-law and when her baby, a healthy boy, made his appearance on Tuesday 11 March between ten and eleven o'clock at night, everyone present in the birth chamber must surely have been silently asking themselves the same question: had the King's sister succeeded where the King's wife had failed? Certainly the Suffolk baby, named, of course, after his uncle Henry, was given a princely baptism, with the King and Cardinal Wolsey as godfathers and his great-aunt Catherine Courtenay, born Catherine Plantagenet, daughter of Edward IV, as godmother.

It had been a good year for babies and that summer there was a family reunion, when Margaret Tudor, the widowed Queen of Scotland, came south on an extended visit, bringing with her another Margaret, Lady Margaret Douglas, her six-month-old baby daughter by her second husband, the Earl of Angus. The sisters had not met for nearly thirteen years, but although they greeted one another with spontaneous pleasure and a show of affection, their ways had long since parted and they had little in common now, apart from some childhood memories. A far stronger bond of friendship and shared experience existed between Mary and her Spanish sister-in-law. When, the following spring, Queen Catherine made a pilgrimage to the shrine of Our Lady of Walsingham to pray for a son, Mary went with her and afterwards the Suffolks entertained her 'with such poor cheer as we could make her grace'.

The unsettled state of European politics caused some domestic anxiety during 1516. French intervention in Scottish affairs and new French triumphs in Italy had combined to cool the Anglo-French *entente* and interrupt the flow of Mary's revenues from France, so that already she was falling behind in the repayment of her debt. It was probably for this reason that she and Suffolk were once again somewhat out of favour and reduced to pleading to be allowed to come to court. But although the debts continued to mount, the cloud seems to have been no more than a passing one. Towards the end of April 1517 both husband and wife were at Richmond, where the court had gone to avoid an outbreak of plague and where, according to the story as related by John Stow, the French Queen, together with her sister and sister-in-law, knelt at Henry's feet to intercede for the lives of the London apprentices condemned to hang after the so-called Evil May Day riots in the city.

The Suffolks stayed on to take part in the festivities which marked the reception of a Hapsburg embassy at the beginning of July, although Mary was now nearing the end of her second pregnancy. She was actually on her way home to East Anglia when her labour began, so that she was obliged to seek the hospitality of the Bishop of Ely's palace at Hatfield, seventeen miles north of London, for her lying-in. Her baby, a daughter this time, was born in the early hours of 16 July, St Francis's Day, and was given the name of Frances in honour either of the saint or, equally possibly, the King of France, whose goodwill was of rather more immediate importance. Marriage and motherhood – her third and last child, another girl christened Eleanor, arrived some time in 1519 and she had also undertaken the upbringing of her stepdaughters Anne and Mary Brandon – appear to have done nothing to quench Mary Tudor's natural gaiety or diminish her zest for the social whirl. Certainly she showed no signs of wanting to retire into domesticity and she and her husband were often at court together during these years, staying either in the royal household itself or at Suffolk Place, Charles Brandon's town house on the south bank of the Thames at Southwark.

In the autumn of 1518 the French Queen was called upon to play a prominent part in the lavish programme of hospitality planned for the entertainment of a high level diplomatic mission from France, headed by an old admirer of hers, the Lord Admiral Guillaume de Bonnivet, with nearly a hundred noblemen and 'young fresh gallants' in his train. The French had come to finalize arrangements for the handing over of Tournai by the English, to sign a new peace treaty and cele-brate the betrothal of the King of England's two-year-old daughter to the King of France's even younger son and heir, and since Queen Catherine was heavily pregnant again the King's sister was the obvi-ous person to act as an extra hostess. On Sunday 3 October she was present at a particularly sumptuous supper party given by Cardinal Wolsey, the like of which, according to the Venetians, had never been surpassed either by Cleopatra or Caligula, and afterwards partnered the King in leading a 'mummery' of twelve masked couples who danced for the delectation of the assembled company. Two days later, the court moved to Greenwich and the Duchess of Suffolk stood with the King and Queen to see her little niece and namesake solemnly espoused to the Dauphin amid all the ceremony and ostentatious display of gold plate that could be contrived.

In the spring of 1520, more elaborate and costly jollifications were laid on for a state visit by Mary's erstwhile fiancé Charles of Castile, who was also, incidentally, the Queen of England's nephew. Following the deaths of those two old partners in crime Ferdinand of Aragon and the Emperor Maximilian, Charles, now nineteen, had succeeded as Holy Roman Emperor, King of Spain, Lord of the Burgundian Netherlands and ruler of all the other widely scattered European fiefs and domains of the Hapsburg family. The attitude likely to be adopted by this important new world leader was naturally a matter of particular interest to his fellow statesmen and Henry and Thomas Wolsey were both eager to make a good impression. For Mary, of course, the interest was purely personal, but we have no record of her reactions on first setting eyes on the man with whom her future had once been so intimately connected.

From a political viewpoint the visit, though brief, was considered a success and no sooner was it over than the King and Queen and the whole court embarked at Dover *en route* for France and a long-planned summit meeting with François, held at Guînes a few miles inland from Calais. The Field of Cloth of Gold – three solid weeks of non-stop dressing up and showing off, over-eating, drinking, dancing, jousting, and socializing – is generally discounted by the history books as a pointless and expensive extravaganza which achieved little or nothing in serious diplomatic terms, but all the same the participants, or most of them, undoubtedly had a very good time. Among the royal ladies – Queen Catherine; Queen Claude, François's good dull plain wife; his mother and his intellectually brilliant sister Marguerite of Navarre – Mary Tudor, Queen Dowager of France, scintillated effortlessly in silver lamé and pearls, in a Genoese gown of white and crimson satin and, of course, cloth of gold. She was twenty-five that summer, her beauty still undimmed. 'Madame,' the Lord Admiral Bonnivet is reputed to have said to her, 'you are the rose of Christendom. You should have stayed in France. We would have appreciated you.'

Back at home, the Suffolks resumed the ordinary routine of life spent partly in East Anglia and partly at court, where Mary had become the acknowledged social leader of a younger set which prided itself on keeping up with the latest developments in French fashion and culture. At the New Year revels of 1522 a newcomer to the circle made her début, dancing with the French Queen and half a dozen other ladies in costumes of yellow satin and cauls, or netted caps, of Venice gold. Anne Boleyn, a lively brunette in her early teens, had just returned from a spell at the French court where she had been a pupil at the select finishing school for young ladies maintained by Queen Claude, and was now seeking to join the ranks of Queen Catherine's maids of honour. The Boleyns, like the Brandons, came from East Anglian farming stock, and Mary knew the family well. Anne's elder sister, another Mary, had been a member of her own entourage when she married King Louis and was one of the handful of English girls allowed to remain with her in France. She may quite likely therefore have put in a word for Anne to help her obtain one of the always much sought-after places in Catherine's household.

As it turned out, Mistress Anne's career at court nearly ended almost as soon as it began, for during the summer she incurred the severe displeasure of the all-powerful Thomas Wolsey by encouraging the attentions of Henry Percy, the Earl of Northumberland's son and heir, who had been sent south to complete his education and acquire some social polish under the Cardinal's eye. The young people soon reached an understanding, but the moment rumours of a secret engagement reached Wolsey's ears he took action to put a stop to such foolishness. The Earl of Northumberland had other plans for his son, while Anne's father was currently negotiating a match for her with one of her Irish Butler cousins. Lord Percy was quickly brought to heel but Anne showed her furious disappointment so openly that she was sent home in disgrace – a banishment which appears to have lasted until the end of 1525 or early 1526.

1525 is sometimes pinpointed as the year when Henry first began to be seriously concerned about the succession to his throne. Certainly by then it had long been obvious that there would be no further children of his marriage to Catherine of Aragon. The young girl who had first come to England nearly a quarter of a century ago to be married to Arthur, Prince of Wales, had been an appealing child, small and well made, with a fine head of thick russet coloured hair 'of a very great length, beautiful and goodly to behold' and a clear pink and white complexion. Now approaching her fortieth birthday, her slender waist thickened by repeated pregnancies, her lovely hair darkened to a muddy brown, she had become a dumpy little woman, 'rather ugly than otherwise', but still with the soft sweet voice which had never entirely lost its trace of foreign accent, and the unshakable dignity which comes from generations of pride of caste. Formidably pious and much preoccupied with the task of bringing up her precious only daughter, Catherine continued to preside smilingly at court functions and festivities, and her influence over her husband remained a factor to be reckoned with, but he no longer shared her bed.

Henry had first taken a mistress back in 1514 and five years later

Bessie Blount had presented him with a fine son. The King had acknowledged the infant with pride and pleasure, had him christened Henry and provided lavishly for his maintenance, but it was not until the summer of 1525 that Henry Fitzroy made his first significant public appearance. On Sunday 18 June an investiture was held at Bridewell Palace by Blackfriars and there the six-year-old child, supported by the Dukes of Norfolk and Suffolk, by Garter King of Arms, the Marquess of Dorset and three earls, was created Duke of Richmond and Somerset; 'and at the conclusion of the ceremonies', says a contemporary description of the event, 'he stood aside in the King's presence above all the other peers of the realm'.

Not surprisingly this sudden and startling elevation of the king's bastard caused a general flurry of interest, especially among the diplomatic corps. There was talk of a possible royal marriage for the new Duke, talk of a separate kingdom to be carved out for him in Ireland, even speculation that this healthy, handsome boy might easily by the King's means be exalted to yet higher things. But although the Duke of Richmond was granted an income of £4,000 a year and established in quasi-royal style with a household of upwards of two hundred and fifty persons at Sherriff Hutton in Yorkshire, nothing more was said officially about his future prospects and international interest gradually faded. The affair had, however, given rise to a certain amount of domestic unpleasantness. Normally far too well bred ever to betray interest in, let alone jealousy of, her husband's extra-marital activities, Queen Catherine had on this occasion been provoked into protesting at what certainly looked like a deliberate insult to her daughter and herself, and the resulting quarrel ended in the dismissal of three of her favourite ladies in waiting, who were accused of having encouraged her unwifely criticism of the King's actions. This, commented a Venetian correspondent, seemed a strong measure, 'but the Queen was obliged to submit and have patience'.

Other family members with an interest in the matter were the parents of the King's nephew, nine-year-old Henry Brandon who had also, incidentally, been honoured on 18 June with the title of Earl of Lincoln. But while the Suffolks might legitimately consider they had cause for concern over the attentions being showered on Henry Fitzroy, they were equally well aware that the succession was becoming a highly sensitive topic and evidently decided that discretion was the better part of valour. An added reason for discretion just then was financial. The recent war with France had caused a prolonged interruption in the payment of Mary's jointure revenues and in 1525 her debt to the crown stood at something not far short of twenty thousand pounds.

In May 1526 the French Queen is reported as having been one of the principal guests at a grand banquet at Greenwich Palace given in honour of the French and Italian ambassadors. In 1527 she was present at the celebrations marking the signing of a new peace with France and was in London again for the Christmas revels, but she came less and less to court during the late 1520s. This progressive withdrawal from public life is usually explained by disapproval of her brother's increasingly blatant infatuation with Mistress Anne Boleyn, sympathy for her sister-in-law, and her own failing health.

Mary had been ill in the spring of 1518 with an acute malarial-type fever, possibly a form of the dreaded sweating sickness which was sweeping the country that year, and in 1520 comes the first reference to a mysterious 'old disease in her side'. In an undated letter to the King, Mary speaks of having been 'very sick and ill at ease' and sending for Master Peter the Fesysyon (physician: like most of her contemporaries, the French Queen's spelling was strictly of the hear-and-write variety). Unhappily, Master Peter's ministrations had left her rather worse than better and she was convinced that only a trip to London would do her any good. Her husband seconded her pleas to be invited to come and consult the royal doctors, drawing a pathetic picture of her plight and assuring Thomas Wolsey that 'her disease showeth that it must ask great counsel'. He rather spoilt the effect by adding plaintively that a lodging of just one chamber in the palace would demonstrate that she was not in worse favour now than she had been on a previous visit to court. It sounds as if this was one of the occasions when the Suffolks were worried about their standing with Henry and were trying the effect of a little moral blackmail. There is, though, no doubt that during the last few years of her life Mary was a sick woman and it seems likely that it was increasing physical debility which kept her away from the bustle and gaiety of court life, rather than any very burning desire to take a high moral tone over her brother's divorce.

The fall-out from Henry VIII's famous scruple of conscience about the validity of his first marriage would overshadow English foreign and domestic politics for nearly a decade, lead directly to the breach with Rome and the establishment of a national Church, and so touch the lives of every man, woman and child in the country, but Mary Tudor Queen of France was to have no part to play in these great and far-reaching convulsions of social change. In the matter of the divorce her personal sympathies naturally lay with Queen Catherine, but Mary, like a true Tudor, always knew how to get her priorities right and in 1527 she was primarily concerned with the niceties of her own marital position.

Three years earlier, Dame Margaret Mortimer – the same who had once lived briefly as Charles Brandon's wife and was now a very old lady – had appealed to the Suffolks for help over a court case in which a pair of grasping relatives were trying to cheat her out of some property. The unwelcome resurrection of this ghost from the past had stirred up an old, long-buried disquiet in Mary's mind and when the King began publicly to question whether he might in fact be living 'abominably and detestably in open adultery' with his brother's widow, his sister began seriously to worry lest doubts could be cast on the legality of her marriage and the legitimacy of her children. After all, if the legitimacy of Henry's daughter and heir presumptive were to be challenged, then the status of Henry Brandon, Earl of Lincoln, would become a matter of considerable constitutional interest. Mary therefore prodded her reluctant spouse into consulting the canon lawyers and applying to Rome for a ruling on the matter. Official support was essential in an undertaking of this nature and while the case was pending was no time to risk antagonizing the King.

The Suffolks presently received the answer they wanted – a papal bull ratifying the original sentence of the Archdeacon of London's court given in 1507 annulling the Brandon–Mortimer marriage. Margaret Mortimer died just about this time which helped to tidy up any loose ends, but all the same the Duke and Duchess took the extra precaution in August 1529 of having the new decree notorially attested before the Bishop of Norwich and a posse of official witnesses.

The King was being noticeably less fortunate in his dealings with canon law, and the adjournment that July of the legatine court at Blackfriars marked the effective defeat of his efforts to obtain a divorce (or, more accurately, a decree of nullity) through the usual channels. Much of the court's time had been taken up with a somewhat distasteful argument as to whether or not the Queen's former marriage to Prince Arthur had been consummated and hearing witnesses who had been present at the public bedding of the Prince and Princess of Wales more than a quarter of a century ago. Among those individuals who obligingly dredged their memories for details suggesting that intercourse had taken place was Charles Brandon, and the arbitrary adjourning of the proceedings by the Italian judge Cardinal Campeggio was the cue for Suffolk's sudden noisy public attack on Thomas Wolsey, banging his fist on the table and shouting that 'it was never merry in England whilst we had cardinals among us'.

According to George Cavendish, Wolsey's gentleman usher (who also recorded his master's dry retort that if it had not been for one cardinal, Charles Brandon might well not have kept his head on his shoulders), this onslaught had been prompted by the King himself, and it is certainly a little difficult to see the duke venturing to set upon such a formidable quarry without being prompted. The truth was, of course, that Wolsey had already been marked down for destruction for his failure to get the King what he wanted, and now the hounds, led by the Dukes of Norfolk and Suffolk joined in temporary alliance and sicked on by Henry, were closing for the kill.

Meanwhile, the battle for the divorce went on, with Queen Catherine fighting every stubborn inch of the way in defence of her marriage, her good name, and her daughter's birthright. Her own conscience was perfectly clear. She believed that she was and always had been the King's true and lawful wife, and so she would continue to believe unless or until Rome ruled otherwise. No amount of bullying or persuasion could budge her and after one such attempt by a pompous delegation of councillors, led again by Norfolk and Suffolk, it was Suffolk who summed the matter up 'in two words', telling Henry that the Queen would obey him in all things 'but there were two that she must first obey. . . . God was the first and her conscience the other.'

Henry was not impressed and in July 1531 he finally banished Catherine from the court. Anne Boleyn was now his constant companion, keeping an estate 'more like a queen than a simple maid' with her own apartments at Greenwich, the favourite royal residence. There was still no sign of any cooling of the King's ardour and he made no secret of his honourable intentions towards his 'Lady' the moment he got his freedom. This was a matter of regret to the great majority of his subjects for, apart from the widespread sympathy felt for Queen Catherine and the natural jealousy her privileged position aroused, few people cared for Mistress Anne. Her bitter tongue had made her a number of unnecessary enemies (she had even managed to offend her influential uncle the Duke of Norfolk) and Eustace Chapuys, the newly arrived Imperial ambassador, wrote that he believed the Duke of Suffolk and his wife would offer every possible resistance to the King's second marriage 'if they dared'.

But although the Suffolks – more especially the duchess – undoubtedly resented and disapproved of the lady, they did not dare very much. In April 1532, the Venetian ambassador reported on an outbreak of fighting in the Sanctuary at Westminster between the followers of the Dukes of Norfolk and Suffolk which had apparently been sparked off by some 'opprobrious language' uttered against Madam Anne by the King's sister, and later that year, when Madam

Anne accompanied the King on a state visit to France, Mary flatly refused to go with them. Suffolk is said to have warned Henry privately that his fiancée had, in all probability, slept with Sir Thomas Wyatt, but that was the nearest he came to making any sort of *démarche*. It was understandable enough. Both he and Mary in their different ways were Henry's creatures, and both had too much to lose now to be able to afford the luxury of moral indignation.

Suffolk owned property at Donnington in Berkshire, at Hognorton and Ewelme near Oxford, Castle Rising in Norfolk and several other places in East Anglia, but most of Mary's time during these years was spent at Westhorpe Hall in Suffolk, the family's principal country seat, a handsome moated manor house, with a cloistered walk and private chapel, some twelve miles from Bury St Edmunds. Here the French Queen lived like any other great lady, teaching her daughters, supervising the household, sitting over her needlework, entertaining the county to dinner, patronizing local events such as the annual Easter fair and market at Edmundsbury, riding out on hunting parties and picnics, or enjoying the hospitality of one or other of the religious foundations in which she and her husband had an interest. Butley Priory, conveniently close to Westhorpe, appears to have been a favourite resort, and the Suffolks' last recorded visit took place in the autumn of 1530 when they stayed with the Austin canons there for nearly two months.

By the beginning of 1533 the family at Westhorpe was breaking up. Charles Brandon's two daughters by his first wife were both married by this time, Anne to Lord Powis and Mary to Thomas Stanley, Baron Monteagle, while that spring arrangements for the betrothal of sixteen-year-old Frances Brandon to her father's ward, Henry Grey third Marquess of Dorset, were being finalized. It seemed a very suitable match. The Greys were an ancient and substantial family whose name is said to have derived from the castle of Croy in Picardy but the first Grey mentioned in Dugdale's *Baronage* is a Henry de Grey who received a grant of land in Essex from Richard the Lionheart. From the sons of this Henry sprang the Greys of Ruthyn and of Wilton. Edward, eldest son by a second marriage of Reginald, third Lord Grey of Ruthyn, married the heiress to the barony of Ferrers of Groby, and it was their son, Sir John Grey of Groby, who, in the middle of the troubled fifteenth century, took to wife Elizabeth, daughter of Richard Woodville of Grafton near Stony Stratford. Sir John was killed in February 1461, fighting on the Lancastrian side at the battle of St Albans, and three years later his widow, a beautiful but designing lady, made such an impression on King Edward IV that he married her – a misalliance generally held to have contributed largely to the eventual downfall of the House of York.

Elizabeth Woodville, as she is always better known, was noted for the strength of her family feelings and she did not hesitate to push the interests of her two sons by her first marriage. Thomas, the elder, was created Marquess of Dorset and *his* son, another Thomas, went soldiering in France with Charles Brandon in 1513 and to Paris with him the following year to help celebrate the Princess Mary's wedding. After his old friend's death in 1530, therefore, it was natural that the Duke of Suffolk should have sought the wardship and marriage of his heir and planned an alliance between the families.

The Grey–Brandon wedding was celebrated in London at Suffolk Place and was the occasion of Mary's last visit to town. She found little temptation to linger. It was an open secret that Henry and Anne Boleyn had been married in a very private ceremony at the end of January and most people also knew by this time that Anne was pregnant. The court was in a turmoil over these latest fascinating developments in the continuing drama of the King's 'great matter' (Eustace Chapuys remarked that even the lady's own supporters hardly knew whether to laugh or cry), and no one had any time or interest to spare for the King's sister. So, as soon as the family gathering at Southwark had dispersed, Mary and her younger daughter Eleanor – now betrothed in her turn to Lord Clifford, son of the great northern magnate Henry, Earl of Cumberland – set out on the familiar journey home through St Albans, Baldock, Royston, Cambridge and Bury St Edmunds.

Suffolk paid a hurried visit to Westhorpe early in May, but he was too busy running the King's errands and superintending the preparations for the new Queen's coronation to be able to spend more than a few days with his ailing wife, nor does he seem to have been with her when she slipped quietly away some time between seven and eight o'clock on the morning of 26 June. She was thirty-eight years old and the exact nature of her long wasting illness remains a matter of speculation. It may have been cancer. It is perhaps more likely, in view of the family medical history, to have been tuberculosis.

In the world outside, the death of Mary Tudor the French Queen caused hardly a ripple. By 1533 her name had ceased to have any significance in diplomatic circles, she had never exerted any political influence over her brother, and socially she had long since been pushed into the background by the Boleyns and their set. In London that summer everyone's attention was taken up with the approaching birth of Anne Boleyn's child and the probable outcome of the approaching confrontation with the papacy, and, apart from ordering requiem masses to be sung in Westminster Abbey, Henry showed little sign of mourning for his favourite sister. The King of France told his ambassador in London that he was 'grieved' but, as Eustace Chapuys did not fail to point out, Mary's death meant he would now be saved the useful sum of 'thirty thousand crowns a year of dower'.

What Charles Brandon felt we do not know. He did not attend his wife's funeral, but that was normal practice and every detail of the ritual pomp and ceremony due to her rank was meticulously observed. The coffin lay in state at Westhorpe for nearly a month before being taken to the abbey of St Edmundsbury for committal. At the head of the cortège walked a hundred poor men in black hoods and gowns and carrying wax tapers. Then came the domestic chaplains with the Westhorpe chapel cross, escorted by a contingent of barons, knights and gentlemen and followed by the officers of the household, Garter and Clarencieux Kings of Arms, and a representative from the French College of Heralds, all mounted on horses trapped to the ground with black. The hearse, or funeral car, was drawn by six horses and draped in black velvet with the dead Queen's motto: *La volonté de Dieu me suffit*, worked in fine gold, while over it was a rich canopy borne by four mounted knights. On the coffin itself lay an effigy of Mary arrayed in the state robes, the crown and panoply of a queen of France, while on either side hung banners painted with the proud escutcheons of her arms as a princess of England and queen dowager of France. Immediately behind the hearse and leading the family mourners rode Frances Grey, supported by her new husband and her brother, the Earl of Lincoln. There followed a cavalcade of noble ladies, each attended by a running footman, two mourning wagons or coaches and, bringing up the rear, the waiting women, yeomen and lesser servants on foot.

Mary, with her beauty, her spontaneous charm and easy kindness, had been much loved in Suffolk and as her funeral procession wound its way through the narrow lanes, the summer dust thrown up by the horses' hooves powdering the sombre mourning hoods and gowns, more and more simple folk from the neighbouring hamlets of Bacton, Wyverstone, Long Thurlow and Crowland, Badwell Ash, Ashfield, Norton and Thurston left their work in the ripening corn fields to trudge after the coffin. True, there would be a coarse black gown, a few pence, free ale and a free meal for all who came to pay their respects, but many of those who answered the call to 'pray for the soul of the right high excellent Princess and right Christian Queen, Mary, late French Queen' would also have been moved by a genuine desire to honour her memory and speed her last journey.

The Right High and Excellent Princess and Christian Queen was laid to rest in the great abbey church at Bury St Edmunds on 22 July and a handsome alabaster monument was presently erected over her tomb. Both abbey and monument were to be destroyed during the period of the dissolution of the monasteries, when so much else of the world Mary had known dissolved into rubble and firewood and shards of broken glass, but her coffin was saved and re-interred in the nearby church of St Mary. In 1784, when it was moved to a new resting place in the north-east corner of the chancel, the coffin was opened and the embalmed corpse found to be in a remarkably good state of preservation. The teeth were complete and undecayed and the hair, almost two feet in length, had retained its red-gold colour – so much so that ghoulish souvenir hunters hurried to cut tresses from it. A piece came into the curious hands of Horace Walpole and another can still be seen in a local museum.

Mary Tudor, Queen and Duchess, was never more than a minor figure on the historical stage. Nothing in her life affected the mainstream of great events, nor did she ever seek to become involved in the dangerous game of high politics. All she ever asked for herself was a measure of personal happiness, and in that respect she was very much more fortunate than most women in her position and her century. Certainly the lovely, spoilt, wilful girl who had defiantly insisted on her right to be allowed to marry the man she loved never seems to have regretted it, and she cannot really be blamed for failing to foresee the deadly inheritance, compounded of her own royal blood and her brother's capricious favouritism, which she was creating for her innocent posterity.

3

The Noble Race of Suffolk

And so from princely Brandon's line,
And Mary did proceed
The noble race of Suffolk's house,
As after did succeed:
And whose high blood the lady Jane,
Lord Guildford Dudley's wife,
Came by descent, who, with her lord,
In London lost her life.

Charles Brandon had made Mary Tudor a faithful and affectionate husband, but he replaced her in his bed within a couple of months of that elaborate funeral. 'The Duke', wrote Eustace Chapuys, 'will have done a service to the ladies who can point to his example when they are reproached, as it is usual, with marrying again immediately after the death of their husbands.' Despite the freely expressed strictures of those moralists who felt that widows at least ought to be content to spend the rest of their lives in prayer and mourning, rapid remarriage by both sexes was the norm in a society which rather prided itself on its unromantic view of the married state; but the fact that the Duke of Suffolk's latest bride was the same age as his daughter Eleanor, fourteen to his forty-eight or -nine, and was already promised to his son, gave the case enough 'novelty', as Chapuys delicately put it, to attract the attention of some political commentators.

Brandon's fourth wife (or fifth, if you count Elizabeth Lisle) was another of his wards, the daughter and heiress of William, Lord Willoughby of Eresby, an important and respected landowner in Suffolk and Lincolnshire, by his second wife Maria de Salinas who had come to England in the train of Queen Catherine of Aragon. Suffolk had invested some two and a half thousand pounds in the wardship of young Catherine Willoughby and she had been living under his roof for the past five years or so, being educated along with his own daughters. She was a graceful, good-looking, well-bred girl, healthy, intelligent and high-spirited, and the Duke may very likely have been fond of her, but his motive for marrying her was pretty certainly financial. He was, as usual, heavily in the red. Frances's wedding had cost him over sixteen hundred pounds, Eleanor's was still to come, and there were numerous other calls on his purse, while Mary's outstanding debts to the Crown were yet to be finally settled. In the circumstances, a rich wife (and the gossipy author of the *Spanish Chronicle* heard that the new Duchess of Suffolk, a baroness in her own right, had an income of 15,000 ducats a year) would obviously be a desirable acquisition. Catherine was conveniently ready to hand and the Duke evidently saw no reason to waste her on his son, who could, after all, be matched easily enough elsewhere.

As it turned out, Henry Brandon, Earl of Lincoln, died the following spring, leaving the gossip-mongers to insinuate that his untimely end was due to grief at having been so heartlessly deprived of his fiancée. Very little, in fact, seems to be known about this young man, who stood so close to the throne. Probably it was ill-health which kept him out of the public eye, for he was barely eighteen when he succumbed, again most probably, to the Tudor family scourge of tuberculosis. His death was, however, regarded as something of a windfall for the King's other nephew, James V of Scotland, as although the Earl of Lincoln's mother had been the younger sister, 'his being a native' – that is, born on English soil – would, thought the pundits, have made him a formidable competitor to the King of Scots in the English succession stakes.

Suffolk survived his second bereavement with tolerable equanimity and six months later, on 18 September 1534, was able to write to Thomas Cromwell (who had replaced Thomas Wolsey at the King's right hand) to tell him that it had pleased God to send him a son another Henry Brandon. 'I beg you will ask the King to make a Christian soul of him', the Duke went on, 'and that you will also be one of the godfathers.' Anne Boleyn is reputed to have commented that 'my lord of Suffolk kills one son to beget another', which, if true, was unnecessarily spiteful, but then Anne Boleyn had been less fortunate in her child-bearing than the Duchess of Suffolk.

The King's domestic affairs remained, in short, in a thoroughly unsatisfactory condition. Henry had turned the world upside down, made powerful enemies at home and abroad, and ruthlessly manipulated the laws of God and man in his determination to ensure that the son he was so confidently expecting should be born in wedlock, and all he had got for his pains was another useless girl. The birth of Elizabeth Tudor in September 1533 had been a black disappoint-

ment to both parents and for Anne Boleyn it brought the beginning
of fear – despite the fact that the revolutionary programme of legislation currently going through Parliament had settled the succession
on her children and made it a treasonable offence to question the validity of the King's divorce and second marriage. Nor was the situation on the home front improved by the uncooperative attitude of the
King's first wife, who was still flatly refusing to recognize the compe-
tence of any English court to judge their matrimonial dispute.

Henry chose to regard his ex-wife's continued intransigence as
deliberate provocation, the more so because it was encouraging the
Princess Mary, his elder daughter and ex-heiress, to adopt a similarly defiant stance. The previous December, therefore, he had
despatched Charles Brandon to conduct another assault on
Catherine, who was then living at Buckden, the Bishop of Lincoln's
isolated palace on the edge of the Fen Country. The Duke's instructions were to re-swear the Queen's remaining servants to her as Princess Dowager – the new title which had been devised for her and
which she passionately rejected – and to arrange her removal to
Somersham in Cambridgeshire, a notoriously damp and unhealthy
spot and even more remote.

There's no reason to doubt that Suffolk had found this errand both
embarrassing and disagreeable – his new wife's mother was, after all,
one of Catherine's oldest and dearest friends – and he had been heard
to wish he might break a leg before being forced to make such a journey. But the family knew there was no question of his refusing to go.
In the event, the encounter proved to be singularly unrewarding, for
Catherine was not about to be bullied by Charles Brandon. After a
brief preliminary skirmish she had barricaded herself into her bedroom and Suffolk told the King that she refused to move to Somersham 'unless we bind her with ropes'. Things hadn't quite come to
that, however, and after a week of face-saving bluster, the Duke and
his colleagues found themselves obliged to retreat in no very good
order.

This was Brandon's last contact with his former sister-in-law, but
no one in public life could avoid active involvement in the moment-
ous happenings of the next few years. The Duke of Suffolk was
among those who attempted to persuade Thomas More to submit to
the King's pleasure in matters relating to papal supremacy and was
among those who subsequently sat with the judges at his trial. He
also sat on the commission of peers who tried Queen Anne Boleyn for
treason, adultery and incest in the early summer of 1536 and was
present on the scaffold to see her beheaded. But his most important
services to the Crown during the mid-1530s were connected with

helping to stamp out civil unrest in Lincolnshire and Yorkshire caused by local irritation over the suppression of the monasteries and the programme of religious innovation being imposed by central government, plus a mixed bag of other grievances both social and economic. In consideration of his energetic devotion to duty, the Duke received, in April 1537, a grant of the castle, lordship and manor of Tattershall, together with the building and site of the former Cistercian abbey of Vaudey, and from now on the Suffolks spent more and more of their time in the country in Lincolnshire, making their home either at Tattershall or Grimsthorpe, which was part of the Willoughby estate.

The Duchess had given her husband a second son, christened Charles, and he was also now beginning to acquire some half-royal grandchildren. Frances Grey had already borne a son and a daughter, both of whom died in infancy, but in 1537 came another daughter who gave promise of survival. The exact birthday of Jane Grey is not recorded, although the month is said to have been October, but in any case interest in the birth of a daughter to Lord and Lady Dorset was naturally eclipsed by the excitement over the birth at Hampton Court Palace, in the early hours of Friday 12 October, of a son to the King and his third wife Jane Seymour. In London solemn Te Deums were sung in St Paul's Cathedral and every parish church in the city. Bells pealed, two thousand rounds were fired from the Tower guns, bonfires blazed up dangerously amid the crowded timber-framed houses, and the citizens shut up shop and surged out of doors to celebrate. Impromptu street parties were organized, bands of musicians went about playing and singing loyal ballads, and everyone drank the new Prince's health in the free wine and beer provided by the civic authorities and other public-spirited individuals. Even the foreign merchants in their headquarters at the Steelyard – which stood on the site of Cannon St. station – joined in the celebrations, burning torches and contributing a hogshead of wine and two barrels of beer for the poor. While the capital rocked and clashed and exploded in a great crescendo of relief and thanksgiving that the King had at last succeeded in begetting a son in indisputably lawful wedlock, messengers were despatched to 'all the estates and cities of the realm' spreading the glad tidings, and the whole country went hysterical with joy. As Bishop Latimer wrote to Thomas Cromwell from his Worcester diocese: 'Here is no less rejoicing in these parts from the birth of our Prince, whom we hungered for so long, than there was, I trow, at the birth of St. John the Baptist. . . . God give us grace to be thankful.'

The christening of England's treasure, 'Prince Edward that

goodly flower', took place in the chapel at Hampton Court amid scenes of suitable splendour with the Dukes of Suffolk and Norfolk and Archbishop Thomas Cranmer as godfathers. Meanwhile, up at Bradgate in Leicestershire, Suffolk's newborn granddaughter was given the name of Jane, presumably in honour of Queen Jane Seymour who, poor lady, was in no condition to appreciate the compliment. Two days after Edward's christening she became so ill that the last sacraments were administered and on 24 October she was dead. According to Cromwell this tragedy was due to the negligence of her attendants who had allowed her to catch cold and eat unsuitable food. In fact, of course, she died of puerperal sepsis, the scourge of all women in child-bed.

The last two years of the eventful 1530s were enlivened by rumours of a 'Yorkist' plot, which gave Henry all the excuse he needed to complete the virtual annihilation of his remaining Plantagenet cousins, and a short-lived but excitable invasion scare, following the Pope's long-threatened promulgation of the Bull of Excommunication deposing the schismatic King of England. The Duke of Suffolk wrote reassuringly from Tattershall that 'the people here will spend life, lands and goods to serve the King, if any chance should happen', and the French ambassador reported that the English were busy strengthening their coastal defences and taking musters of all men able to bear arms. The biggest of these musters took place in London on 8 May 1539, when a citizen army fifteen thousand strong assembled at the villages of Mile End and Stepney before marching through the City to Westminster. The Dukes of Norfolk and Suffolk, as the country's senior military leaders, watched the parade from Suffolk's house at Charing Cross (for which he had exchanged Suffolk Place in Southwark) and both men were closely involved in co-ordinating the various anti-invasion measures being undertaken that summer.

The late 1530s and early 1540s were good years for Charles Brandon. He was happily married with two sturdy sons growing up to carry on his name. He had kept the King's trust and friendship throughout all the extraordinary vicissitudes of the past decade, and although he never held one of the great political offices of state, he was now firmly established as a respected and influential public figure standing among the greatest in the land, not to mention as one of the greatest land-owners, especially in East Anglia and Lincolnshire. In 1540 further grants of monastic property came his way – including Butley, where he and Mary Tudor had once spent so many pleasant lazy days – and also in 1540 he was appointed to the prestigious post of Great Master of the royal household. The following

August he and his wife had the honour of entertaining the King and his current Queen, Catherine Howard, at Grimsthorpe, now enlarged and rebuilt with stone from Vaudey Abbey. The court was on a progress north to York and the visit was repeated on the homeward journey in October. It was on his return to London about a fortnight later that the King was first informed that his young wife, his 'Rose Without a Thorn' had been unchaste when he married her and had since been deceiving him with Master Thomas Culpeper of the Privy Chamber – a disillusionment which caused him to shed tears of self-pity over his 'ill-luck in meeting with such ill-conditioned wives'. Needless to say, there was no pity for Catherine Howard and it was all part of the rich pageant of Tudor court life that in February 1542 the Duke of Suffolk should have found himself deputed, with the Earl of Southampton, to extract a confession from the erring queen and later to command the armed escort which convoyed her down-river from Syon House to the Tower.

Suffolk was absent on the war-torn Scottish border when Henry made his sixth and last marriage in a quiet ceremony at Hampton Court in July 1543, and in 1544, despite his advancing age, the Duke was once more on active service in France, commanding the army besieging Boulogne. He was back in England by the end of the year, but 1545 was also taken up with military matters. The latest French war had been going badly and the summer saw Suffolk travelling with the King round the south-eastern counties and again busy co-ordinating home defence.

In July came news that a French fleet had been sighted in the Solent. It presently had the impertinence to land, albeit briefly, on the Isle of Wight and raided the coast of Sussex, burning the village of Brighton. Worse than this was the disaster which had overtaken one of the King's biggest and most important warships, the *Mary Rose*, which capsized and sank with all hands under the King's very eyes in Portsmouth harbour while attempting to manoeuvre in the confined waters of the haven. At first it was hoped that she might be recovered, and Suffolk came hurrying over from his temporary base at Rochester to help organize the salvage operation. On 1 August he was writing to Secretary William Paget with a 'remembrance of things necessary for the recovery with the help of God, of the Marie Rose'. These included two of the greatest hulks that may be gotten, four of the greatest buoys, and five of the greatest cables that may be had, plus thirty Venetian mariners and a Venetian carpenter. But all efforts to raise the *Mary Rose* in 1545 proved unavailing and this was, in fact, to be the last piece of official business in which Charles Brandon was involved.

During the third week of August he was with the King at Guildford attending a series of crisis council meetings, until, hearing that the French fleet had withdrawn, Henry and his entourage moved on to Woking. The Duke, perhaps feeling the strain of his recent exertions, was reported to be unwell and then, suddenly, on 23 August, the Council was writing to the Earl of Hertford in Scotland: 'We pray you to pray with us for my lord of Suffolk, who died yesterday at four o'clock.'

My lord of Suffolk was sixty years old. He had been a constant feature of the royal landscape for the better part of half a century and for the King his going left a void which no one else could fill. Charles Brandon had been one of the few men still living who could remember the lusty and courageous Prince Harry the Eighth in the days of his youthful glory, and those far-off golden summers when life had been spent in 'continual festival'. He was also one of the select few whose devotion to his lord and master had been unquestioning and unquestioned – his one stunning act of disobedience having been long since forgiven and forgotten – and at a council meeting shortly after his death Henry paid his old friend a rare public tribute, remarking that for as long as the Duke had served him, he had never known him betray a friend or seek to take unfair advantage of an enemy, and 'is there any of you, my lords, who can say as much?' In his will the Duke had asked to be buried at Tattershall 'without any pomp or outward pride of the world', but this was not good enough for the King and on royal instructions and at royal expense, the son of the sturdy Suffolk yeoman who had died for the Tudors at Bosworth Field was given a grand funeral in St George's Chapel, Windsor.

Although several years younger than Charles Brandon, Henry himself was now becoming increasingly aware of his own age and infirmities, suffering great pain and recurrent attacks of fever caused by the inflammation of his notorious 'sorre legge'. He did his best to conceal his disabilities and continued to hunt and travel round the Home Counties, but those closest to him could see a steady deterioration and some people were already looking towards the future. Already the jockeying for position during the forthcoming royal minority had begun, and by the summer of 1545 the outlines of two opposing parties were becoming clearly discernible. On one side of the throne stood the conservatives, led by the Howard family and the right-wing churchmen; on the other the progressives, led by young Prince Edward's maternal uncle, Edward Seymour Earl of Hertford, and John Dudley Viscount Lisle, two thrustingly ambitious characters with distinguished reputations as soldiers and diplomats.

Inevitably the developing conflict over who would inherit the realities of power was fought out on the contentious issue of religious reform – between those who felt that this had already gone quite far enough and those eager to see a more radical break with the superstitious past than anything the King had yet been prepared to sanction. A natural dyed-in-the-wool conservative himself, it is unlikely that the King would ever have sanctioned any break with the past if the Pope had not been so disobliging over his divorce – although the material advantages in terms of increased revenue and personal status soon became irresistibly apparent. Nevertheless, Henry remained a conservative at heart, insisting on the retention of so much of the dogma of Catholic orthodoxy that it is still sometimes said that his Reformation was no more than 'Catholicism without the Pope'. This is both an over-simplification and an underestimate. The King may not have intended to start a revolution when he resigned from the Church of Rome but that, in effect, was what he had done.

There was in England a long tradition of anti-clerical feeling and smouldering religious radicalism going back two hundred years to John Wycliffe and the Lollards, and Henry's quarrel with the Pope had served as the catalyst for a chain reaction which proved unexpectedly difficult to control, especially after 1538 when an English Bible was made available to the general public. Every concerned and educated layman was now, for the first time, in a position to study and interpret the word of God for himself and this, in the increasingly literate and sophisticated society of the late 1530s and early 1540s, was the very stuff of revolution. It led naturally to the spread of revolutionary ideas; to the exhilarating realization that it was possible for an individual to hold direct communion with God, that the ordinary layman was no longer totally dependent on the priest to act as his intermediary; and a conviction was growing among thoughtful men and women that the priests could offer no scriptural authority for their time-honoured claim to be the only channel through which the laity could hope to receive divine grace. The priesthood, led by hard-line bishops like Gardiner of Winchester and Bonner of London, reacted vigorously against a heresy which struck at the very roots of its power, but without the support of the King in his new and revolutionary capacity of Supreme Head of the Church in England it was labouring under a considerable handicap.

Henry's attitude towards the force he had unleashed remained ambivalent. As long as it seemed politically expedient he had encouraged or, at any rate, had not seriously discouraged a limited amount of progressive thinking. Himself an enthusiastic amateur theologian, he took a keen if rather spasmodic interest in doctrinal matters and had given his blessing to a moderate programme of liturgical reform. On the other hand, he had no intention of allowing the radicals to get above themselves. Generally speaking, his policy was to hold a balance between the rival factions and, with splendid impartiality, he hanged Catholics for treason and burnt Protestants for heresy. But during the mid-1540s in the aftermath of Catherine Howard's disgrace, the progressive party appeared to be having things pretty much its own way. Very few heresy prosecutions were brought during 1544 and 1545 and in London especially the law was being openly flouted.

The climate began to show signs of change in the autumn of 1545 and the Duke of Suffolk's death was held to have been a grievous loss for all friends of the Gospel. But while it is true that the Duke had become closely associated with the progressives in recent years (he played a leading part in the unsuccessful attempt to bring down Stephen Gardiner in 1544), it is somehow difficult to visualize that hard-bitten, experienced old courtier-soldier in the role of a born-again Christian – far more readily can one see the impetus behind the Suffolks' patronage of the New Religion as coming from the Duchess.

Although still only in her mid-twenties, Catherine Suffolk was already established as a personality to be reckoned with: 'a lady of a sharp wit and sure hand to thrust it home and make it pierce where she pleased'. As well as her sarcastic tongue and a tendency to 'frowardness' deplored by her masculine acquaintance, my lady of Suffolk possessed a good brain, a lively and enquiring mind eagerly receptive of new ideas and an ardent nature. It was for just such women that the discovery of the Scriptures brought release for otherwise frustrated emotional and intellectual energies and opened up a whole new world of delights in which the spirit could find its own refreshment. Together with the Countess of Sussex, Joan Denny, Anne Herbert, Lady Lane, Jane Dudley, the Countess of Hertford and other like-minded ladies, the Duchess of Suffolk joined an influential group at court which studied and discussed the Gospels and listened to discourses by avant-garde preachers such as Nicholas Ridley, Nicholas Shaxton and Hugh Latimer – a group which met under the sponsorship of the King's latest wife, a committed convert to the new humanistic brand of piety.

In many ways Henry's sixth Queen was his most successful choice, and as a loyal, sympathetic companion for his declining years he could hardly have done better. Lady Latymer of Snape Hall, born Catherine Parr, the daughter of a Northamptonshire knight, had already been twice married to men much older than herself and twice widowed. In her early thirties she was still a pretty woman, but more importantly she was a mature, well-educated, serious-minded woman. According to the author of the *Spanish Chronicle*, she was 'quieter than any of the young wives the King had had, and as she knew more of the world she always got on pleasantly with the King and had no caprices'.

The new Queen was no stranger to royal circles. Like Catherine Suffolk, her mother had been one of Queen Catherine of Aragon's senior ladies and the two were close friends. The Queen had also taken steps to renew her childhood acquaintance with the King's elder daughter and she is remembered for being a good stepmother as well as a good wife, taking a conscientious and constructive interest in the welfare of her husband's oddly assorted brood and creating a comfortable domestic enclave at court where the royal family could be almost cosy. An active patron of the New Learning as well as the New Religion, Catherine Parr encouraged the Princess Mary to exercise her mind and use her Latin by translating Erasmus's paraphrase of the Gospel of St John. She is generally credited with helping to secure the appointment of John Cheke, leading Greek scholar and intellectual trend-setter from St John's College, Cambridge, to be principal tutor to Prince Edward; and it was almost certainly Catherine Parr who picked William Grindal, another Cambridge man, to tutor the ten-year-old Princess Elizabeth.

The Queen's benign influence was quickly noted in the outside world as a significant new factor on the English political scene and worthy of comment in ambassadorial despatches, while at home she was winning golden opinions among the liberal intelligentsia. Every day at court was like a Sunday, enthused one of the scholars she patronized, adding that this was something hitherto unheard of, especially in a royal palace. Nicholas Udall, master at Eton College and editor of the volume of translations to which the Princess Mary was contributing, wrote approvingly in his preface that it was now no strange thing to hear gentlewomen use grave and substantial talk in Greek or Latin with their husbands on godly matters. 'It is now no news in England', he went on, 'to see young damsels in noble houses and in the courts of princes, instead of cards and other instruments of vain trifling, to have continually in their hands either psalms, homilies or other devout meditations.'

This was all very well, but the right-wing faction on the Council, alarmed by the spread of heresy, suspected that dangerously subversive elements both inside and outside the Church were being encouraged by the Queen's study groups and her interests in 'godly mat-

ters'. Bishops Gardiner and Bonner in particular had no hesitation
in laying the blame for the growth of religious dissent in high places
at the Queen's door, and there were personal animosities involved as
well. Catherine herself was always tactful but some members of her
circle were not. The Duchess of Suffolk, for example, had named her
pet spaniel 'Gardiner' in a deliberately provocative gesture and
made no attempt to conceal her low opinion of his grace of Winchester; while Lady Hertford, arrogant and quarrelsome by nature,
never experienced any difficulty in getting herself disliked.

By the early spring of 1546 the King had become sufficiently per-
turbed by the uninhibited manner in which that precious jewel, the
word of God, was being 'disputed, rhymed, sung and jangled in
every alehouse and tavern' that he had been persuaded to authorize
a full-scale anti-heresy drive, but Gardiner and his principal ally on
the Council, the Lord Chancellor Thomas Wriothesley, remained
convinced that the key to the situation lay with the Queen; that the
way to bring down the leaders of the radical party was to attack them
through their wives. Opportunity presented itself in midsummer in
the person of Anne Kyme, better known by her maiden name of
Anne Askew or Asycough, a notorious heretic already convicted and
condemned.

Anne was an interesting example of an articulate, highly intelligent and passionate woman destined to become a victim of the society in which she lived – a woman who could not reconcile herself to
her circumstances but fought an angry, hopeless battle against them.
To Thomas Wriothesley and Stephen Gardiner, though, the most
interesting thing about her was her association with the court; she
had almost certainly attended some of those scriptural seminars held
in the Queen's apartments and was quite certainly acquainted with
several of the Queen's ladies. If it could now be proved that any of
these ladies had been in touch with her in prison, encouraging her to
stand firm in her heresy, then there might well be grounds for a
dramatic series of further arrests.

Anne was therefore transferred to the Tower and examined by
Wriothesley and his henchman the Solicitor General, the unappealing Richard Rich, about the identity of the other members of her
'sect'. She was asked specifically about my lady of Suffolk, my lady of
Sussex, my lady of Hertford and Lady Denny but, apart from admitting that she had received small sums of money from servants wearing the liveries of Lady Denny and Lady Hertford, Anne told her
interrogators nothing usable. Convinced that she could have given
them a long list of interesting names (coming as she did from a
respected old Lincolnshire family she would undoubtedly have

known the Duchess of Suffolk), Wriothesley ordered her to be 'pinched' on the rack. This was not only illegal without a warrant from the Privy Council, it was unheard of to apply torture to a gentlewoman like Anne Askew. It was also counter-productive. The Chancellor got no further information out of his prisoner and, as soon as the story got round, she became a popular heroine.

Anne Askew's ordeal was closely connected with the famous abortive attack on Catherine Parr, related with so much glee and circumstantial detail in the pages of John Foxe's *Acts and Monuments*. Her martyrdom at Smithfield on 16 July 1546 also marked the effective end of the right-wing resurgence on the Council. That autumn the conservatives were devastated by the imprisonment and attainder of the Duke of Norfolk, the execution of the Earl of Surrey and the abrupt exclusion of Bishop Gardiner from the magic inner circle of royal goodwill. Although it was no coincidence that the progressive leaders, Hertford and Lisle, had now returned from military service abroad, the motivation behind the King's eleventh-hour assault on the conservative party has always been a little obscure. Possibly he doubted whether either Norfolk or Gardiner, both old-fashioned Catholics at heart, could be trusted to remain sound on the question of royal supremacy, and with men like Edward Seymour and John Dudley in the saddle there would certainly be no danger of any return to papal domination – if nothing else the spectre of popery would be held at bay. Henry has been accused by some historians of attempting to rule from beyond the grave but there is no question that it was he who, in the closing months of his life, ensured that in his son's reign the balance of power would be decisively tilted in favour of the party of reform.

The old King died at the end of January 1547 and on 16 February he was laid to rest in St George's Chapel, Windsor, beside Queen Jane Seymour, the only one of his wives who had satisfactorily fulfilled her primary function, and not far from Charles Brandon, who had so satisfactorily filled the role of comrade and friend. Jane Seymour's nine-year-old son now succeeded as Edward VI, while the eleven-year-old Henry, Duke of Suffolk, Charles Brandon's son by Catherine Willoughby, carried the orb at the coronation on 20 February, and he and his younger brother were created Knights of the Bath in the coronation honours.

One way and another, the future looked bright for the noble house of Suffolk in those early months of the new reign. The young Duke, by all accounts an exceptionally gifted and attractive child, was already installed as a member of the elite group of high-born youths hand-picked as companions for the King and would thus be getting the best possible start in life; that 'devout woman of God' his mother was happily occupied applying her considerable talents and local influence to spreading the word in Lincolnshire and helping the liberal reformist regime of her friend Edward Seymour, now Duke of Somerset, in its campaign to root out idolatry and superstition, while the other Suffolk family had acquired a special and unexpected dynastic distinction by the terms of the late King's will.

The milestones of Henry VIII's matrimonial marathon had been marked by a series of Acts of Succession. The first, in 1534, had bastardized and disinherited the Princess Mary. The second, in 1536, had similarly disabled Anne Boleyn's daughter and, at a time when lawful heirs had been a more than usually scarce commodity, had empowered the King if need be to bequeath the Crown as he thought best, like any other piece of real estate. The third Succession Act, passed in 1544, confirmed Henry's right to dispose of the crown by will, but at the same time made it clear that should Edward die without heirs, and failing any children of the Catherine Parr marriage, the throne would pass first to Mary and her children and then to Elizabeth, subject to certain conditions to be laid down by their father in his will.

The will itself, a controversial and hotly debated document which was to be a contributory cause of much grief, bitterness, and confusion in time to come, recapitulated the provisions of the 1544 Act and went on to stipulate that if either Mary or Elizabeth (neither of whom, incidentally, had been re-legitimated) were to marry without the consent of their brother's Council, they would forfeit their restored places in the succession. Should the direct line fail altogether, then the Crown was to come not to the descendants of Henry's elder sister Margaret, she who had married King James IV of Scotland, but instead:

> to the heirs of the body of the lady Frances our niece, eldest daughter to our late sister the French Queen lawfully begotten; and for default of such issue of the body of the said Lady Frances, we will that the said imperial crown . . . shall wholly remain and come to the heirs of the body of the Lady Eleanor, our niece, second daughter to our said late sister the French Queen.

Only if both Frances and Eleanor failed to leave issue would the imperial Crown 'wholly remain and come to the next rightful heirs', unspecified but presumably the royal Stewarts, currently represented by Margaret Tudor's granddaughter Mary Queen of Scots, born in 1542, and her daughter by her second marriage – Margaret

Douglas, who had married into a collateral branch of the Stewart family and was now Countess of Lennox and the mother of a son, Henry, Lord Darnley.

The motive for this deliberate act of discrimination against the Scottish line has been attributed to Henry's very proper desire to prevent the realm of England from falling into the predatory hands of the Kings of Scotland, a contingent danger which had been raised by his father's advisers back in the days when his elder sister's marriage was under discussion. There was also, of course, the common law decree that no foreigner could wear the English crown and the strong English national prejudice against the Scots. This prejudice was fully shared by the King and there's little doubt that he had been to some extent influenced by personalities when drawing up his will. Henry had been on bad terms with Margaret for several years before her death, and had never forgiven her son James for failing to turn up at the summit meeting planned to take place at York in the autumn of 1541. In 1544, too, the King of England was still seething over the malice, the perfidy and wicked ingratitude of the Scots in refusing to deliver their little Queen into his hands as a bride for Prince Edward. Anglo-Scottish relations remained actively hostile until the spring of 1548, when England's so-called 'Rough Wooing' with fire and sword was brought to an end by the removal of five-year-old Mary Stewart to the more civilized environment of the French court.

In 1547, though, the various eventualities provided for in the old King's will still seemed reasonably remote. Everyone naturally hoped that young Edward would grow rapidly to manhood and prove more fortunate than his father when it came to getting sons. Equally naturally, any reference to the wretched survival record of Tudor boys was taboo in polite society, where the new King was being hailed as a miracle of precocity, learning, gravity, wit and gentleness, and compared in sermon after sermon to such scriptural paladins as David, Josiah and the young Solomon. If anyone noticed an ominous physical likeness between the small, serious, blond Edward and his long-dead uncle Arthur, or remembered Henry Brandon, Earl of Lincoln, and Henry Fitzroy, Duke of Richmond, both more recently dead in their teens, no one said so, and the most immediate consequence of Henry VIII's eccentric testamentary arrangements was the enhanced social status conferred on the children of Frances and Eleanor Brandon.

Neither sister had succeeded in raising a son. Eleanor had lost two boy babies and did not herself long survive her uncle Henry, dying in November 1547 at the age of twenty-eight, leaving a seven-year-old daughter, Lady Margaret Clifford, as her only posterity. Following the birth of Jane, Frances had produced two more daughters, the Ladies Catherine and Mary Grey, now aged seven and two respectively, so that these four little girls between them represented the royal Suffolk line.

The Grey sisters spent their first years at Bradgate, the principal family home on the edge of Charnwood Forest, a large and luxurious red-brick, stone-turreted mansion with every modern convenience, built by their grandfather, the second Marquess of Dorset and further enlarged and improved by the third Marquess their father. Surrounded by formal pleasure gardens and set in rolling, well-wooded country teeming with game and offering some of the best sport in England, Bradgate was a delightful place to live and, when the Dorsets were in residence, a very grand one. Frances Grey, a buxom, energetic, high-coloured, hard-riding woman who, as she grew older, began to bear an unnerving resemblance to her late uncle Henry, was exceedingly conscious of her exalted rank and took care that her neighbours should appreciate it as well. Semi-regal state was therefore maintained at Bradgate and when the family dined in public in the great hall they kept open house, with covers laid for two hundred persons, musicians playing in the gallery and each course served to the accompaniment of a fanfare of trumpets. When my lady Marchioness condescended to pay a visit to the nearby town of Leicester, she was ceremonially welcomed and entertained by the mayor and corporation. In 1540 it is recorded that the strawberries and wine provided for her refreshment cost two shillings and sixpence, while another time four shillings was paid for mulled and spiced wine, served with a collation of wafers, apples, pears and walnuts.

The principal pastimes at Bradgate were hunting and hawking, but although her ladyship was a well-known sporting enthusiast, she and her husband spent more time in London and at court than they did in Leicestershire, and were content to leave their daughters' early upbringing in the hands of servants. We know that Lady Jane's nurse was a Mrs Ellen who stayed with her for the rest of her life, and that her first tutor was probably the domestic chaplain, Dr Harding, but we know very little else about the years up to 1547. We can guess that she received the usual elementary training which laid great emphasis on formal good manners and the inculcation of the feminine virtues of docility, obedience and passivity, but it seems unlikely that her education during this time extended further than the usual basic Latin, French, needlework, music, dancing and household management. Neither of the Dorsets were scholars themselves and the revolutionary notion that girls as well as boys might benefit from an academic classical training had not yet penetrated to rural Leicestershire. It was, in fact, still largely confined to rarefied intellectual circles in London and the universities, especially Cambridge, being a by-product of that great rebirth – or renaissance – of intellectual curiosity which had sprung to life in fourteenth- and fifteenth-century Italy and spread slowly northwards.

Paradoxically the New Learning, as the movement became known in England, had its roots in nostalgia for the past. Like most reformers, the scholars of the Renaissance wanted to go back to the beginning: to revive the classical culture of the ancient world and, in northern Europe at least, to return to the purity of the early Apostolic Church. They turned to the study of Greek partly to rediscover the pre-Christian philosophers but also to read the Gospels in their original form, so that the New Learning had helped to open the door to the New Religion. In England, too, the new wave of scholars had from the beginning taken a particular interest in the education of the rising generation. William Lily of *Lily's Latin Grammar*, John Colet, founder of St Paul's School, Thomas Linacre the physician, William Grocyn the Greek scholar and Thomas More the lawyer were all eager to disseminate their ideas for the introduction of a wider and more liberal curriculum in the schools and universities, but it was Thomas More, using his own daughters as guinea pigs, who conducted the first serious experiment with the novel idea that girls could be educated too.

By no means everyone was convinced that this was either wise or feasible. Even More's old friend and admirer Desiderius Erasmus had been sceptical. But the Sage of Rotterdam was so impressed by the mini-Utopia of the household at Chelsea, which he described enthusiastically as 'Plato's Academy on a Christian footing', where the More girls studied Latin and Greek, logic, philosophy and theology, mathematics and astronomy, that he was quite won over and predicted that his friend's example would be imitated far and wide. In fact, of course, it was not, and women like More's eldest daughter Margaret, who became an internationally respected scholar in her own right, remained the exception rather than the rule. Sir Thomas did, however, have an influential supporter in Queen Catherine of Aragon who, in 1523, invited another well-known educationalist, her compatriot Juan Luis Vives, to draw up a plan of studies for the seven-year-old Princess Mary which would help her to grow in learning and virtue. Among other things, Vives recommended that Mary should have companions at her lessons, for it was not good for any child to be taught alone, and for a time at least one of the carefully selected young girls sharing the resources of the royal schoolroom was the young Catherine Parr, who grew up to carry on a tradition of female learning and piety at the Tudor court which had begun with the foundress of the dynasty, Lady Margaret Beaufort herself.

But when Lord and Lady Dorset arranged to place their eldest daughter in Queen Catherine Parr's charge they were undoubtedly thinking in terms of worldly rather than scholarly or spiritual advantage. The custom of 'placing out' – that is, of sending one's children away to learn virtue and good manners in a family better circumstanced than one's own – was an old one which seems to have had its origin in the feudal practice of sending a boy to serve as a page in his lord's household as the first step in his progression towards knighthood. For girls, even if in some cases they paid for their keep by performing domestic duties or acting as 'waiting gentlewomen' to their hostesses, it offered a practical opportunity to acquire accomplishments and social polish and, of course, a better chance of making a good marriage.

For the Grey sisters the only possible 'place' was the royal household, but by the time Jane was old enough to leave home the King was dying and life at court was in a state of suspended animation. Henry left his wife generously provided for, but with no share in the regency and no further say in the upbringing of her stepson, and at the beginning of March 1547 François van der Delft, the Imperial ambassador in London, reported that the Queen Dowager was shortly going to reside in the suburbs. Until the young King married, however, the Queen Dowager would remain the first lady in the land, taking precedence even over the princesses; Edward was known to be very much attached to her and she continued to command a great deal of influence and respect. When she moved into her dower manor at Chelsea, a comfortable, up-to-date, brick-built house standing on the site of the present Cheyne Walk, she took with her the thirteen-year-old Lady Elizabeth who, it had been decided, would stay with the Queen until she had finished her education. And on an unrecorded date, probably no later than the end of March, the establishment was joined by nine-year-old Jane Grey.

This was pretty certainly not Jane's first introduction to court circles. Pretty certainly she would have been brought on visits to London before this, to stay at her parents' house, Dorset Place in Westminster, and taken to meet her royal relations – especially Prince Edward. But like the other details of her early childhood, this is largely a matter of guesswork. It was not until the spring of 1547 that Jane Grey emerges into full historical daylight and, ironically enough, her future prospects at that time looked extremely rosy. She might not be a beauty, with her red hair and freckles, but although she was very small for her age she was apparently quite healthy, a bright, promising child whose Tudor blood would add considerably to her value on the marriage market. After all, if the provisions of King Henry's will were followed, Jane, as his eldest English great-niece, stood presumptively third in line of succession to the throne.

For Jane herself her translation into Queen Catherine's care meant nothing but good. She had not been happy at home and her parents, her mother in particular, never seem to have shown her any affection. Not that this was necessarily unusual, though the Dorsets do appear to have been rather more unfeeling than most – unless it is that their harshness has been better publicized. But the sixteenth century practised no sentimental cult of childhood, something widely regarded as an irritating prelude to useful adult life, a period of physical and mental infirmity to be got over as quickly as possible and for which few allowances were made. Even that enlightened scholar Luis Vives had disapproved of 'cockering', or indeed of any outward display of maternal love, 'lest the children become emboldened to do whatever they like'. He was of the opinion that daughters especially should be handled without cherishing, for while indulgence was bad for sons 'it utterly destroyeth daughters'.

It is unlikely that Frances Dorset had read Vives's somewhat turgid manual *The Education of a Christian Woman*, but she would certainly have agreed with this precept, and her daughters at least were never in any danger of being destroyed by cherishing. Catherine Parr's generous, warm-hearted kindness must therefore have come as a revelation. In the Queen's household Jane was petted and praised; her cleverness, 'towardness' and piety were openly discussed and admired, her brilliant prospects whispered over and, in this congenial atmosphere, she naturally began to blossom.

Catherine, too, was blooming that spring. With the King and his government safely in the hands of the progressive party, the Queen, like her friend Catherine Suffolk, was now free to indulge her devotional and intellectual interests without fear or need for concealment, and the palace at Chelsea soon became a recognized centre of advanced godliness, where the minds of some potentially very important wives and mothers were being moulded. The Queen Dowager was also now for the first time free to arrange her private life as she chose, and within a very few weeks of King Henry's death she was engaged to be married to Sir Thomas Seymour, younger brother of the new Lord Protector Somerset.

This was not quite so impetuous as it looked, for the couple had been planning to wed four years earlier, at the time of Catherine's second widowhood in the brief period before the King declared his interest; as the Queen wrote to her fiancé from Chelsea: 'I would not have you think that this mine honest good will towards you to proceed of any sudden motion of passion; for, as truly as God is God, my mind was fully bent the other time I was at liberty, to marry you before any man I knew.' On that occasion the Almighty, in the formidable guise of Henry VIII, had withstood her will 'most vehemently' but now, at last, she was to have her reward for patient self-abnegation and at thirty-four was as radiant as a teenager over this late chance of romance. 'I can say nothing', she wrote, 'but as my Lady of Suffolk saith, "God is a marvellous man".'

The lovers were married very privately, so privately in fact that the date of the ceremony is not known, although it probably took place no later than April or early May, but for Catherine Parr, as for Jane Grey, this happy time was destined to be pathetically short.

4

So Divine a Maid

Go on thus, O best adorned virgin! to the honour of thy country, the delight of thy parents, thy own glory, the praise of thy preceptor, the comfort of thy relatives, and the admiration of all.

Henry VIII's will had provided for a council of sixteen executors, each 'with like and equal charge', to govern the country during his son's minority – an arrangement so patently unworkable that it had been set aside within a week of the old King's death. When the executors, or those thirteen of them who were in London, met formally for the first time on 31 January 1547, it was unanimously agreed that some 'special man' of their number would have to be preferred in name and place before the rest: in other words, that someone would have to be nominated as acting head of state if a system of government geared to personal rule was to be carried on with any degree of efficiency. The choice was an obvious one and the assembled councillors proceeded to confer on Edward Seymour Earl of Hertford 'the name and title of Protector of all the realms and dominions of the King's majesty that now is, and of the Governor of his most royal person'.

There were plenty of precedents (admittedly not all of them entirely reassuring) for appointing the uncle of a child king to be his regent and guardian, and Edward Seymour was a man of proven ability, generally respected by his peers, who had been trusted by the late King. But he was not of the blood royal. Eldest surviving son of a well-to-do Wiltshire squire, he owed his earldom in part to his own efforts but rather more to the fact that his sister had been fortunate enough to become Queen and give the King a male heir. His present elevation to vice-regal status would inevitably give rise to jealousy and faction, and it remained to be seen whether or not he possessed the necessary ruthlessness to fight off competition.

He had begun promisingly. Guided by his friend and ally that shrewd political operator Secretary of State William Paget, Hertford had slipped unobtrusively out of Whitehall to seize custody of the new King almost before the breath had left the old King's body, and the *coup* was so skilfully managed that by the time the council met on the thirty-first the transference of power was an accomplished fact needing only to be rubber-stamped.

Just over a fortnight later the new rulers of England were treating themselves to their first taste of the sweets of power. Edward Seymour was created Duke of Somerset to underline the dignity of his position, and John Dudley became Earl of Warwick. The younger Seymour brother got a barony, a seat on the Council, and the office of Lord Admiral, but he was very far from being satisfied. On the contrary, the new Lord Seymour of Sudeley took bitter exception to an arrangement which allowed one of the King's uncles to enjoy all the advantages of their valuable relationship while leaving the other to be fobbed off with mere consolation prizes, and he had every intention of redressing the balance the moment he was in a position to do so.

As an eligible bachelor, his first step in this direction had been his whirlwind courtship of the unsuspecting Catherine Parr, though the word soon went that if my lord – always more noted for optimism than common sense – 'might have had his own will', he would have married the Lady Elizabeth before he married the Queen. Physically a most attractive man – 'fierce in courage, courtly in fashion; in personage stately, in voice magnificent, but somewhat empty of matter' – the Admiral was also vain, shallow and greedy, the classic confidence trickster, quite unscrupulous in his exploitation of man, woman or child, but especially woman or child, and possessing just the sort of easy surface charm calculated to fascinate his victims.

Aware that their marriage would not be popular in some quarters – the Lord Protector was in fact 'much displeased' when the news leaked out – the newly wedded pair were at pains to keep it quiet until Catherine had been able to explain to Edward that no disrespect was intended to his father's memory. Reassured on this point, the little King was graciously pleased to give them his blessing and by mid-summer the Admiral had moved in with his wife, his boisterous loud-voiced personality blowing like a gale through the cosy, rather oppressively pious atmosphere of Chelsea.

Thomas Seymour took no interest in the New Learning or in advanced Protestant thought. His all-consuming interest in the advancement of his own career left very little room for anything else, and it was even noted with regret that my lord soon developed a habit of remembering important business elsewhere whenever it was time for family prayers. His other habit of bursting in on the Lady Elizabeth in the early morning, still in his nightgown and slippers, to 'bid her good morrow', to tickle her and smack her familiarly on her behind, or play hide-and-seek round the bedcurtains amid much giggling and squealing, was also regarded with deep and understandable disapproval by Elizabeth's governess.

The Admiral never appears to have indulged his taste for horseplay with the other young girl living under the Queen's protection, but Jane Grey was too undeveloped physically to give any spice to slap and tickle and, besides, he had other plans in mind for her. With his usual opportunism, he had wasted no time in furthering his acquaintance with the Greys after the publication of King Henry's will, sending his most trusted friend and confidential servant, John Harington, to talk to the Marquess of Dorset. Harington's instructions were to use 'all the persuasions he could' to get Dorset to agree to put Jane's future in his master's hands, promising that the Admiral would see her placed in marriage much to her father's comfort. When Dorset hedged, asking for more details, Harington, at least according to his own later recollection, replied discreetly that Jane was 'as handsome a lady as any in England' and worthy to be the wife of any prince in Christendom; that if the King's majesty, when he came of age, should decide to marry within the realm, he was as likely to choose his cousin as anyone else and that, in any case, living in my lord's house, who was uncle to the King, must greatly improve her chances.

Lord Dorset was to remember the conversation rather differently, swearing Harington had given him a firm guarantee that the Admiral would arrange to marry his daughter to the King, and there's no doubt that it was on this understanding that a bargain was presently struck and 'certain covenants' entered into. Put at its crudest, the Marquess agreed to sell his daughter's wardship and marriage to Thomas Seymour for the sum of two thousand pounds; the Admiral handed over a few hundred on account and the Lady Jane passed into his custody.

No one, of course, saw any reason to consult Jane herself, nor would she have expected it. She was, it may safely be assumed, happy in her new surroundings, either at Chelsea, at Catherine's other house at Hanworth in Middlesex, or else at Seymour Place in London, being launched on a programme of studies which now included Greek and modern languages as well as Latin, and absorbing the evangelical Protestantism of the Queen's circle with all the eager response to be expected of an intelligent, sensitive child previously starved of both affection and mental stimulus.

But in the world outside, relations between the Seymour brothers were deteriorating. A particularly acrimonious dispute blew up in the autumn of 1547 over some pieces of the Queen Dowager's jewellery held by the Protector. Catherine claimed these were her own property, gifts from the late King. But the Protector refused to give them up, insisting they belonged to the Crown. He had also installed a tenant against her wishes in one of her dower manors, and the normally sunny-tempered Catherine was furious. Nor were matters improved by the attitude of the Duchess of Somerset, 'a woman for many imperfections intolerable but for pride monstrous', who angrily resented the fact that the Queen was entitled to take precedence over her at social functions and made no secret of her feelings on the subject of presumptuous wives of younger sons. The first Parliament of the new reign was due to meet in November and the Admiral, imbued with a fresh sense of his various grievances, stamped about shouting that by God's precious soul he would make this the blackest Parliament that ever was in England. When his cronies tried to calm him down, he roared defiantly that he could live better without the Protector than the Protector without him, and that if anyone went about to speak evil of the Queen he would take his fist to their ears, from the highest to the lowest.

Thomas Seymour had tried to persuade his nephew to sign a letter to be presented to the House of Lords, asking them to favour a suit which he meant to bring before them. According to the Admiral, this was a perfectly harmless petition for the recovery of the Queen's jewellery – more probably he was hoping to gather support for his pet scheme to have the offices of Protector of the Realm and Governor of the King's Person divided between his brother and himself. Edward, however, took the advice of his tutor, Sir John Cheke, who warned him seriously about the dangers of becoming compromised in the Admiral's intrigues, and wisely refused to sign anything he might be made to regret. Frustrated, the Admiral took to prowling the corridors of St James's Palace, remarking wistfully that he wished the King were at home with him in his house and speculating on how easy it would be to steal the boy away. But even Tom Seymour could see the folly of attempting to kidnap the King without the assurance of some very solid backing in the country. He patched up his quarrel with his brother and subsided – for the time being at any rate.

The following spring the trouble brewing in his own house over his teasing pursuit of the Lady Elizabeth threatened to break out in open scandal. It seems that the Queen, 'suspecting the often access of the Admiral to the Lady Elizabeth's grace, came suddenly upon them, when they were alone (he having her in his arms)'. At the sight of her husband and stepdaughter locked in an embrace which did not look in the least playful, 'the Queen fell out, both with the Lord Admiral and with her grace also. . . . And hereupon . . .' this same account continues, 'there was much displeasure.'

Catherine's initial reaction to her betrayal by the husband she loved and the girl she had tried to mother was natural enough, especially as she was now more than half-way through her first pregnancy; but it was also entirely due to her tact, generosity, and presence of mind that the affair was successfully hushed up and an ugly scandal averted. In the week after Whitsun, Elizabeth, with her governess and other household staff, was sent off to Cheshunt on a protracted visit to Sir Anthony and Lady Denny, both old and trusted friends of the royal family. The Queen and Princess parted affectionately and, except for those immediately concerned, no one appears to have had any inkling of the real reason for her going.

Jane Grey stayed with Catherine and there is nothing to indicate that she was at all affected by the tensions in her guardians' marriage, or that she missed Elizabeth's companionship. Although the two girls had spent more than a year together under the same roof, very likely sharing some of the same lessons and certainly seeing a good deal of one another at meals, at prayers and in general daily intercourse, there is no evidence of any friendly relationship having developed between them; nor does there at any time appear to have been any correspondence, any exchange of gifts, the loan of a servant with some special skill or indeed any of the small mutual courtesies usual between two ladies so nearly related. The four-year difference in their ages would, of course, have meant most at the time when they were physically closest – the gulf between nine and thirteen can be a wide one – and years later Henry Clifford, writing the biography of his mistress Jane Dormer, once a maid of honour to Queen Mary Tudor, remarked of Elizabeth that 'a great lady who knew her well, being a girl of twelve or thirteen, told me that she was proud and disdainful, and related to me some particulars of her scornful behaviour, which much blemished the handsomeness and beauty of her person'. There may also have been some jealousy. Jane Grey might have been only King Henry's great-niece, but no one could cast doubt on her legitimacy or on her mother's virtue, while Elizabeth was still legally the bastard of a notorious adulteress and this fact may have been mentioned from time to time in the privacy of the household.

On 13 June 1548 the Queen Dowager and her husband set out for Sudeley, their Gloucestershire estate, accompanied by a princely retinue and taking Lady Jane Grey with them. It was at Sudeley, on

30 August, that Catherine's baby was born: a girl, christened Mary. At first all seemed to be well. The Admiral wrote off enthusiastically to his brother with the good news and the Protector responded with a congratulatory note. 'We are right glad', he wrote, 'to understand by your letters that the Queen, your bedfellow, hath had a happy hour; and escaping all danger, hath made you the father of so pretty a daughter.' But sadly the rejoicings were premature. Catherine developed the dreaded symptoms of child-bed fever and within a week she was dead. She was buried in the chapel at Sudeley Castle with all the pomp and ceremony due to a Queen Dowager of England. Miles Coverdale, the biblical translator, preached the sermon and Jane Grey, a diminutive figure in deepest black, acted as chief mourner for the only person ever to show her disinterested kindness.

Thomas Seymour was sufficiently shaken by his wife's death to suggest returning Lady Jane to her parents, but this uncharacteristic loss of confidence soon passed. On 17 September, ten days after the funeral, he was able to tell Lord Dorset that, having taken stock of his position, he found he would not, after all, be obliged to break up his household and had changed his mind about sending Jane home. He now intended to retain the services of all the late Queen's ladies, together with 'the maids which waited at large and other women being about her grace in her life time'. As well as this, his own mother was coming to take charge and would be 'as dear unto her [Jane] as though she were her own daughter'.

But the Dorsets were growing restive. More than a year had gone by with no sign of any of Tom Seymour's 'fair promises' being fulfilled, and although Lord Dorset assured Lord Seymour that he was still ready to be guided by him in the matter of his daughter's 'bestowing', the Marquess was plainly looking for an excuse to wriggle out of his previous undertakings. Jane, he wrote, was too young to be left to rule herself without a guide and he feared lest, for want of a bridle, she might take too much head and forget all the good behaviour she had learned from Queen Catherine. His lordship therefore felt strongly that she should be returned to the governance of her mother, to be 'framed and ruled towards virtue' and her mind, in these so important formative years, addressed to humility, soberness and obedience. Frances Dorset added her voice in a letter enclosed with her lord's, in which she thanked her 'good brother' the Admiral for all his gentleness, but begged him to trust her and to believe that a mother knew what was best for her own child.

This sudden access of concern for their daughter's moral welfare imperfectly concealed the Dorsets' ruthless determination to sell her to the highest bidder and they were, in fact, beginning to wonder whether, in the circumstances, it might not be wiser to settle for a match with the Lord Protector's son, which had already been tentatively discussed. But although Jane did go home for a while towards the end of September, Thomas Seymour had no intention of giving up his claim to her without a struggle. He sent his crony William Sherington of Lacock Abbey to work on Frances Dorset and himself paid a visit to London when, according to the Marquess, he was 'so earnestly in hand with me and my wife' over the custody of Lady Jane that in the end, 'because he would have no nay, we were contented she should again return to his house' though not, it seems, without 'much sticking of our sides'.

During the negotiations, conducted by Lord and Lady Dorset on one side and Sherington and the Admiral on the other, the Admiral had renewed his promises that if only 'he might once get the King at liberty' he would ensure that his majesty married none other than Jane. He also agreed to advance another five hundred pounds of the two thousand he was 'lending' Jane's parents. No need for a bond, declared Tom Seymour expansively, the Lady Jane's presence in his house was more than adequate security. The Dorsets, greedy, foolish and chronically hard-up, rose to the bait and in October 1548, round about the date of her eleventh birthday, Jane went back to live at Hanworth or Seymour Place under the indulgent chaperonage of old Lady Seymour.

By this time the Admiral was scarcely bothering to conceal his eagerness to put an end to his brother's protectorate, dropping broad hints about his plans and boasting of his strength in the country to anyone who would listen. Actually, of course, he was no nearer to getting his hands on Edward than he had ever been. Elizabeth, too, remained out of his reach. But in the princess's household, now established at the old palace at Hatfield, there was excited speculation about his intentions and gossip had begun to circulate that the real reason why the Lord Admiral had kept Queen Catherine's maids together was to wait on the Lady Elizabeth after they were married. Rather less credibly, gossip was also linking his name with the Lady Jane – a titbit which his lordship passed on to one of his confidants as a joke, 'I tell you this merrily.'

Several people, including the venerable and highly respected Lord Privy Seal John Russell, tried to warn him of the extraordinary risks he was running – especially with regard to his pursuit of Elizabeth. Any Englishman who sought to marry either of the Princesses would be asking for trouble, remarked Lord Russell judiciously, but Thomas Seymour who was so closely related to the King would be particularly vulnerable, for if one of his uncles married one of the heirs to his crown all Edward's worst suspicions would naturally be aroused. But it seems that Thomas Seymour, for whatever reason, believed himself to be fire-proof. The New Year came in and his career approached its all too predictable conclusion.

As evidence of his various 'disloyal practices' became more and more circumstantial, the faction headed by John Dudley, Earl of Warwick, which had been waiting patiently for the Seymour brothers to destroy one another, decided that the time had come to start applying pressure on the Duke of Somerset. The Protector made a last ditch attempt to save the situation by trying to send Thomas abroad, but it was too late. Lord Seymour of Sudeley had already tied a noose round his neck with the rope so generously paid out to him. He was arrested at Seymour Place on 17 January and the Council proceeded to the not very onerous task of rounding up his associates.

John Fowler of the Privy Chamber, who had carried notes and gifts of pocket money between the Lord Admiral and his nephew, John Harington, William Sherington, and Catherine Ashley and Thomas Parry, the Lady Elizabeth's governess and steward, were taken away for questioning, while Sir Robert Tyrwhit was despatched to Hatfield to extract a 'confession' from the Princess. Embarrassing details of those early morning romps at Chelsea were dragged into the open, even the shameful reason why Queen Catherine had had to send her away the previous Whitsun, but Elizabeth resolutely denied that she had ever for a moment contemplated marrying the Admiral, or anyone else, without the consent of the King and his Council. No trick of the interrogator's trade could trap her into any damaging admission and Tyrwhit was finally obliged to concede defeat: 'I . . . have practised with my lady's grace by all means and policies to cause her to confess more than she hath already done; wherein she doth plainly deny that she knoweth any more than she hath already opened to me.' Even at fifteen Elizabeth Tudor knew how to look after herself.

Jane Grey, of course, was not involved in any of these slightly discreditable proceedings. She had been hurriedly reclaimed by her parents after the Admiral's arrest and was now back at Bradgate out of harm's way, while Lord Dorset, in a series of self-exculpatory statements, was busy helping the government with its enquiries by explaining fluently how he had been 'seduced and aveugled', much against his better judgement, into co-operating with Seymour's plans for his daughter's future. Nor was there any lack of evidence from other sources about Tom Seymour's vaunting ambition, his want of brotherly love towards the Protector, and general treasonable intent. His ultimate fate was never in doubt but since Parliament was in session it was decided not even to accord him the courtesy of a trial. Instead, a bill of attainder – always a cheap and convenient method of dealing with troublemakers – was drawn up, and passed both Houses early in March. The Protector, though, as head of state, still had to take the final decision on his brother's life. There was silence for nearly a week and then the Council, nudged by the Earl of Warwick, sent a deputation to wait on the King to suggest that they be authorized to proceed without further troubling or molesting the Lord Protector or himself. Edward, who did not greatly care for either of his uncles, was quite willing to allow the law to take its course and Thomas Seymour went to keep his appointment with the executioner on Tower Hill on 20 March 1549.

One innocent and often forgotten victim of this unfortunate affair was little Mary Seymour, now just seven months old. At her father's special request she was to be confided to the care of the Duchess of Suffolk, once Queen Catherine Parr's dearest friend, but as an attainted traitor all the Admiral's property had been automatically confiscated, and my lady of Suffolk took a notably unsentimental attitude towards the penniless infant dumped on her at Grimsthorpe that spring. The Protector had apparently promised that suitable financial arrangements would be made but, despite frequent applications to the Somersets, these did not materialize and in July the Duchess wrote to her friend and near neighbour in Lincolnshire, young Mr William Cecil, now beginning his political career as the Protector's secretary, regarding her problem over the late Queen's child: 'for now she with a dozen persons lyeth all together at my charge, the continuance whereof will not bring me out of debt this year'. Her ladyship, it seems, was planning to transfer the charge to the Lord Marquess of Northampton, Catherine Parr's brother, but he had 'as weak a back for such a burden as I have. And he would receive her but more willingly if he might receive her with the appurtenances. Thus groweth matters; you must help us beggars and I pray you that you may.'

In fact, of course, neither the Duchess nor the Marquess could truthfully be described as poverty stricken and the cost of Mary Seymour's maintenance would not have beggared either of them, but they were understandably determined to try and make the Duke of Somerset at least share the burden of supporting his brother's child. A rather meagre amount of nursery equipment was sent up to Grimsthorpe: plate, including three silver pots, three goblets and a set of spoons; some bedding – quilts, pillows, a scarlet embroidered tester, bed curtains of crimson taffeta and 'two counter-points of imagery for the nurse's bed'. There were six pairs of sheets, but 'of little worth', some curtains and other soft furnishings, cushions, a chair, two 'wrought stools', a bedstead and two milch cows, which were to be bestowed as wedding presents upon two of the nursery maids. But still no money was forthcoming and in August the Duchess wrote again to Master Cecil complaining that 'the Queen's child . . . still doth lie at my house, with her company about her, wholly at my charges'. The company, too, were clamouring for their wages, 'whose voices my ears hardly bear, but my coffers much worse'.

Whether my lady of Suffolk ever won her campaign to extort an allowance from the Somersets is not recorded, but there are no more letters from her on the subject and no further mention of Mary Seymour. One authority says she died young, but there is a tradition, preserved by Agnes Strickland in her biography of Catherine Parr, that she survived to become the wife of Sir Edward Bushel, a gentleman in the household of James I's Queen, Anne of Denmark.

As it happened, his niece's affairs would have been one of the least of the Lord Protector's worries in 1549, which was a year marked by general and increasing popular discontent: due in part to economic hardship caused by rising prices and widespread unemployment, and in part to an angry reaction against the sweeping religious changes introduced since Henry VIII's death. This discontent presently erupted into two quite serious popular revolts, one in the West Country and the other in Norfolk, both of which aroused correspondingly serious alarm in the minds of the property-owning classes. Somerset's high-minded liberalism might have earned him the title of 'the Good Duke' among certain sections of the common people, but it did nothing to endear him to the nobility and gentry, who turned instead towards the Earl of Warwick – a reassuringly tough and capable soldier untroubled by any dangerous notions about the rights of the poor. Meanwhile, the Protector's growing sense of insecurity was being reflected in a show of arrogance and intolerance of opposition which had the effect of alienating his remaining support on the Council. His public image, too, had been fatally damaged by his brother's death – just as Warwick had known it would be. The Duke was a naturally reserved, undemonstrative character and his seemingly cold-blooded reaction to the Admiral's execution had repelled a lot of people who now, unfairly, stigmatized him as a fratricide, 'a blood-sucker and a ravenous wolf'.

In mid-September the Earl of Warwick returned triumphantly to London after putting down the rebellion in East Anglia. As well as being the hero of the hour, he now had a well-trained, experienced body of troops ready at his command and the moment was clearly ripe for a move to dislodge the Lord Protector from his shaky throne. Towards the end of the month the citizens were surprised to see those members of the Privy Council who followed Warwick's lead going armed about the streets with 'their servants likewise weaponed attending upon them in new liveries'. There was a lot of coming and going at the Earl's house in Holborn and rumours that the confederates were planning to seize the Tower went flying round the city. Somerset, who had been at Hampton Court with Edward, hurriedly retreated to the greater security of Windsor, but the London Lords, as Warwick's faction was known, pursued him there and on 10 October he was arrested and taken away under guard. The second *coup* of the reign was thus accomplished with a minimum of fuss and no bloodshed, and the Earl of Warwick became one of the six lords attendant on the King with all the power but wisely without the title of Lord Protector.

The new strong man was in his late forties with a commanding presence and magnetic personality, whose career to date had set a perfect pattern of the rise of the Tudor meritocracy. The Dudleys were a respectably old and well-connected baronial family, deriving their surname from the castle and town in the West Midlands, but John Dudley was descended from a junior branch of the tree and his father, Edmund, a clever lawyer with a first-class financial brain, had served Henry VII in the capacity of fiscal adviser rather too efficiently for his own good. One of the first acts of the young Henry VIII had been to offer Edmund Dudley, together with his colleague Richard Empson, as sacrifices on the altar of public opinion and both men were executed on charges of treason which the administration hardly bothered to pretend were other than contrived to appease the outraged taxpayers of England. John Dudley, who was nine years old at the time, became the ward of his father's friend Sir Edward Guildford, a prosperous land-owner in Kent and Sussex, and later married Guildford's daughter Jane.

A darkly handsome athletic boy, gifted, vital and aggressively ambitious, young John was clearly destined to be a high-flier and by the early 1520s was beginning to make a name for himself in military circles. He was knighted by the Duke of Suffolk during the brief and not very glorious French expedition of 1523, while his spectacular feats of courage and skill in the tiltyard earned him royal esteem and the sort of glamour usually associated with a sporting superstar. By the next decade he had progressed to more serious things, proving that he could offer a wide range of political, diplomatic and administrative talents in total commitment to the King's service. In 1533 he became Master of the Tower armoury in succession to his former guardian Edward Guildford. Other appointments, grants and offices followed, including the deputy governorship of Calais, and in 1542 John Dudley was entrusted with the responsible job of Warden of the Scottish Marches and raised to the peerage as Viscount Lisle – a title which devolved from his mother, born Elizabeth Grey, aunt of that other Elizabeth Grey once briefly betrothed to Charles Brandon and who had died in 1519. (It is always as well to remember that the Tudor ruling class comprised a very small and intricately inter-related society.) Throughout the remainder of the 1540s Lord Lisle, and later the Earl of Warwick, continued to enhance his reputation as a first-rank military commander in both the French and Scottish campaigns. In 1543 he was appointed Lord High Admiral, another prestigious post which he only reluctantly relinquished to the unworthy Seymour and resumed again in 1549, and his name of course had figured high on the magic list of executors of King Henry's will.

Throughout his career Warwick had made a careful study of Tudor psychology and he had been a particular favourite with the old King – especially after Charles Brandon's death. His plan in the winter of 1549–50 seems to have been to use the still malleable Edward as a screen behind which further to consolidate his own pos-ition and secure the future of his numerous sons. In private life the Earl was an affectionate family man with plenty of experience of bringing up boys, but he never made the mistake of treating Edward like a child. Instead he treated him as a king who should now be old enough to start taking an active part in the business of government, and Edward at just twelve years old naturally responded eagerly to this calculated form of flattery.

It often used to be said that Warwick took the pale consumptive little boy out of the stuffy atmosphere of the schoolroom and brought him into the fresh air. In fact, the King's timetable had always included provision for plenty of outdoor exercise and physical train-ing. The 1549 coup just happened to have coincided with that stage of his development when, growing bigger and stronger, he was able to participate more fully in such strenuous pursuits as tilting and riding at the ring. At the same time, it was undoubtedly an important part of the Earl's general strategy to bring him forward, introduce him to the more exciting aspects of kingship and ensure that he was kept happy and entertained. Edward still followed a regular study prog-ramme, but under his new guardian's tactful regime his horizons were widening daily and like a true Tudor he thoroughly appreciated all the treats and attentions being showered on him.

Up in Leicestershire his cousin Jane, who had now been back in the bosom of her family for nearly a year, had no such cause for cheerfulness. After her brief spell of comparative emancipation she was finding it understandably hard to readjust to the repressive atmosphere of home. But she did still have the solace of that inner world to which Catherine Parr had given her the key and which she was able to explore in the company of her much-loved tutor John Aylmer, a Norfolk man and protégé of Lord Dorset, who had sponsored the promising young scholar to university and subsequently employed him to instruct his daughters.

Some time in the late summer of 1550 Roger Ascham, formerly tutor to the Princess Elizabeth, who had been a member of the circle at Chelsea and Hanworth and a friend and admirer of both Aylmer and Lady Jane, came up to Bradgate to pay his respects to the family before leaving on a visit to Germany. He found the Dorsets, with all the ladies and gentlemen of the household, out hunting in the park – all that is except the Lady Jane, who was alone in her chamber reading Phaedon Platonis in Greek 'and that with as much delight as some gentlemen would read a merry tale in Boccaccio'.

When he asked why she was not out enjoying herself with her parents and their friends, Jane replied:

'I wisse [know] all their sport in the park is but a shadow to that pleasure that I find in Plato. Alas! good folk, they never felt what true pleasure meant.'

'And how came you, madam, to this deep knowledge of pleasure, and what did chiefly allure you into it,' enquired Ascham, 'seeing not many women, but very few men, have attained thereunto?'

'I will tell you,' exclaimed Lady Jane, 'and tell you a truth which perchance ye will marvel at. One of the greatest benefits that ever God gave me is that he sent me so sharp and severe parents and so gentle a schoolmaster. For when I am in presence of either Father or Mother, whether I speak, keep silence, sit, stand or go, eat, drink, be merry or sad, be sewing, playing, dancing, or doing anything else, I must do it as it were in such weight, measure and number, even so perfectly as God made the world; or else I am so sharply taunted, so cruelly threatened, yea presently sometimes with pinches, nips and bobs and other ways (which I will not name for the honour I bear them), so without measure misordered, that I think myself in hell, till time come that I must go to Mr Aylmer, who teacheth me so gently, so pleasantly, with such fair allurements to learning, that I think all the time nothing whiles I am with him. And when I am called from him, I fall on weeping because whatsoever I do else but learning is full of grief, trouble, fear and wholly misliking to me.'

Ascham was so impressed by this remarkable outburst that he remembered and later preserved it for posterity in his famous manual *The Scholemaster*, using it as another illustration of his constant plea for the adoption of more humane methods of educating the young. It has also been used by generations of Protestant propagandists to illustrate not only Lady Jane's praiseworthy application to her lessons, but her parents' shocking treatment of her.

Neither of these assumptions has been questioned until the present century, when Jane's biographers first began to wonder just why the Dorsets should have been so especially hard on their blameless eldest daughter. The answer is really that they were not – or at any rate not by the standards of an age which believed implicitly that to spare the rod was to spoil the child, and expected unquestioning, reverential obedience from child to parent as a matter of course. Jane was not yet, after all, the Protestant saint and martyr celebrated by John Foxe and his like. At thirteen she was a stubborn, unusually bright, articulate and opinionated adolescent who did not hesitate to inform sympathetic visitors that she regarded her parents' company as hellish and whose youthful self-righteousness must often have irritated her father and mother profoundly. Like all their set the Dorsets were compulsive gamblers, playing for high stakes at both cards and dice, a practice much deplored by the godly. James Haddon, resident chaplain at Bradgate, fought a losing battle with his employers over this issue, for although quite willing to forbid their domestics to play, my lord and his lady reserved the right to do as they pleased themselves among their own friends and turned quite nasty when Haddon insisted on delivering a public reproof from the pulpit. Needless to say the chaplain was supported by John Aylmer and by Lady Jane, which did nothing to lessen the tensions of family life.

Meanwhile, Jane's intellectual and spiritual horizons were continuing to widen and Roger Ascham, with fond recollections of the 'so divine a maid' he had found so engrossed in Plato, wrote urging her to: 'Go on thus, O best adorned virgin! to the honour of thy country, the delight of thy parents, thy own glory, the praise of thy preceptor, the comfort of thy relatives, and the admiration of all.' Ascham, feeling very much out of his element in a quarrelsome Germany preoccupied with rumours of wars and commotions, was frankly envious of Aylmer. 'Oh, happy Aylmer! to have such a scholar and to be her tutor. I congratulate both you who teach and she who learns.' He begged that Jane would keep her promise to write to him in Greek and added that if she were to take the trouble to write a letter in Greek to his friend John Sturm, the Protestant guru of Strasbourg University, neither she nor Aylmer would regret it.

Ascham is also sometimes credited with first bringing Jane to the notice of Henry Bullinger, chief pastor of the radical church of Zürich, but her connection with the Continental reformers was actually initiated in the spring of 1550 after a visit to Bradgate by John ab Ulmis, or Ulmer, an impecunious Swiss student who had come over to England to seek his fortune and contrived to ingratiate himself with the Marquess of Dorset, 'the protector of all students and the refuge of foreigners'. This noble personage, Ulmer informed Bullinger, had a daughter, 'pious and accomplished beyond what can be expressed', to whom he intended to present a copy of Bullinger's book on the holy marriage of Christians; and so began a correspondence conducted, naturally, in Latin which continued sporadically over the next two and a half years.

In July 1551, Jane is thanking Bullinger for sending her father and herself his treatise on Christian Perfection – that little volume of 'pure and unsophisticated religion' from which she is daily gathering the sweetest flowers, as out of a beautiful garden. Her most noble father, she adds hastily, would have written himself had he not been so busy with public affairs and will do so as soon as he has leisure from his other weighty engagements. As for Jane, she is now beginning to learn Hebrew and would be greatly obliged if Bullinger would advise her and 'point out some way and method of pursuing this study to the greatest advantage'.

Prompted by John ab Ulmis, who was determined to keep his toehold on Bradgate and the comforts to be enjoyed there, Aylmer and Haddon were now also writing to Bullinger. In a series of letters which forms a small part of the vast bulk of Bullinger's correspondence – the so-called Zürich Letters – they poured out their hopes and fears for their prize pupil and asked for help in the anxious task of guiding her along the paths of learning and piety and away from those temptations of the world, the flesh and the devil, so dangerous for any high-born young girl, but especially one who, for all her rare qualities and virtues, was just a little inclined to be headstrong.

At one time Aylmer seems to have been afraid that the teenage Jane was showing signs of taking too much interest in her appearance – dress, jewels and braidings of the hair – and spending too much time on her music. 'It now remains for me to request', he wrote solemnly to the middle-aged Swiss pastor, 'that you will instruct my pupil in your next letter as to what embellishment and adornment of person is becoming in young women professing godliness. . . . Moreover, I wish you would prescribe to her the length of time she may properly devote to the study of music.'

Communication between Leicestershire and Zürich was necessarily slow and further impeded by a shortage of reliable postmen, but in another letter from Jane to Bullinger, dated from Bradgate in the summer of 1552, she speaks of having received as much benefit from his excellent and truly divine precepts as from her daily reading of the best authors, and goes on with characteristic cautious honesty:

> You exhort me to embrace a genuine and sincere faith in Christ my Saviour. I will endeavour to satisfy you in this respect, as far as God shall enable me to do; but as I acknowledge faith to be his gift, I ought therefore only to promise so far as he may see fit to bestow it upon me. I shall not however cease to pray, with the apostles, that he may of his goodness daily increase it in me. . . . Do you, meanwhile, with your wonted kindness, make daily mention of me in your prayers. In the study of Hebrew I shall pursue that method which you so clearly point out.

Despite the gulf of age, sex and geographical distance which separated them, the curious penfriendship persisted. 'Were I indeed to extol you as truth requires', wrote Jane in the third and last of her surviving letters, 'I should need either the oratorical powers of Demosthenes, or the eloquence of Cicero.' She herself was fully conscious of her own inadequacy:

> In writing to you in this manner I have exhibited more boldness than prudence: but so great has been your kindness towards me, in condescending to write to me, a stranger, and in supplying the necessary instruction for the adornment of my understanding and the improvement of my mind, that I should justly appear chargeable with neglect and forgetfulness of duty, were I not to show myself mindful of you and of your deservings in every possible way. Besides, I entertain the hope that you will excuse the more than feminine boldness of me, who, girlish and unlearned as I am, presume to write to a man who is the father of learning; and that you will pardon that rudeness which has made me not hesitate to interrupt your more important occupations with my vain trifles. . . . My mind is fluctuating and undecided; for while I consider my age, sex and mediocrity, or rather infancy in learning, each of these things deters me from writing; but when I call to mind the eminence of your virtues, the celebrity of your character, and the magnitude of your favours towards me, the higher consideration yields to the inferior; a sense of what is becoming me gives way to your worth, and the respect which your merits demand usually prevails over all other considerations. . . . As long as I shall be permitted to live, I shall not cease to offer you my good wishes, to thank you for the kindness you have showed me, and to pray for your welfare. Farewell, learned sir. Your piety's most devoted,
> Jane Grey.

Much of the flattering interest in Jane shown by the European reformers stemmed from their hopes that she and Edward might yet make a match of it. 'A report has prevailed . . . that this most noble virgin is to be betrothed and given in marriage to the King's majesty', John Ulmer told Bullinger with more optimism than accuracy in May 1551. 'Oh, if that event should take place, how happy would be the union and how beneficial to the church!' But as the noble virgin approached her fourteenth birthday and with it the end of childhood, she was still unspoken for and negotiations were currently well advanced for the betrothal of the King of England to the French (and popish) princess Elisabeth.

Since the fall of ex-Protector Somerset nothing more had been heard of a possible marriage between the Lady Jane and his son, but there had been talk of an alliance between Henry Brandon, the young Duke of Suffolk – who, with his brother Charles, was now a student at St John's College, Cambridge – and Somerset's daughter Anne. The Duchess of Suffolk, who counted the Seymour family among her closest friends, would certainly have welcomed such a match: 'I know none this day living that I rather wish my son than she.' However, in a letter to William Cecil dated 9 May 1550, my lady of Suffolk displayed an unusual degree of broadmindedness on the subject of the arranged marriage in general, stating her belief that the young people concerned should be given the chance to mature, to get to know one another and to 'begin their love themselves' without forcing or being hurried into a decision which might lead to a lifetime of unhappiness.

> No unadvised bonds between a boy and a girl can give such assurance of good will as has been tried already. And now, they, marrying by our orders and without their consents, as they be yet without judgement to give such consent as ought to be given to matrimony, I cannot tell what more unkindness one of us might show one another, or wherein we might work more wickedly, than to bring our children into so miserable a state not to choose by their own likings.

Duchess Catherine's enlightened attitude was not shared by the Somersets (though, to be fair, the Duke was scarcely in a position just then to afford the luxury of very much enlightenment) and, on 3 June, Anne Seymour married the Earl of Warwick's eldest son another John Dudley – a union apparently intended to seal the patched-up reconciliation between their respective fathers. The wedding was a grand affair with a dinner, a dance and a tournament attended by the King, and on the following day another of Warwick's sons, Robert, married his sweetheart Amy Robsart of Wymondham in a ceremony also honoured by the royal presence.

Catherine Suffolk's reaction is not recorded, but she was probably not particularly surprised, or downcast. Her son was still full young and with his wealth, background and connections – not to mention his personal attributes – she cannot have anticipated much difficulty in finding him a suitable bride when the time came. Catherine, though, was in no hurry, being chiefly preoccupied with ensuring that both boys received the best possible Christian education, and she had taken a house in the village of Kingston, a few miles outside Cambridge, in order to be near them and keep a discreet eye on their progress.

The brothers were then living in college, as required by university regulations, and following the fairly rigorous routine of sixteenth-century undergraduates: getting up between four and five o'clock, spending an hour in chapel and then studying, either privately with their tutor or else attending 'common lectures'. Dinner was at ten and might be no more than a penny piece of beef stewed in a broth thickened with oatmeal and shared among four. The young Duke and his brother are likely to have fared rather better than this, but their tutor – he was the brilliant young don Thomas Wilson, author of *The Arte of Rhetorique* and later one of Queen Elizabeth's Secretaries of State – reports that his pupils were expected to read a chapter of the Greek testament during dinner and later to translate it into English. 'They then said Grace in turns; and did afterwards propound questions, either in philosophy or divinity; and so spent all the time at meat in Latin disputation.'

The Brandons apparently throve on this indigestible sounding mixture and they certainly got plenty of it. Again according to their tutor, they were always present at any public disputation – that is, a formal exercise in debating a thesis – and every morning read and translated a passage of Plato, to be presented at supper, the only other meal of the day, which was at five o'clock. After supper there would be more study or the intellectual athletics of 'reasonings in problems' until about nine or ten, when those students unable to afford a fire in their lodgings would go for a walk or run up and down for half an hour to get warm before going to bed.

Thomas Wilson could never speak highly enough of the attainments, 'towardness' and general promise shown by Henry, Duke of Suffolk, and his brother. Henry Brandon's nature was such 'that he thought himself best when he was among the wisest, and yet contemned none but thankfully used all, gentle in behaviour without childishness, stout of stomach without all pride, bold without all wariness and friendly without good advisement'. Lord Charles, 'being not so ripe in years, was not so grave in look, rather cheerful than sad, rather quick than ancient; but yet, if his brother were set aside not one that went beyond him'. Even allowing for Wilson's natural desire to flatter noble and influential patrons, there seems little reason to doubt that these were agreeable, intelligent, serious-minded boys who had been fortunate enough to inherit their mother's brains and personality along with their father's good looks and easy-going charm.

Disaster struck the family in July 1551, when the university and town of Cambridge were visited by an outbreak of the dreaded sweating sickness. This mysterious disease, often fatal within hours, had first appeared in England in 1485, brought, so it was said, by the French mercenaries who accompanied Henry VII from Brittany, and remained a scourge throughout the first half of the Tudor century, when it suddenly vanished or mutated. The 'sweat' which, with its accompanying symptoms of chills, tremors, raging fever, severe headache, backache and vomiting, sounds like a virulent form of influenza but was probably caused by a virus unconnected with any modern strain, was also notorious for the terrifying speed of its onset – a man could sit down to dinner apparently in the best of health and be dead by suppertime. Nor was it any respecter of persons. On the contrary, the comfortable classes seem to have been most at risk. The moment the contagion was reported in the town, therefore, the Brandon boys were hurried away to Buckden – that same isolated house where once their father had gone so reluctantly to harass Catherine of Aragon – but it was already too late. The sixteen-year-old Duke sickened and died almost immediately and by the time his distraught mother had reached him, Lord Charles, too, was dying.

Catherine of Suffolk retired alone to Grimsthorpe while she struggled to come to terms with her grief and the inscrutable will of a deity who could take both her beautiful sons from her within the space of a single day. This battle had to be won if her life was to retain any meaning but it was early September before she was able to write to William Cecil in a mood of Christian resignation.

> I give God thanks, good Master Cecil, for all his benefits which it hath pleased him to heap upon me; and truly I take this last (and to the first sight most sharp and bitter) punishment not for the least of his benefits, inasmuch as I have never been so well taught by any other before to know his power, his love and mercy, mine own weakness and that wretched state that without him I should endure here.

The Duchess went on to say that although she would like to see her old friends she had to confess herself 'no better than flesh' and could not yet trust herself to behold them 'without some parts of those vile dregs of Adam to seem sorry for that whereof I know I ought rather to rejoice'.

In the first traumatic shock of her sons' deaths Catherine had felt herself quite unable to cope with funeral arrangements and the boys were buried very quietly and privately at Buckden. It was not until nearly the end of September that the eulogies were made, the epitaphs written and the banners and escutcheons of arms set up over the tomb in Buckden church. The Duchess endowed four scholarships at St John's in memory of those two model students and the London funeral furnisher Henry Machyn commented in his Diary that 'it was great pity of their death, and it had pleased God, of so noble a stock they were, for there is no more left of them'.

5

The King's Device

For lack of issue male of my body to the issue male coming of the issue female. . . . To the Lady Frances' heirs male . . . to the Lady Jane's [and her] heirs male.

The death of her two half-brothers left Frances Dorset sole surviving heir to the Brandon estates. The Brandon dukedom of Suffolk had become extinct but on 4 October 1551 a new peerage of the same title was conferred on the Marquess of Dorset *jure uxoris*, that is, in right of his wife. Henry Grey was not the only new duke at court that autumn. After two years in power the Earl of Warwick felt sufficiently secure to petition the King on his own account and on 11 October was created Duke of Northumberland – thus becoming the first Englishman having no ties of blood or marriage with the royal house ever to bear a ducal title.

The Greys and the Dudleys had both received their promotion by the time Mary of Guise, mother of Mary Queen of Scots and regent of Scotland, paid a visit to the English court on her way home from a protracted stay with her young daughter in France. The Scottish Queen Regent was escorted in style from Portsmouth to Hampton Court, where she spent two nights at the beginning of November, and among those members of the royal family summoned to meet her were the new Duke and Duchess of Suffolk with their fourteen-year-old daughter Jane, who was making what amounted to her début in grown-up circles.

Jane's cousins, the Ladies Mary and Elizabeth, were not present at the state banquet given for Mary of Guise, and indeed Edward's half-sisters played hardly any part in the life of his court. Mary Tudor, now in her mid-thirties and still unmarried, had suffered bitterly as a result of her parents' divorce and still bore the scars of those sufferings. Forcibly separated from her much loved mother, viciously humiliated by her father's second wife and finally bullied by her father into signing a document repudiating the Bishop of Rome's 'pretended authority' and acknowledging her own illegitimacy, she had, not surprisingly, developed into a nervous, unhappy, dyspeptic woman with little taste for socializing and, in any case, in the autumn of 1551 the unfortunate Princess was once more at loggerheads with the authorities over her religious beliefs.

Trouble had begun in the spring of 1549 when Thomas Cranmer's *Book of Common Prayer*, replacing the Latin mass with a new-fangled Anglican service of communion, was introduced as the only legal order of service in the Church of England. Faced with the threatened proscription of the Catholic faith which was her only consolation, Mary had appealed to her powerful kinsman the Holy Roman Emperor himself, and Charles had responded by demanding a written undertaking from the Duke of Somerset that his cousin would be allowed to continue to practise her religion unmolested. This was refused, but Somerset did reluctantly concede that Mary might do as she thought best in the privacy of her own house until such time as the King came of age. But then came the October coup and early in 1550 Mary was warned that her breathing space would soon be over. During that summer a warrant was issued for the arrest of one of her chaplains and by the autumn the battle of the Lady Mary's mass was fairly joined, the new government maintaining that any promises made by the former Lord Protector had been strictly temporary and provisional and applied only to Mary herself; certainly the fifty-odd members of her household staff could claim no privilege and must obey the King's laws or suffer the consequences. By the following January the King himself had taken a hand in the affair, adding a personal postscript to one of the Council's hectoring letters. 'Truly, sister,' he wrote,

> I will not say more and worse things, because my duty would compel me to use harsher and angrier words. But this I will say with certain intention, that I will see my laws strictly obeyed, and those who break them shall be watched and denounced, even as some are ready to trouble my subjects by their obstinate resistance.

This unequivocal statement of the King's position came to Mary as a bitter revelation of the gulf which yawned between them. Until now she had been able to comfort herself with the thought that her little brother was still a helpless tool in the hands of men like John Dudley and his cronies – that it was they, not he, who were her enemies. But in Edward's letter the echo of their father's voice was too unmistakable to be denied. Mary had been avoiding the court deliberately, keeping her occasional visits as brief and as private as possible for fear that she would somehow be tricked or forced into attending one of the new services and so appear to be lending her countenance to the hated New Religion. But in March 1551 she did go up to town to try the effect of a plea for brotherly tolerance and consideration. 'The lady Mary my sister came to me at Westminster . . .' recorded Edward with characteristic terseness,

> where it was declared how long I had suffered her mass *against my will* [he later crossed out these words] in hope of her reconciliation, and how now . . . except I saw some short amendment, I could not bear it. She answered that her soul was God's and her faith she would not change, nor dissemble her opinion with contrary doings. It was said I constrained not her faith, but willed her as a subject to obey.

The King took his responsibilities as the keeper of his people's conscience with great seriousness, and yet it seems likely that the question of his sister's awkward conscience did not at this time worry him too extremely. Mary, by contemporary standards, was already middle-aged. To Edward at thirteen, she must have seemed already old – she was, after all, more than old enough to be his mother – and her health was known to be poor. The King, a notably unsentimental child, may well have reflected that the problem would surely soon go away of its own accord and the indications are that, left to himself, he would have been prepared, reluctantly, to let the matter rest.

But unhappily for the Princess, she was now once again heiress presumptive and her actions and beliefs consequently held political significance. John Dudley had found it expedient to form an alliance with the extreme radical wing of the Protestant party, which stood far to the left of moderates like Archbishop Cranmer. At the same time, he knew that the conservative bulk of the English people disliked the noisy violence of the militant reformers and their spoilation of the parish churches, that the silent majority agreed in their hearts with the Lady Mary when she wished aloud that everything could have remained as it was at the time of her father's death. Her example and her influence were important and so, as once before in her life, it was necessary to compel her submission. And, as once before, Mary finally surrendered. By the end of the year, mass was no longer being celebrated in her private chapel where, of course, any of her neighbours who wished to come and worship in the old familiar way had always been welcome. Mary herself continued to seek the consolations of her religion, but in fear and secrecy behind the locked doors of her own apartments.

Edward's relations with his younger sister were uncomplicated by theological divergences. On the contrary, Elizabeth was always 'most honourably received' when she came to court, in order, reported the Imperial ambassador, 'to show the people how much glory belongs to her who has embraced the new religion and is become a very great lady'. Nevertheless, the great lady, determined as far as possible to avoid involvement with any factional interests, kept her public appearances to a minimum, and her failure to greet Mary of Guise was probably not unconnected with the fact that the French were already insinuating that, as the late King's bastard, she had no right to her place in the succession. Since his domestic policies had brought him into collision with the Emperor, the Duke of Northumberland had been forced to cultivate the French, and Elizabeth would naturally have been unwilling to run the risk of a snub. She had therefore stayed at home, ostentatiously ignoring the interest in French fashions which the visit had reawakened among her contemporaries. Elizabeth at this time affected a severely plain style of dress which had won her golden opinions from the reforming party, and John Aylmer commented approvingly on her refusal to alter any of her 'maiden shamefastness' while all the other ladies were going about 'dressed and painted like peacocks'.

Elizabeth was, of course, setting a fashion of her own to be copied by other high-born Protestant maidens. When Jane Grey received a present from Mary of a dress of 'tinsel cloth of gold and velvet, laid on with parchment lace of gold', she is said to have complained:

'What shall I do with it?'

'Marry, wear it!' answered one of her ladies in surprise.

'Nay,' said Jane, never noted for her tact, 'that were a shame to follow my Lady Mary against God's word, and leave my Lady Elizabeth, which followeth God's word.'

In spite of the religious divide, however, there was far more in the way of regular friendly intercourse between the Suffolks and the Lady Mary than with Elizabeth. Mary and Frances Grey were very much of an age, sharing much the same childhood memories and social background, and they saw quite a lot of one another. For instance, it is recorded that in November 1551 Frances and all three of her daughters stayed with Mary for several weeks at the Princess's town house, the former Priory of St John of Jerusalem at Clerkenwell, and this may have been the occasion when Mary gave 'my cousin Frances' a pair of beads (that is, a rosary) of crystal trimmed with a tassel of goldsmith's work, and 'to my cousin Jane' a necklace set with small rubies and pearls, a suitable trinket for a young girl.

The Duke and Duchess, their three daughters and the Duke's two younger brothers, Lord Thomas and Lord John Grey, spent that Christmas at Tylsey, or Tilty, in Essex, home of the Willoughbys of Woollaton. The Duke's aunt, Lady Anne Grey, had married Sir Henry Willoughby and on their deaths Suffolk had become the guardian of their children. Also present, despite her recent bereavement, was Catherine, now strictly speaking the Dowager Duchess of Suffolk, although she was never referred to as such but simply as 'my lady of Suffolk'. Open house was kept at Tylsey throughout the festive season, with lavish quantities of food and drink laid on for all the neighbourhood, plus entertainment by tumblers, jugglers and singing boys – the local talent being supplemented by the Earl of Oxford's company of professional actors.

James Haddon, needless to say, disapproved profoundly of these mummeries, which seemed to him to serve the devil by imitating a pagan saturnalia, and he lamented the manner in which uninstructed country folk regarded it as almost a part of their religion to make merry after this unwholesome fashion 'on account of the birth of our Lord'. The nobility, it was true, were beginning to understand that it was not part of their duty so to conduct themselves:

> yet partly from the force of habit, and a desire not to appear stupid, and not good fellows as they call it, but partly and principally, as I think, from their not having yet so far advanced as to be able perfectly to hate the garment spotted by the flesh . . . they have no settled intention, much less any desire, to conquer and crucify themselves.

The godly Dr Haddon discoursed long-windedly on this head in a letter to Henry Bullinger, but appears to have had little or no success in persuading his own unregenerate flock to crucify themselves by giving up their accustomed Christmas revels. The party at Tylsey did not break up until nearly the end of January, when the Suffolks went on to visit the Duke's sister, Lady Audley, at nearby Walden.

All this junketing about, though, had been rather too much for the Lady Jane, for in February John Ulmer was reporting to Zürich that she had but recently recovered from 'a severe and dangerous illness'. But she was still engrossed in scholarly pursuits and was currently engaged in 'some extraordinary production which will very soon be brought to light'. Ulmer does not give any further details but perhaps the extraordinary production was connected with the recent discovery of 'a great treasure of valuable books: Basil on Isaiah and the Psalms in Greek . . . Chrysostom on the gospels in Greek; the whole of Proclus; the Platonists etc.', which had apparently been found in some parcels of books acquired for the Duke of Suffolk from an Italian dealer. Jane was also still corresponding with Bullinger and other German-Swiss doctors of the so-called Genevan, or Calvinist sect, and in the spring of 1552 sent a present of a pair of gloves to Bullinger's wife. But although her enthusiasm remained as strong as ever, she had less time to devote to her academic interests. Her parents had never objected to these – they were fashionable and therefore desirable. All the same, now that Lady Jane was growing up they expected her to take her place in society and not spend all day immured in the study. Learning and piety were all very well, but the Suffolks had certainly not abandoned their hopes of exploiting their daughter's dynastic potential by seeing her make a great marriage.

During that summer of her fifteenth year she went with her mother and father to stay with the Princess Mary at Newhall Boreham in Essex, Mary's favourite country house. It was there, according to the story handed down by Protestant tradition, that Jane once more displayed the sort of fearless honesty – or offensive bigotry, according to point of view – not calculated to endear her to her more politic elders. She was, so the story goes, walking through the chapel at Newhall with Lady Wharton, the wife of one of Mary's officers and, naturally, a devout Roman Catholic.

Seeing her companion curtsy to the altar, where the Host was exposed, Jane enquired guilelessly if the Lady Mary had come in.

'No,' answered Lady Wharton, 'I made my curtsy to Him that made us all.'

'Why,' said Jane, 'how can that be, when the baker made him?'

This exchange was, of course, promptly repeated back to Mary who 'never after loved the Lady Jane as she had before'. But the argument over the Real Presence in the Eucharist – whether the bread and wine miraculously assumed the substance of Christ's body and blood at the moment of consecration, or whether they were merely the hallowed symbols of the communicant's means of redemption – lay at the very heart of the ideological conflict dividing Catholic and Protestant. In Jane Grey's world it was a fundamental point of principle for which thousands of committed men and women were ready to, and did, suffer martyrdom, and in this context her reaction to the tacit challenge offered by Anne Wharton was perfectly in character.

The year 1552 saw the introduction of the second English prayer book, in which the words of the administration of communion now ran uncompromisingly: 'Take and eat this in remembrance that Christ died for thee, and feed on him in thy heart by faith with thanksgiving.' The communion tables, already replacing the altars in parish churches, were now to be 'had down into the body of the church . . . and set in the mid-aisle among the people'. The use of the old priestly vestments associated with the celebration of mass was no longer permissible; even the act of kneeling to receive the sacrament became hedged about with anxious denials that any form of adoration was intended. The result of these latest innovations was to bring the English Church still further into line with the austere Genevan or Calvinist model so admired by Lady Jane Grey and her mentors, but whether this trend would be maintained obviously depended very largely on the King who, if he survived, would soon be casting off the tutelage of his Council.

If he survived. . . . Edward was not the big, strong-looking boy his father had been and his fair colouring and slender physique promoted an impression of fragility, encouraging the emissaries of those Catholic powers alarmed by evidence of his increasingly belligerent Protestantism to drop hopeful hints in their letters home that the King of England was not likely to live long. In fact, at fourteen Edward seemed healthy enough, spending every spare moment on the tennis court, in the tiltyard or shooting at the butts. The Spanish ambassador reported that the King was beginning to exercise himself in the use of arms and enjoyed it heartily. The French ambassador complimented him on the dexterity of his sword-play, declaring that his majesty had 'borne himself right well' and receiving the modest reply from Edward that it was a small beginning, but as time passed he hoped to do his duty better.

Then, on 2 April 1552, the King went down with a high temperature and a rash. He himself recorded: 'I fell sike of the mesels and the smallpokkes.' This would surely have been a lethal combination and Edward's illness was probably a sharp attack of measles. He made a good recovery and was well enough to attend a St George's Day service at Westminster Abbey, wearing his Garter robes. At the end of the month the court moved to Greenwich, where the King reviewed his men-at-arms on Blackheath and ran at the rings with the lords and knights in his company. On 27 June, apparently in his usual health and spirits, he set out on the first stage of an ambitious progress through the south and west which took him to Portsmouth, Southampton, the New Forest, Salisbury and home by way of Winchester, Newbury and Reading.

The progress was a triumphant personal success for the king, who had never travelled so far afield before and thoroughly enjoyed himself. But the programme was an exhausting one and people noticed that he was looking pale and thin. That unlucky bout of measles, coming just at the most dangerous age for Tudor boys and followed by a strenuous summer, had fatally weakened him and by the time he got back to Windsor in mid-September tuberculosis was already established. By Christmas it was obvious that he was far from well and a more than usually elaborate round of festivities was arranged to distract attention from this disturbing fact. When Mary came to London early in February, Edward was running a fever and it was three days before he was able to see her. The Emperor's ambassador, Jehan de Scheyfve, reported that the Princess was received with noticeably greater attention and courtesy that on previous occasions, the Duke of Northumberland himself going down to the outer gates of the Palace of Westminster to welcome her. No one had yet admitted that there was anything seriously wrong with the King, but the significance of the new respect being shown to his heir was unmistakable. Edward was still in bed and Mary sat beside him while they chatted amicably about safe subjects. The thorny topic of religion was not mentioned.

Edward stayed in his room for the rest of the month. He seemed, wrote de Scheyfve, 'to be sensitive to the slightest indisposition or change' and suffered a good deal when the fever was on him. In March he rallied temporarily, enough to be able to open the new session of Parliament, although the Lords and Commons had to go to him and a much curtailed ceremony was performed within the precincts of the palace. The doctors, who remained in constant attendance, made reassuring noises, but those courtiers who had not seen the King since Christmas were horrified by the change in him. He had become thin to the point of emaciation and his left shoulder seemed higher than his right. On 11 April he was moved back to Greenwich, always his favourite residence, but de Scheyfve wrote that he was no better and the ambassador heard from 'a trustworthy source' that his sputum was 'sometimes coloured a greenish yellow and black, sometimes pink, like the colour of blood'. A month later de Scheyfve had another gruesome bulletin for the Emperor: 'The physicians are now all agreed that he [Edward] is suffering from a suppurating tumour on the lung. . . . He is beginning to break out in ulcers; he is vexed by a harsh, continuous cough, his body is dry and burning, his belly is swollen, he has a slow fever upon him that never leaves him.' The government was still making every effort to conceal the gravity of the King's condition from the public but, of course, it was impossible to stop the rumours spreading. Everyone knew that Northumberland's power would end with Edward's death and, since no one believed the Duke would give up without a struggle, the court and city seethed with excited speculation.

Northumberland himself appears to have been gripped by a curious lethargy during the early months of 1553. He was no longer a young man. He seemed tired, depressed and out of sorts and spoke of his desire for retirement after a long life of service. But there could be no retirement for a man in John Dudley's place – having once mounted the tiger of ambition there was no way to go but on, for the sake of his family if for no other reason, and John Dudley was nothing if not a devoted husband and father.

It is impossible to be certain when he finally came to terms with the fact that the King was dying, and the inference is that he clung to a desperate hope of his recovery for far longer than was reasonable. By early May, however, at the latest the future had had to be faced, the options weighed. These were limited. If Henry VIII's will were followed and Mary succeeded, the best the Duke could hope for would be total political extinction; the worst (and most likely) bodily extinction at the headsman's hands – he had made too many bitter enemies among the Catholics and other right-wingers who would surround the new Queen. Elizabeth, now in her twentieth year and uncommitted except, perhaps, to the more moderate Protestants, looked a more hopeful prospect. Jehan de Scheyfve believed for a time that Northumberland intended to use her as his instrument in furthering the pretensions of the house of Dudley, either by marrying her to his eldest son, after first causing him to divorce his wife, or else 'that he might find it expedient to get rid of his own wife and marry the said Elizabeth himself'. But the Duke had no time to waste on such elaborate manoeuvres and, in any case, was well enough acquainted with Elizabeth Tudor to know that she would be nobody's cat's-paw. The Princess had always been careful to keep on friendly terms with Northumberland, but there is absolutely no evidence that she ever even considered linking her fortunes with him, or indeed that he ever approached her on the subject. There remained the Suffolk girls.

The previous year Northumberland had proposed his only remaining unmarried son, Guildford, as a match for Margaret Clifford, daughter of Eleanor Brandon, but had been turned down by the young lady's father. Now, on a date at the end of April or beginning of May 1553, he announced the betrothal of Guildford and Jane Grey. Lady Jane, it seems, had also attempted to reject Guildford but had been forced to consent to the marriage 'by the urgency of her mother and the violence of her father' who, between them, set on her with a mixture of verbal and physical abuse.

The authority for this incident, faithfully and circumstantially retailed by all Jane's biographers, is a contemporary though second-hand report by two Italians, one of whom, Raviglio Rosso, visited England the following year on a courtesy mission from the Duke of

Ferrara, while the other was Federigo Baoardo, or Badoer, resident Venetian ambassador at the court of Charles V in Brussels. The Italians, especially the Venetians, were usually well informed, but they were also great gossips and both these accounts are necessarily based on gossip and hearsay – not that there is anything inherently improbable about the story if Jane really did attempt to defy her parents over her marriage. Once the Suffolks had dreamt of seeing their eldest daughter become Queen Consort of England. Now that an unimaginably greater prize was being dangled before them they would certainly have dealt ruthlessly with any opposition.

The reason given for Jane's alleged recalcitrance is that she considered herself already contracted to Edward Seymour Earl of Hertford, an attractive and serious-minded youth but whose eligibility had died with his father – the Protector Somerset having been finally liquidated in the usual manner in February 1552. She is also said to have disliked Guildford Dudley, then about seventeen or eighteen years old. As the youngest of a large family and reputedly his mother's favourite, Guildford may have been a little spoilt. A handsome boy, he may also have been a little conceited – though all the Dudleys were good-looking. Apart from this, there seems to have been nothing very serious known against him; and marriage, as Jane was well aware, offered the only possible avenue of escape from the tyranny of home. Her recoil was, therefore, more likely motivated by fear and distrust of her prospective father-in-law than any special repugnance for her prospective husband. It was noticeable that outside his immediate family circle most people, even his political allies, disliked and distrusted John Dudley, Duke of Northumberland.

Whatever the truth of the matter, any rebellion was quickly suppressed and thereafter Jane's attitude towards her fiancé appeared correct, if unenthusiastic. Despite the convention that there should at least be some 'liking' between an engaged couple, no one ever pretended that this was anything but an alliance cold-bloodedly arranged for the political, financial and dynastic advantage of the families concerned. (William Cecil heard that the Marchioness of Northampton, wife of Catherine Parr's brother, had been employed as go-between.) Arrangements for two other significant family alliances were also concluded at this time. Catherine Grey, now thirteen, was to be betrothed to Lord Herbert, the Earl of Pembroke's heir, and a Dudley daughter, another Catherine, to Lord Hastings, son of the Earl of Huntingdon and doubly descended from the Plantagenet stock. Thus Northumberland and Suffolk hoped to secure the future support of Pembroke and Huntingdon – both influential figures on the political scene. Thus, too, the Dudleys had finally succeeded in breaking into the magic circle of royal kinship.

Lady Jane was married on 25 May 1553 at Durham House, the Duke of Northumberland's London residence, one of the great riverside mansions lying between Temple Bar and Charing Cross – the millionaire's row of Tudor London. It was, in fact, a triple wedding, creating a triple-strength line of defence, for Catherine Grey was married on the same day to the young Lord Herbert and Catherine Dudley to Henry Hastings. In spite of the speed with which the occasion had had to be organized, every effort was made to create an atmosphere of relaxed grandeur. Warrants had been despatched to the Master of the Wardrobe authorizing him to issue all manner of rich stuffs and jewels from the royal store to provide wedding finery for the three brides, their mothers and for Lord Guildford Dudley – stuff which included 'certain parcels of cloth of gold and silver' once, ironically enough, the property of the Duke and Duchess of Somerset. And, says Raviglio Rosso, the festivities were attended by 'a great concourse of the principal persons of the kingdom'.

There were, however, some notable absentees. Neither of the Princesses had been invited and, although it had been announced that the king would be present, Edward was in no condition now to grace any more Dudley weddings. Nor were either the French or the Imperial ambassadors among those summoned to Durham House on that Whitsunday to see Jane Grey, her hair braided with pearls, being led, literally, as a sacrifice to the altar. This is not to say that the two major European powers were not taking a close interest in the progress of events in London: on the contrary. Claude de l'Aubespine, a secretary often employed by the French king on high level diplomatic missions, had recently arrived in England and despite the secrecy which surrounded his visit de Scheyfve heard that he had come to offer his master's services to the Duke of Northumberland in the event of King Edward's death. De Scheyfve also believed that the French intended to try and prevent Mary from succeeding her brother.

Certainly the French had good reasons for preferring to keep the princess off the English throne – as the Emperor's cousin she would naturally take her country back into the Imperial camp – and in the early 1550s the French happened to be particularly well placed for intervention in English affairs. As a result of gross mishandling of Scottish affairs by both the late King and the Protector Somerset, the 'Auld Alliance' between France and Scotland had been revived and refurbished to the extent that Scotland was currently being governed very much as a province of France, with a strong French military presence established on the other side of England's vulnerable land frontier. Henri II, the new King of France, also held a potential ace in the international poker game in the person of the little Queen of Scotland, now a pretty and promising ten-year-old being brought up at his court as the future wife of his son and heir the dauphin François. Mary Stewart might have been arbitrarily excluded from her place in the English succession by the terms of Henry VIII's will; but by all the commonly accepted laws of primogeniture her claim was unquestionably superior to that of her Suffolk cousins and, in the eyes of all orthodox Catholics, to that of her cousin Elizabeth who, as everyone knew, was a bastard born in the lifetime of King Henry's first wife. A case could also be made out to show that the Queen of Scots' claim was superior to that of her cousin Mary Tudor, on whose legitimacy such grave doubts had been cast at the time of the great Divorce. Their father's will regardless, the point could reasonably be made that both the Tudor sisters were still illegitimate by English Act of Parliament. The situation, in short, fairly bristled with nice points of constitutional and canon law and, for the French, was fraught with interesting possibilities – always provided, of course, that the Duke of Northumberland could organize another successful *coup d'état.*

Jane Grey's marriage had signalled the opening moves in the campaign to set aside the established line of the succession, but for some months before this King Edward had been pondering ways and means of depriving his elder sister of her birthright. Edward's motives appear to have been quite straightforwardly ideological. He had, after all, been trained in the purest Cambridge school of advanced intellectual and evangelical Protestantism and believed just as rigidly as Mary did that his was the only way of salvation for both himself and his people, for whose salvation he had always been taught he was personally responsible under God. Conviction of this kind naturally overrode all considerations of earthly justice and legality, and as soon as he began to realize that he might not live to provide heirs of his own body, Edward knew that if he valued his immortal soul he must take every precaution to guard against the overthrow of the Protestant revolution.

In his famous Device for the Succession, a draft memorandum written in his own hand probably at the beginning of 1553, possibly even earlier, he had already fixed on the Suffolk line, bequeathing the throne first to the Lady Frances's (that is, the Duchess of Suffolk's) notional 'heires masles', then to the Lady Jane's 'heires masles' and so on through the family. But as his condition deteriorated and the fact had to be faced that neither his aunt Frances nor any of his so regrettably female cousins were going to produce heirs male in the foreseeable future, the king made a simple but radical change to his Device, leaving the throne to 'the Lady Jane *and* her heires masles'.

Why he chose to exclude his Protestant sister, to whom he was supposedly so attached, as well as his Catholic one we do not know. He may have felt it would be inequitable and impractical to deprive one of the princesses and not the other; he may have feared that Elizabeth, however good her intentions, might find herself obliged to marry some Catholic prince; or he may have sensed that she would have rejected any bequest based on such obvious injustice. The official reasons as set out in the Letters Patent for the Limitation of the Crown – the Device in its final form – were that the Ladies Mary and Elizabeth were 'illegitimate and not lawfully begotten', related to the king by half-blood only and therefore not entitled to succeed him, and liable to marry foreign husbands who would take control of the government and thus 'tend to the utter subversion of the commonwealth of this our realm'. The question of whether or not either or both of Henry VIII's daughters could properly be regarded as having been born in wedlock was and remains debatable. The other grounds alleged for their exclusion from the succession were constitutionally merely frivolous. In any case, no will, Device or Letters Patent issued by Edward could have any validity in law as long as the 1544 Act of Succession remained on the Statute Book. But for the dying King, for the Duke of Northumberland, now committed beyond the point of no return, for the King of France waiting hopefully in the wings, the legality of the scheme mattered very much less than the speed and efficiency with which it could be put into practice.

First it was necessary to carry the Privy Council, the judiciary and the bishops, and the struggle went on through most of that tense, uneasy month of June. The strongest opposition came from the Lord Chief Justice, Sir Edward Montague, who pointed out that without another Act of Parliament the King had no power to alter his father's testamentary dispositions, and from Archbishop Cranmer, whose conscience troubled him deeply. Montague, to his credit, put up a spirited fight but he was an elderly man conditioned to obey royal commands and frightened of Northumberland who, in a fit of rage, had called him a traitor before all the Council and said 'that in the quarrel of that matter he would fight in his shirt with any man living'. What with John Dudley's bullying and the King ordering him 'with sharp words and angry countenance' to obey on his allegiance, small wonder that he gave in and agreed to draw up the necessary documents.

The Limitation of the Crown passed the Great Seal on 21 June and by the end of the month it had been endorsed, more or less reluctantly, by the Lord Chancellor, the Privy Councillors, twenty-two peers of the realm, the Lord Mayor of London, the aldermen and sheriffs of Middlesex, Surrey and Kent, the officers of the royal household, the Secretaries of State (even that super-cautious individual William Cecil had been obliged to add his signature), the judges and the bishops, headed by Thomas Cranmer. More than anything else the compassionate Archbishop wanted to see his much loved godson die in peace – happy in the belief that he had ensured the continuance of the true Protestant religion.

Edward, who was suffering as much if not more from the remedies being inflicted on him as from his disease, had now taken no solid food for nearly three weeks; his sputum was black, fetid and stinking; his fingers and toes were becoming gangrenous, and the boy born in such joy and wondrous hope fifteen years and nine months earlier longed only for death. Release came in the early evening of Thursday 6 July, when the last Tudor King died in the arms of his friend Henry Sidney.

The six weeks which had passed since her marriage had not been happy ones for Lady Jane Dudley and she seems to have developed such an aversion to her husband's family that even her own mother's company was preferable. Apparently she had been promised that she could continue to live at home after the wedding and immediately after the ceremony had gone back first to Suffolk Place at Westminster and then to her parents' new suburban residence, converted from the former Carthusian monastery on the south bank of the river Thames at Sheen. But the Duchess of Northumberland, who did not get on with the Duchess of Suffolk, soon became impatient with this foolishness. She told Jane that the King was dying and that she must hold herself in readiness for a summons at any moment because he had made her the heir to his dominions.

According to Jane's own account, this was the first she had heard of the seriousness of Edward's illness and the news, flung at her without warning, caused her the greatest stupefaction and agitation of spirit, but she put it down to 'boasting' and an excuse to separate her from her mother. Being Jane, she probably said as much, for the result was a furious quarrel, with the Duchess of Northumberland accusing the Duchess of Suffolk of deliberately trying to keep the newly-weds apart and insisting that whatever happened Jane's place was with her husband. This argument was unanswerable and Jane was forced to join Guildford at Durham House where, possibly, the marriage was consummated.

But the reluctant bride stayed only a few days with her in-laws. She had become ill – probably some form of dysentery or summer complaint aggravated by nervous strain – and, with a surprising lack of logic, was convinced that the Dudleys were poisoning her. In fact, of course, her health and well-being were crucial to the Dudleys just then, and they sent her out to Chelsea, with its happy memories of Queen Catherine Parr, to rest and recuperate. She was still there on the afternoon of 9 July when her sister-in-law, Northumberland's eldest daughter Mary Sidney, came to fetch her to go to Syon House, another former convent on the banks of the Thames, which had been commandeered by the Duke.

At Syon, Jane found her parents, her husband, her mother-in-law, the Marquess of Northampton, the Earls of Arundel, Huntington and Pembroke, and the Duke of Northumberland, in his capacity of President of the Council. These distinguished personages greeted her with 'unwonted caresses and pleasantness' and, to her acute embarrassment, proceeded to kneel before her and do her reverences which she considered most unsuitable to her estate. Her father-in-law then broke the news of Edward's death, declaring that 'everyone had reason to rejoice in the virtuous life he had led and the good death he had died' and drawing comfort from the fact that at the end of his life he had taken such good care of his kingdom. The exact nature of his late Majesty's care was now officially disclosed to his heiress, as Northumberland announced the terms of the King's Device, how he had decided for good and sufficient reasons that neither of his sisters was worthy to succeed him and how – 'he being in every way able to disinherit them' – he had instead nominated his cousin Jane to follow him on to the throne of England.

It has always been accepted that this was the first Jane knew of the deadly inheritance thrust upon her, and certainly she had taken no part in the internecine manoeuvrings of the past few months. But at the same time it is a little hard to credit that this highly intelligent, highly educated young woman can really have been so unworldly as not to have grasped the underlying significance of her hastily arranged marriage; or that she had not at least guessed something of what was being planned for her. Not, of course, that prior knowledge would in any way have affected the helplessness of her position. On the contrary, Jane's nightmare lay in her awareness that she had become the prisoner of a power-hungry, unscrupulous junta, led by the man whom she feared above all others. She managed to gasp out something about her 'insufficiency' and, as the Lords of the Council solemnly swore to shed their blood in defence of her right, muttered a hasty prayer that if to succeed to the throne was indeed her duty and her right, God would help her to govern the realm to his glory. God, that traumatic Sunday evening, seemed to be her only friend.

Next day, the new Queen was taken in full state down-river from Syon to Westminster. The royal party probably dined at Durham House and then entered their barges again to complete the journey to the Tower, the great fortress-palace where, according to ancient custom, all new sovereigns came to take possession at the beginning of their reigns. Jane and her entourage arrived at about three o'clock in the afternoon and the Genoese merchant Baptista Spinola, who was standing among a group of spectators waiting outside the main gates to see the procession disembark, took the trouble to describe her appearance in considerable detail. 'This Jane', he wrote,

> is very short and thin [all three Grey sisters were tiny – Mary, the youngest, to the point of deformity], but prettily shaped and graceful. She has small features and a well-made nose, the mouth flexible and the lips red. The eyebrows are arched and darker than her hair, which is nearly red. Her eyes are sparkling and reddish brown in colour.

Spinola was standing so close to Jane that he noticed her complexion was good but freckled and her teeth, when she smiled, white and sharp. She had been put into chopines – shoes with a specially raised cork sole – to make her look taller and more visible and was wearing a gown of green velvet stamped with gold; while Guildford, 'a very tall strong boy with light hair' resplendent in a suit of white and silver preened himself at her side and 'paid her much attention'.

Guildford was enjoying himself. He made no pretence of loving his wife – he probably regarded her as a tiresome little prig – but he was quite prepared to be polite to her in public in return for the golden stream of social and material benefits which would flow from her. Unfortunately these happy expectations were about to receive a severe set-back. No sooner was Jane installed in the now vanished royal apartments than she was visited by the Lord Treasurer, the old Marquess of Winchester, bringing a selection of royal jewels for her inspection. He also brought the crown itself although, as Jane was later careful to stress, she had not asked for it. In what was most likely an attempt to force her into committing herself beyond any possibility of retreat, Winchester urged her to try it on to see if it fitted her. Jane recoiled in horror. In her eyes the crown represented the ultimate symbol of sanctified early power: to treat it as a plaything, a sort of extra-special headdress, would be tantamount to violating a sacred mystery. But Winchester failed to recognize the storm signals. She could take it without fear he told her, adding casually that another would be made to crown her husband withal.

This was the final straw. It was perhaps only then that Jane realized, 'with infinite grief and displeasure of heart', the full extent of the cynical trick which had been played on her. Despite all their pious speeches, no one cared a snap of their fingers about fulfilling the dead King's wishes, about maintaining the gospel and the true Protestant faith, or even whether the throne was rightfully hers. The plot was simply to use her and her royal blood to elevate a plebeian Dudley to a throne to which he had no shadow of right, so that his father could continue to rule. Jane possessed her full share of Tudor family pride and now that pride was outraged. Small, stubborn, terrified and furious, she laid back her ears and dug in her heels. She would make her husband a duke but never, never would she agree to make him King. In any case, she pointed out coldly, nothing could be done without the consent of Parliament.

This *démarche* precipitated another full-scale family row. Guildford rushed away to fetch his mother and together they launched an all-out assault on their victim – he whining that he didn't want to be a duke, he wanted to be King; she scolding like a fishwife. At last, finding Jane immovable, they stormed out of her presence, the Duchess of Northumberland swearing that her precious son should not stay another moment with his unnatural and ungrateful wife but would return immediately to Syon. Jane watched them go and then summoned the Earls of Arundel and Pembroke. Little though she cared for Guildford's company, she had no intention of allowing him to put such a public slight on her, and she instructed Arundel and Pembroke to prevent him from leaving. Their positions were now, somewhat ironically, reversed. Whether Guildford shared her bed or not, his place was at her side and there he must remain. Guildford sulked, but he did as he was told; 'and thus', Jane was to write, 'I was compelled to act as a woman who is obliged to live on good terms with her husband; nevertheless I was not only deluded by the Duke and the Council, but maltreated by my husband and his mother'.

While these domestic battles were raging inside the Tower, the Sheriff of London, Sir William Garrard, with three heralds, a trumpeter and an escort of the guard, had made his way to the Cross in Cheapside to proclaim Jane, the Duke of Suffolk's daughter, to be Queen of England. But, noted the *Greyfriars Chronicle* ominously, 'few or none said God save her'.

6

Jane the Quene

This virtuous lady the queen's highness, who . . . is rather of force placed therein than by her own seeking and request.

On paper John Dudley's ascendancy looked to be absolute. The reign of his daughter-in-law and puppet had begun; he controlled the capital, the Tower with its armoury, the treasury and the navy, while the great lords of the Council, apparently hypnotized by his powerful charisma, waited meekly to do his bidding. His only opponent was a frail, sickly woman of thirty-seven, without money, influence, professional advice or organized support of any kind. No informed observer of the political scene believed that Mary Tudor stood a chance of enforcing her claims against a man like Northumberland, and the Emperor could only urge his envoys to recommend his cousin to the Duke's protection and to try and win the confidence of England's strong man.

Yet even as these somewhat pusillanimous instructions were being penned, control was starting to slide out of the Duke's hands. The English people knew nothing and cared less about Jane Grey, but they had always had a soft spot for the Lady Mary and over the last few years many of them had come to loathe the whole tribe of Dudley for a parcel of greedy, overbearing upstarts. Gilbert Pot or Potter, tapster at the St John's Head tavern within Ludgate and a member of that silent crowd standing in Cheapside to hear Queen Jane proclaimed, had remarked that the Lady Mary had the better title. Gilbert was unlucky enough to be reported to the authorities, who promptly set him in the pillory and cut his ears clean off, but it was not possible to silence Stephen Amory, clothier of Norfolk, or Richard Troughton, bailiff of South Witham in Lincolnshire, who was told of Mary's plight by his friend James Pratt as they stood together by the cattle drinking-place called hedgedyke, and cried aloud: 'Then it is the Duke's doing and woe worth him that ever he was born, for he will go about to destroy all the noble blood of England.' And drew his dagger and 'wished it at the villain's heart'.

Gilbert Potter and Richard Troughton spoke with the authentic voice of England and although the great Duke of Northumberland was never one to take much account of public opinion, he knew well enough how narrow his power base actually was. Certainly he harboured no illusions about the loyalty of his confederates if the going were to get rough. Survival would depend on a swift, bloodless success, which in turn depended on the swift and silent elimination of all opposition.

During Edward's last illness Northumberland had continued to correspond with Mary, sending her regular and on the whole accurate bulletins about her brother's condition, but Jehan de Scheyfve believed these niceties were no more than a smokescreen designed to conceal the real intentions of the ruling junta and told the Emperor bluntly, 'it is to be feared that as soon as the King is dead they will attempt to seize the Princess'.

Mary was staying at the old nursery palace at Hunsdon, near Ware in Hertfordshire, when, on or about 5 July, she received a summons to the King's deathbed and set out, albeit hesitantly, on the journey. She had not gone far, no further than Hoddesdon on the London road, before warning reached her that the government's message was a trap – Nicholas Throckmorton later claimed the credit for having despatched the Princess's goldsmith on this vital errand. Reacting with uncharacteristic decisiveness, Mary at once turned round and, accompanied by no more than half a dozen trusted aides, made for Kenninghall, the Howard family stronghold in Norfolk. She had some good friends in East Anglia and there, if the worst came to the worst, she would be within reach of the coast and escape to the Spanish Netherlands.

Meanwhile, in London, the King's death was being kept a close secret, or as close as it was possible to keep any secret in a royal household. The three special envoys sent by the Emperor Charles V ostensibly to enquire after King Edward's health, and who had arrived, ironically enough, on 6 July, quickly picked up the news from an informant in the palace. During the course of the next few days the regime did all the expectable things. The ports were closed and the Lord Treasurer Winchester, the Marquess of Northampton, the Earl of Shrewsbury and the Lord Admiral, Lord Clinton, all known allies of Northumberland, came up from Greenwich to 'inspect' the Tower of London, key fortress of the realm. Clinton was installed as Constable and the garrison could be seen hauling out the heavy guns and mounting them ready for immediate use. On Saturday the eighth, the Lord Mayor with a delegation of aldermen and other leaders of the mercantile community were summoned to court to be told, in strict confidence, of Edward's death and his provisions for the succession, 'to the which they were sworn and charged to keep it secret'.

Northumberland would naturally have preferred to go on keeping it secret until such time as he had got his hands on any rival claimants. He had already despatched his son Robert with a party of horse and urgent orders to pursue and capture the Lady Mary, but as it became apparent that she had, temporarily at least, slipped through the net, he could wait no longer and on Sunday 9 July he was forced to show his hand. Nicholas Ridley, Bishop of London, preaching at St Paul's Cross, referred to both the Princesses explicitly as bastards and fulminated especially against Mary as a stiff papist who, if she became Queen, would not only overturn the true religion so happily established under King Edward, but betray the country to a foreign power. After this, of course, there could be no going back. Jane was duly proclaimed on the following day and the proclamation printed in black letter by Richard Grafton, ready to be posted up in the city of London and in church porches and market crosses up and down the land.

But on that same eventful Monday 10 July a letter had been delivered to the Lords of the Council from the Lady Mary, now in temporary sanctuary at Kenninghall, expressing dignified surprise that they had failed to inform her of 'so weighty a matter' as her brother's death and commanding them forthwith to proclaim *her* right and title in her city of London. Their lordships, it seems, were 'greatly astonished and troubled' by the unwelcome news that Mary was still at large and showing fight and, so they heard at the Imperial embassy, the Duchesses of Suffolk and Northumberland both shed tears of mortification. At the Imperial embassy, though, the new arrivals were still confidently expecting the worst. They had not ventured to make any direct contact with Mary or to answer her anguished appeals for help, and could only deplore her stubborn refusal to admit defeat.

Inside the Tower, an air of carefully studied calm prevailed. The Council wrote sternly back to Mary, reminding her of the sundry Acts of Parliament by which she was 'justly made illegitimate and uninheritable to the Crown Imperial of this realm' and adjuring her not by any pretext to continue to vex and molest the loyal subjects of 'our Sovereign Lady Queen Jane'. If she showed herself quiet and obedient, as she ought, then the lords would be glad to do her any service consonant with their duty; if not, they indicated, she would be sorry. The Council also despatched Richard Shelley to Brussels with a letter authorizing him to inform the Emperor of King Edward's death and another letter, over the sign manual of 'Jane the Quene', instructing Sir Philip Hoby to continue in his post of resident ambassador at the Imperial court, while young Guildford Dudley amused himself by drafting a document giving Sir Philip full powers to deal in *his* affairs. A requisition was sent to the Master of the Wardrobe in the name of Queen Jane ordering twenty yards of velvet, twenty-five ells of fine Holland, or linen cloth and thirty-three ells of coarser material for lining to make robes. More boxes of jewels had now been delivered to the Tower, but unfortunately they seem mostly to have contained a curious miscellany of odds and ends, such as every household accumulates, including amongst other things a toothpick in the shape of a fish, an assortment of buttons, semi-precious stones and trinkets, a selection of the jewelled borders worn on ladies' hoods and a clock of damascened work made in the shape of a book. There was a prayer book, a leather purse, some coins, eyebrow tweezers and even some old shaving cloths, presumably a relic of King Henry VIII.

So far the determination to present a confident face to the outside world was holding. The French ambassador in London, Antoine de Noailles, had written an optimistic report after seeing the Council on 7 July and generously offering the assistance of the French King should need arise. Both de Noailles and the Emperor's envoys believed that 'the actual possession of power' was nine points of the law, especially among barbarians like the English, and the Imperial ambassadors were so nervous that they scarcely dared to go out for a walk. But it was the Imperialists who detected the first signs of a crack in the façade when, on Wednesday 12 July, they received a visit from Lord Cobham and Sir John Mason on behalf of Northumberland.

Of the three envoys sent over by Charles V, it was Simon Renard, a native of the Franche Comté and a brilliant, hard-working, subtle career diplomat, who had taken the lead. When Cobham and Mason began in a hectoring manner, telling them that their credentials were no longer valid now that Edward was dead, forbidding them to attempt to communicate with Mary and threatening them with England's 'barbarous laws' if they gave any cause for suspicion, it was Renard who replied, tactfully assuring the councillors of the Emperor's goodwill and urging them rather to welcome the advances of old friends than seek new alliances with those who had always been their enemies. The French, he pointed out, had a vested interest in stirring up trouble, their object being 'to seek to gain a foothold in England for their own ends and to the advantage of the Queen of Scotland and that of her affianced spouse, the Dauphin of France'. When the Emperor heard that his cousin had been declared a bastard and of the violence openly said to be intended against her person, he would naturally conclude that French intrigues had pre-vailed and that the rights long recognized by the international com-munity as belonging to Mary had been snatched away to gain the crown for the Queen of Scots, under colour of conferring it upon the Duke of Suffolk's daughter.

Renard and his colleagues had the satisfaction of seeing Cobham and Mason reduced to pensive silence. Nor did they miss the shifty exchange of glances between the two men as they began to back-pedal, murmuring that of course it had been a mistake to say the ambassadors' commission had expired and hoping their excellencies would not feel obliged to ask for their passports until the full Council had had an opportunity to consider the Imperial position. 'So they left us in suspense', wrote Renard, 'waiting to see what they would say or do.'

Antoine de Noailles was casually describing Guildford Dudley as 'the new King' and Simon Renard was still gloomily convinced that Mary would be a prisoner in Dudley hands within a matter of days, but in fact the whole flimsy edifice of Dudley power was about to fall apart. On that Wednesday some very disquieting news had come in of the support rallying to Mary. The Earl of Bath, the Earl of Sussex and his son, Sir William Drury, Sir John Shelton, Sir Thomas Whar-ton and Sir John Mordaunt, together with substantial families like the Bedingfields, Bacons, Jerninghams and Cornwallises, were already with her or on their way. A letter had been prepared by the Duke of Northumberland for circulation to the Lieutenants and sheriffs of the counties announcing Jane's accession and calling on them to repel and resist the feigned and untrue claim of the Lady Mary, bastard daughter to Henry VIII of famous memory, to the utmost of their power; but it was obvious now that a full-scale exped-ition would have to be mounted from London 'to fetch in the Lady Mary'. All hope of presenting a grumbling but acquiescent nation with a *fait accompli* had vanished and the issue would instead have to be decided openly on the field of battle.

There was no time to be lost and a muster was ordered to be held in Tothill Fields that same day, the unusually high rates of pay offered, ten pence a day, being a measure of the administration's con-cern. It had been intended to put the Duke of Suffolk in command of the army but when this information was conveyed to Queen Jane on the evening of 12 July she promptly burst into tears and begged that her father 'might tarry at home in her company'. Jane seems to have forgotten that she had once thought it hell to be in her parents' company, but she hadn't known the Dudley family then.

The lords of the Council gazed thoughtfully at their weeping sovereign lady and then at one another, an idea forming or, more likely, already formed in their collective mind. This idea they presently propounded to the Duke of Northumberland. It would be so much better, they suggested, if he took command himself. No other man was so well fitted for the task, especially since he had already successfully suppressed one rebellion in East Anglia and was therefore so feared in those parts that no one would dare offer him resistance. Besides, was he not 'the best man of war in the realm'? Then there was the matter of the Queen's distress, and the fact that she would 'in no wise grant that her father should take it on him'. So it was really up to the Duke, remarked someone, a note of steel suddenly clearly audible beneath the flattery and the subservience, it was up to the Duke 'to remedy the matter'. And the Duke gave way. 'Since ye think it good,' he said, 'I and mine will go, not doubting of your fidelity to the Queen's majesty which I leave in your custody.'

The fidelity of his associates to anything but their own best interests was, of course, more than doubtful, and it was a lively fear of what they might do as soon as his back was turned which lay behind John Dudley's reluctance to take the field himself. He knew that he was being manoeuvred into the role of scapegoat, but there was no turning back now. Even as they sat talking round the council table in the summer dusk the sound of heavy wagons laden with weapons and supplies – 'great guns and small, bows, bills, spears, morris pikes, harness, arrows, gunpowder and victuals' – could be heard rattling eastward through the city streets 'for a great army towards Cambridge'.

Preparations continued all next day. Early in the morning the Duke called for his personal armour and saw it made ready, before appointing his own retinue to meet him at Durham Place. Then, his arrangements made, he addressed the assembled Council for the last time. After urging that reinforcements should be sent without fail to join him at Newmarket, he made a last effort to assert the old dominant force of his personality. He and his companions, he said, were going forth to adventure their bodies and lives 'amongst the bloody strokes and cruel assaults' of the enemy, trusting themselves and their wives and children at home to the faith and truth of those they left behind. If anyone present was planning to violate that trust and 'to leave us your friends in the briars and betray us', let them remember that treachery could be a two-handed game. Let them also reflect on God's vengeance and the sacred oath of allegiance they had taken 'to this virtuous lady the Queen's highness, who by your and our enticement is rather of force placed therein than by her own seeking and request'. There was, too, the matter of God's cause. The fear of papistry's re-entry had, after all, been the original ground on which everyone had agreed and 'even at the first motion granted your good wills and consents thereto, as by your hands' writing evidently appeareth'. John Dudley could say no more, but in this troublesome time wish his hearers 'to use constant hearts, abandoning all malice, envy and private affections'.

'And this I pray you,' he ended; 'wish me no worse speed in this journey than ye would have to yourselves.'

'My lord,' said someone – it may have been Winchester, the eldest of the peers – 'if ye mistrust any of us in this matter, your grace is far deceived; for which of us can wipe his hands clean thereof?' While they were still talking the servants had come in with the first course of dinner and were laying the table, but Winchester (if it were he) went on: 'If we should shrink from you as one that were culpable, which of us can excuse himself as guiltless? Therefore herein your doubt is too far cast.'

'I pray God it be so,' answered Northumberland abruptly. 'Let us go to dinner.'

After the lords had eaten, the Duke went to take his formal leave of the Queen and to receive from her his signed and sealed commission as Lieutenant of her army. Jane thanked him 'humbly' for allowing her father to stay at home and asked him to use all his diligence. 'I will do what in me lies,' he said, looking down at the thin, red-headed slip of a girl to whom he was now bound by the unbreakable kinship of mutual destruction. Coming out through the council chamber he encountered the Earl of Arundel, 'who prayed God be with his grace; saying he was very sorry it was not his chance to go with him and bear him company, in whose presence he could find in his heart to spend his blood, even at his foot'. Henry Fitzalan did not add that he, together with the Earls of Shrewsbury and Pembroke, the Lord Privy Seal John Russell, Lord Cobham, John Mason and Secretary William Petre, were having a very private meeting with the Imperial ambassadors that day. But then nor was Northumberland advertising the fact that he had just despatched his cousin Henry Dudley on an urgent and secret mission to the King of France, offering, so it is said, to trade Ireland and Calais in exchange for immediate French military aid.

The situation remained extremely volatile and, in an atmosphere thick with suspicion and distrust, rumour and counter-rumour bred and multiplied. Reports were coming in that the gentry were up proclaiming Queen Mary in Buckinghamshire but Renard, in a despatch dated 14 July, continued to predict her imminent subjugation. Mary herself, who had now retreated to Framlingham Castle in Suffolk, a stronger place than Kenninghall and nearer the coast, sent a courier to the Imperial embassy with a verbal message that 'she saw destruction hanging over her' unless the Emperor helped her quickly.

Northumberland, meanwhile, had succeeded in raising an army of around three thousand horse and foot and early on the morning of Friday 14 July he rode out of Durham Place and turned east down the Strand towards the Cambridge road and 'towards my Lady Mary's grace to destroy her grace'. But as his cavalcade passed through the village of Shoreditch, where the way was lined with silent, staring crowds, the Duke turned to Lord Grey of Wilton who was riding alongside him and observed sourly, 'The people press to see us, but not one sayeth God speed us.'

During the next few days the faces of those left cooped up in the Tower grew steadily longer as word arrived that Mary had been proclaimed in Norwich and that the town, one of the largest and richest in the country, was sending her men and supplies. Colchester had also declared for her, and in places as far apart as Devon and Oxfordshire the leaders of the local community were following suit. More and more gentlemen 'with their powers', that is, their tenantry and dependants, were voting with their feet by joining the growing camp at Framlingham, while the noblemen's tenants showed ominous signs of refusing to serve their lords against Queen Mary, and the Duke's own army was plagued by internal dissension and desertion.

Then came a really shattering piece of news. The crews of the six royal ships which had been sent to watch the port of Yarmouth and cut off Mary's escape route to the Low Countries had gone over to her in a body, taking their captains and their heavy guns with them. 'After once the submission of the ships was known in the Tower', wrote an eyewitness, 'each man then began to pluck in his horns'; and when Northumberland wrote querulously from his command post in the old Brandon territory of Bury St Edmunds complaining about the non-arrival of his promised and much-needed reinforcements, he received 'but a slender answer'. This was hardly surprising, since from the moment of the navy's defection it had been a question not of whether but when the lords of the Council would follow the sailors' example. Already certain individuals, notably the Earl of Pembroke and the Lord Warden of the Cinque Ports Thomas Cheyne, were looking for an excuse to go out and 'consult' in London and on the sixteenth there was an alarm at about seven o'clock in the evening, when the main gates of the Tower were suddenly locked and the keys carried up to Queen Jane. It was given out that a seal had gone missing, but the author of the *Chronicle of Queen Jane* believed the truth of the matter was that her highness suspected the Lord Treasurer of some evil intent. Old Winchester had apparently sneaked out to his own house during the day and had to be fetched back at midnight – the other lords were not risking any one of their number stealing a march at this stage.

Inside the Tower they were still going through the motions. Jane was still solemnly signing letters addressed to the sheriffs and justices of the peace requiring them to take steps to suppress the 'rebellion' of the Lady Mary, but there was of course no question of her being able to stem the tide: she had neither the experience nor the authority – nor did her father command the respect of his peers. By the eighteenth the Earls of Arundel, Bedford, Pembroke, Shrewsbury and Worcester, the Lords Paget and Cobham and about half a dozen others were ready to move, leaving the Tower *en masse* on the not very convincing pretext of having urgent business to discuss with the French ambassador. Instead, they assembled for a conference at Pembroke's house, Baynard's Castle on the riverbank below Ludgate Hill, and the following afternoon it was the Imperial embassy which received a visit from the Earl of Shrewsbury and Sir John Mason. They came to explain to the Emperor's representatives how reluctant they and their fellow councillors had been to subscribe to King Edward's Device, but really they had had no choice, for they had been so bullied by Northumberland and treated almost as if they were prisoners. Of course they had always believed in their hearts that Mary was the rightful Queen and they were going to proclaim her in London that very day.

And so they did, between five and six o'clock in the evening of Thursday 19 July, at the Cross in Cheapside amid scenes of wild popular excitement. People with money in their pockets flung it out of windows into the cheering, yelling crowds below. The Earl of Pembroke was seen to throw a whole capful of gold angels and no doubt regarded it as a good investment. Sober citizens wrenched off their gowns and capered in the streets like children. Church bells rang a joyful peal in a forest of steeples. Bonfires blazed up on every corner and all that night the people of London sang and danced and feasted, drinking the health of the rightful Queen, God bless her! and destruction to her enemies.

Simon Renard and his companions could hardly believe the evidence of their own eyes, fearing that this astonishing change of front must conceal some especially diabolical piece of heretical treachery, while the French ambassador wrote: 'the atmosphere of this country and the nature of its people are so changeable that I am compelled to make my despatches correspondingly wavering and contradictory'. Both sides were agreed in attributing the sudden transformation of Mary's prospects to the intervention of divine Providence, although de Noailles made it plain that he for one thought poorly of divine judgement in this instance.

Faint echoes of the general rejoicing could be heard even in the Tower where, so it is said, the Duke of Suffolk presently came to break the news of her deposition to his daughter as she sat at supper, and with his own hands helped to tear down the cloth of estate from above her head. Then, ordering his men to leave their weapons behind, he went out on to Tower Hill, saying helplessly, 'I am but one man', and proclaimed the Lady Mary's grace to be Queen of England before scuttling away to his house at Sheen. Jane was left alone in the stripped and silent rooms to listen to the distant clamour of the bells – for her there would be no going home. When Lady Throckmorton, one of the ladies of the household who had gone out that afternoon to attend a christening, returned to her post she found the royal apartments deserted and, asking for the Queen's grace, was told that the Lady Jane was now a prisoner detained in the Deputy Lieutenant's house.

It was there, the next day, that Jane suffered a visit from the Marquess of Winchester peremptorily demanding the return of all the jewels and other 'stuff' she had received from the royal stores during her nine days' reign. The Lord Treasurer went through her and Guildford's wardrobes with a fishy pawnbroker's eye, confiscating jewellery, furs, hats, a velvet and sable muffler and all the money in their possession. In spite of this, a peevish inter-departmental correspondence about the unexplained disappearance of 'a square coffer covered with fustian of Naples', a leather box marked with Henry VIII's broad arrow and containing, among other things, thirteen pairs of worn leather gloves, and another box labelled 'the Queen's jewels' dragged on into the autumn.

While Winchester was busy covering his tracks, Mr Secretary Cecil was doing the filing, methodically endorsing the office copy of a letter signed 'Jane the Quene' on 10 July with the words 'Jana non Regina', and the Earl of Arundel and William Paget were riding hard for Framlingham to lay their allegiance and their excuses at Mary Tudor's feet. Mary accepted them both. She had no choice, for, like it or not, she was going to have to rule the country with their help, and on Saturday the twenty-first they went on to Cambridge to arrest the Duke of Northumberland in the Queen's name.

'I beseech you, my lord of Arundel, use mercy towards me, know-ing the case as it is,' said John Dudley to the man who barely a week before had wished he might die at his feet.

'My lord,' answered Arundel tiredly, 'ye should have sought for mercy sooner; I must do according to my commandment.'

Although Mary had wanted the prisoners to be allowed to pass peaceably, some disgraceful scenes took place when Northumber-land, his three elder sons, his brother Andrew and some half a dozen others were brought into London through Bishopsgate four days later. Armed men had been posted in the streets to keep the crowds in order and the Duke's escort made him take off the conspicuous red cloak he wore, but he was quickly recognized and pelted with insults, filth and stones. 'A dreadful sight it was', wrote Simon Renard, 'and a strange mutation for those who, a few days before, had seen the Duke enter London Tower with great pomp and magnificence when the Lady Jane went there to take possession, and now saw him led like a criminal and dubbed traitor.'

The entire Dudley family, the Duke, the Duchess and their five sons, were now safely under lock and key, but the Duchess of North-umberland was soon released – 'sooner than expected', reported Renard – and, like the devoted wife and mother she was, at once hur-ried off to meet the Queen to try 'to move her to compassion towards her children'. This was being too optimistic and Mary ordered her back to London, refusing to let her approach closer than five miles. The Duchess of Suffolk was more fortunate. Although Suffolk had been arrested at Sheen and returned to the Tower on 28 July, the Queen readily granted her cousin Frances a private audience and the Duke suffered no more than a few token days in detention.

Mary made her state entry into London on 3 August. Wearing a gown of purple velvet over a kirtle 'all thick set with goldsmith's work and great pearl', King Henry's daughter rode in triumph through newly gravelled streets hung with banners and streamers and lined with cheering crowds, the trumpets blowing proudly before her. Once she had been pretty – small and finely made with a delicate pink and white complexion and the Tudor family's red-gold hair. Now she was painfully thin, indelibly marked by the long years of unhappiness, ill-health and disappointment. Impartial observers still described her as 'fresh coloured' but the pink and gold had long since faded, leaving a sandy-haired, tight-lipped little woman, with myopic grey eyes, no eyebrows and a surprisingly deep, gruff voice.

When her procession reached the Tower, the guns thundering a salute, the new Queen was greeted by three kneeling figures: the old

Duke of Norfolk, who had been lying under suspended sentence of death ever since 1547; Stephen Gardiner, who had spent most of Edward's reign in prison for his unfashionable religious opinions; and young Edward Courtenay, grandson of Catherine Courtenay née Plantagenet, who had spent most of his life in prison for that reason alone. Mary raised the suppliants, kissed them, saying smilingly, 'These are my prisoners', and ordered their immediate release. Other, more recent and more controversial prisoners were not in evidence on this auspicious occasion. The Duke of Northumberland was quartered in the Garden Tower – later popularly dubbed the Bloody Tower – and his sons were crowded together in the Beauchamp Tower, while Jane had now been moved into the Gentleman Gaoler's house next door.

No one, it appears, had made any attempt to intercede for Jane. If her mother had taken the opportunity to speak up for her when she saw the Queen at Newhall on 30 July, it was not reported, and Jane now proceeded to write to Mary herself. It was a long letter of which the original has disappeared – it survives only in an Italian translation re-translated into English – and gives Jane's version of events from her marriage to Guildford Dudley to her early days in the Tower. She freely admitted having done very wrong in accepting the crown and having listened to the persuasions of those who appeared at the time to be wise but who had since proved the contrary. Indeed, her fault was so serious that she quite understood that, 'but for the goodness and clemency of the Queen', she could have no hope of pardon. She did, however, deny that she had either consented or been a party to Northumberland's conspiracy at any stage. 'For whereas I might have taken upon me that of which I was not worthy, yet no one can ever say either that I sought it . . . or that I was pleased with it.'

Mary believed her. She had always been fond of her little cousin in spite of her heresy – the child couldn't help the way she had been brought up – and her blunt outspokenness. At least you always knew exactly where you stood with Jane, and Mary, transparently honest herself, appreciated that quality in others. In fact, while her brief, incredulous glow of happiness lasted, the Queen was ready to call the whole world her friend, innocently believing that the country in general hated the new ways as much as she did and that the great mass of the people were only waiting for a lead to return thankfully to the fold of the true Roman Church. Living for so many years in rural retreat surrounded by her Catholic household, Mary had completely failed to realize how strongly a nationalistic form of Protestantism had taken root in London and the south-east during the past decade; and had completely misinterpreted the nature of the popular support she had been given. The people were delighted to be rid of the Dudleys and genuinely glad to see the true line of the Tudor succession re-established, but this did not mean they were necessarily prepared to submit once more to the authority of the Bishop of Rome.

For a time Mary clung to her hopes of a peaceful reconciliation. She told the Council on 12 August that she did not wish to 'compel or constrain other men's consciences', trusting God would put a persuasion of the truth into their hearts, and shortly afterwards a proclamation was issued in which the Queen expressed her desire that the religion she herself had professed from infancy would now be quietly and charitably embraced by all her subjects. Mass, although still officially illegal, was being celebrated at court with the Privy Councillors (whose consciences were apparently as elastic as their loyalty) attending in a body but within a month of Northumberland's débâcle ominous signs of a Protestant backlash had begun to manifest themselves in the streets of the capital.

The chances of continuing harmony between the Catholic Queen and her independently minded subjects were not improved by Mary's obvious, understandable but injudicious reliance on Simon Renard (who had now taken over from Jehan de Scheyfve as the Emperor's resident ambassador) in preference to her English councillors. Renard's real business, of course, was to see off the French and rebuild the Anglo-Imperial alliance by negotiating the notorious Spanish marriage which, in the event, not only poisoned the political atmosphere beyond recovery but finally wrecked Mary's personal life as well. First, though, it was necessary to steer the inexperienced Queen through the tricky opening weeks of her reign, and Renard soon discovered she was quite unlike any ruler he had ever had dealings with before.

The Emperor had sent instructions that, for the sake of England's internal peace and quiet, his good sister and cousin must be dissuaded from taking too harsh a revenge on her enemies, but it seemed that Mary had no appetite for vengeance. On the contrary, she would have been ready to pardon the Duke of Northumberland himself if the Emperor had wished it and, wrote Renard, suppressing his exasperation with some difficulty: 'As to Jane of Suffolk, whom they tried to make Queen, she [Mary] could not be induced to consent that she should die.' All the more so because Mary apparently believed that Jane's marriage to Guildford Dudley was invalid, 'as she was previously betrothed by a binding promise . . . to a servitor of the Bishop of Winchester'. The identity of this mysterious fiancé remains unclear, unless it may have been a mistake for the Earl of Hertford, but in any case Mary was firmly convinced of Jane's innocence of any complicity in Northumberland's intrigues and her conscience would not permit her to have a blameless young creature put to death.

Appalled, the ambassador pointed out as forcefully as he dared that, while Jane might be morally innocent, the fact remained that she had actually borne the title of Queen – a title which could always be revived at some future date to trouble the succession to the crown. It was also necessary to remember that, in affairs of state, power and tyranny unfortunately sometimes achieved better results than right or justice, and Renard hastily dredged up a precedent from Roman history when the Emperor Theodosius had felt obliged to order the death of Maximus and Victor his son, 'notwithstanding his tender age'. But Mary was not to be moved, although she did promise to take every possible precaution before setting the Lady Jane at liberty! Defeated, Simon Renard could only shrug up his shoulders and hope, without much conviction, that the Queen would not soon have cause to regret her extraordinary clemency.

Not even Mary could forgive the Duke of Northumberland, and on 18 August he and his eldest son and William Parr, Marquess of Northampton, were tried and convicted by their peers in Westminster Hall. Next day another, lesser batch of conspirators – Andrew Dudley, Sir John Gates, once Edward VI's Captain of the Guard, his brother Henry and Thomas Palmer, Northumberland's instrument in the original attack on the Protector Somerset – were also tried and convicted, but only the Duke, 'the great wheel' of the attempted coup, John Gates and Thomas Palmer actually suffered the penalty of high treason. The execution date was fixed for Monday 21 August and all the preparations had been made when John Dudley, whether from a genuine concern for his immortal soul or a last minute hope of pardon, suddenly indicated that he wished to be reconciled to the Catholic faith. Sentence was therefore respited for twenty-four hours to allow the Duke to make his peace with God and the government to make the most of this unexpected and valuable propaganda point. At nine o'clock on the Monday morning, in a carefully staged public spectacle, Northumberland, the Marquess of Northampton, Andrew Dudley, Henry Gates and Thomas Palmer were escorted to the chapel of St Peter-ad-Vincula by Tower Green to attend mass which, according to one rather scornful witness, was celebrated with all the elaborate business of elevation of the Host, pax giving, blessing, crossing, 'breathing', turning about, 'and all the other rites and accidents of old time appertaining'. When the time came for the prisoners to receive the sacrament, Northumberland turned to the congregation saying:

My masters, I let you all to understand that I do most faithfully believe this is the very right and true way, out of the which true religion you and I have been seduced these sixteen years past, by the false and erroneous preaching of the new preachers. . . . And I do believe the holy sacrament here most assuredly to be our Saviour and Redeemer Jesus Christ; and this I pray you all to testify and pray for me.

Next morning, standing on the scaffold on Tower Hill, forty-three years almost to the day, so the chroniclers noted, since his father had stood in the same place for the same reason, John Dudley repeated his solemn apostasy in the presence of a crowd of several thousand spectators and there were, it was thought, 'a large number turned with his words'.

Just a week later, on Tuesday 29 August, the author of the *Chronicle of Queen Jane* (generally thought to have been one Rowland Lea, an official of the royal mint living in the Tower), dropped in to dine at the house of his friend Partridge the Gentleman Gaoler and found the Lady Jane, who had chosen to eat with the family that day, sitting in the place of honour 'at the board's end', attended by her page and one of her ladies. Gracious and self-possessed, Jane gave the Gaoler and his guest permission to remain covered in her presence, 'commanding Partridge and me to put on our caps', drank the visitor's health and bade him heartily welcome.

Talk at the dinner table naturally turned to current affairs. 'The Queen's majesty is a merciful Princess,' said Jane, who knew by this time that she was not to be executed; 'I beseech God she may long continue and send his bountiful grace upon her.' After this, recorded the diarist, 'we fell in discourse of matters of religion'. Jane wanted to know who had preached at St Paul's Cross the previous Sunday. Then she asked:

'Have they mass in London?'

Yes, answered Lea cautiously, 'in some places'.

'It may be so,' said Jane. 'It is not so strange as the sudden conversion of the late Duke; for who would have thought he would have done so?'

'Perchance he thereby hoped to have had his pardon,' suggested someone and thus released the floodgates of Jane's eloquence.

'Pardon?' she cried. 'Woe worth him! he hath brought me and our stock in most miserable calamity and misery by his exceeding ambition. But for the answering that he hoped for life by his turning, though other men be of that opinion, I utterly am not; for what man is there living, I pray you, although he had been innocent, that would hope of life in that case; being in the field against the Queen in person as general, and after his taking so hated and evil spoken of by the commons? and at his coming into prison so wondered at [reviled] as the like was never heard by any man's time. Who was judge that he should hope for pardon, whose life was odious to all men? But what will ye more? Like as his life was wicked and full of dissimulation, so was his end thereafter. I pray God, I, nor no friend of mine, die so. Should I, who am young and in my few years, forsake my faith for the love of life? Nay, God forbid! Much more he should not, whose fatal course, although he had lived his just number of years, could not have long continued. But life was sweet, it appeared; so he might have lived, you will say, he did not care how. Indeed the reason is good; for he that would have lived in chains to have had his life, by like would leave no other mean [un]attempted. But God be merciful to us, for he sayeth, Whoso denieth him before men, he will not know him in his Father's Kingdom.'

'With this and much like talk the dinner passed away', wrote Rowland Lea, to whom we are indebted for a splendid and revealing account of Jane Grey in full and vigorous flow. The party ended in a polite exchange of compliments, Lea thanking Lady Jane for condescending to accept him in her company and Jane thanking Partridge for bringing 'this gentleman' to dinner.

'Well, madam,' responded the Gaoler apologetically, 'we were somewhat bold, not knowing that your ladyship dined below until we found your ladyship there.' On this note of mutual courtesy the two men took their leave, Rowland Lea surely hurrying away to record his interesting experience while it was fresh in his mind.

As well as vividly illustrating Lady Jane's opinion of the late Duke of Northumberland and her own stern religious philosophy, Lea's account makes it clear that the physical circumstances of her imprisonment were not too disagreeable. She was, in fact, permitted a staff of four – two waiting gentlewomen, Mrs Tilney and Mrs Jacob, a manservant and her old nurse, Mrs Ellen – while the generous sum of ninety-odd shillings a week had been allocated out of government funds for her board and lodging, with a further allowance of twenty shillings a week for each of the servants. Partridge and his wife treated her with respectful consideration. She was allowed to walk in the Queen's garden. Nobody was bullying her and she no longer had to cope with the oppressive demands of her parents, her husband or her in-laws. She had books, peace and quiet and leisure for study, plus the Queen's assurance of life and eventual liberty. Jane would not have needed telling that, all things considered, she had escaped exceedingly lightly. Her pleasure at seeing a new face at the dinner table indicates that she was beginning to suffer the boredom which is the inevitable lot of every prisoner and no doubt she especially missed the stimulus of intellectual companionship and conversation. But that was a relatively trivial and, hopefully, temporary deprivation, and she was able to alleviate the monotony a little round about this time by composing a long and forthright denunciation of Dr Harding, once a chaplain at Bradgate and her own first tutor, now unhappily 'fallen from the truth of God's most Holy Word'.

In the new, chilly political climate Dr Harding had hastened to follow his more prudent brethren back into the shelter of the Roman fold, to the fluently expressed disgust of his former pupil who had no patience with such chicken-hearted behaviour. 'I cannot but marvel at thee and lament thy case', she wrote,

> who seemed sometime to be the lively member of Christ, but now the deformed imp of the devil; sometime the beautiful temple of God, but now the stinking and filthy kennel of Satan; sometime the unspotted spouse of Christ, but now the unshamefaced paramour of Antichrist; sometime my faithful brother, but now a stranger and apostate; sometime a stout Christian soldier, but now a cowardly runaway. Yea, when I consider these things, I cannot but speak to thee, and cry out upon thee, thou seed of Satan.

Nineteenth-century biographers of Jane Grey had some trouble with this sustained piece of invective, which does not exactly fit the image of gentle Jane meek and mild, that model of Christian forbearance fashioned for the edification of Victorian schoolrooms; and they made strenuous efforts to dissociate their heroine from the 'vulgar polemic' of this 'coarsely violent epistle', refusing to believe that such unbecoming language could have issued from the mind or pen of an amiable young female. Jane's own contemporaries took a more robust view and welcomed the Harding letter – which was later printed both as a popular pamphlet and in John Foxe's best-selling *Book of Martyrs* – as proceeding from the zealous heart of a justly aggrieved Christian lady. The Elizabethans saw nothing unbecoming in such epithets as 'sink of sin', 'child of perdition' or even 'white-livered milksop' being applied to someone who had let the side down as badly as poor Harding had done.

'Oh wretched and unhappy man, what art thou but dust and ashes?' continued the aggrieved Christian lady:

> And wilt thou resist thy Maker that fashioned thee and framed thee? Wilt thou now forsake Him, that called thee . . . to be an ambassador and messenger of his eternal word? . . . How canst thou, having knowledge, or how darest thou neglect the law of the Lord and follow

the vain traditions of men; and whereas thou hast been a public professor of his name, become now a defacer of his glory? Wilt thou refuse the true God, and worship the invention of man, the golden calf, the whore of Babylon, the Romish religion, the abominable idol, the most wicked mass? Wilt thou torment again, rend and tear the most precious body of our Saviour Christ with thy bodily and fleshly teeth? . . . Can neither the punishment of the Israelites . . . nor the terrible threatenings of the prophets, nor the curses of God's own mouth, fear thee to honour any other god than him?

Jane went on to batter her target with fusillades of texts from the Old and New Testaments, before exhorting him to repentance:

Disdain not to come again with the lost son, seeing you have so wandered with him. Be not ashamed to turn again with him from the swill of strangers . . . acknowledging that you have sinned against heaven and earth. . . . Be not abashed to come home again with Mary, and weep bitterly with Peter, not only with shedding the tears of your bodily eyes, but also pouring out the streams of your heart – to wash away, out of the sight of God, the filth and mire of your offensive fall. Be not abashed to say with the publican, 'Lord be merciful unto me a sinner.'. . . Last of all, let the lively remembrance of the last day be always before your eyes, remembering the terror that such shall be in at that time, with the runagates and fugitives from Christ . . . and contrariwise, the inestimable joys prepared for them, that fearing no peril, nor dreading death, have manfully fought and victoriously triumphed over all power of darkness, over hell, death and damnation through their most redoubted captain, Christ, who now stretcheth out his arms to receive you.

The effect of all this on Dr Harding does not appear to be recorded, but it is difficult to avoid the impression that Jane had relished the opportunity of letting off mental steam.

Meanwhile, life in the Gentleman Gaoler's house continued on its uneventful course. In the Tower some prisoners were released, among them King Edward's old tutor the famous Greek scholar Sir John Cheke, and a couple of judges, Sir Roger Cholmley and Sir Edward Montague; while two churchmen, Bishop Hugh Latimer and Archbishop Thomas Cranmer, were brought in. Some of the Dudley wives were given leave to visit their husbands, while the Dudley brothers were now being allowed to exercise on the leads – that is, the roof – of their prison in the Beauchamp Tower. At the end of September there was a renewed flurry of activity in the royal apartments as the court came briefly back into residence preparatory to the Queen's coronation and the traditional eve-of-coronation Recognition Procession through the city to Westminster. None of this had anything to do with Jane. Her sixteenth birthday came and went and she remained, apparently forgotten, in her quarters in the Gentleman Gaoler's house looking out on to Tower Green.

The first Parliament of the new reign met on 5 October and one of its first acts was to repeal the divorce of Henry VIII and Catherine of Aragon, pronouncing the marriage of the Queen's father and mother to have been good and lawful. It also repealed all the religious legislation passed in her brother's time, thus in effect returning the English Church to the state in which Henry VIII had left it – an arrangement which well suited all those members of both houses who had done so nicely out of the general share-out of church property in the 1530s, and 1540s. It was less acceptable to the militant Protestants, and already there had been violent demonstrations at the weekly sermons at Paul's Cross, necessitating strong counter-measures by government and civic authorities. Also, as Renard had feared, the Queen's moderation and policy of substituting fines for executions were being interpreted as weakness. 'Her authority', he wrote, 'has suffered from the pecuniary compositions for offences, and people have come to judge her actions so freely that they go so far as to laugh at them.' It was for this reason, so the ambassador heard, that Mary had now agreed to take a different course, 'and to order the four sons of the Duke of Northumberland, and Jane of Suffolk, to be tried and sentenced to receive capital punishment for the crimes they have committed'. This despatch was dated 19 September, but it was mid-November before Jane finally stood trial, and her co-defendants were her husband, two of his brothers, Ambrose and Henry, and Thomas Cranmer.

The five were led out of the Tower on foot to be arraigned at the Guildhall, the executioner, as was customary, carrying the axe before them. Jane, dressed entirely in black – black cloth gown, a cape lined and trimmed with velvet, a French hood also in black with a velvet billament or border, a prayer book bound in black velvet hanging from her girdle and another book of devotions held open in her hands – walked behind Guildford in the procession, attended by her two ladies. The proceedings, held before Richard Morgan, newly appointed Justice of the Common Pleas, were brief and formal. The defendants pleaded guilty to the charges of high treason brought against them, and sentence – hanging, drawing and quartering for men, burning or beheading at the Queen's pleasure for Lady Jane – was pronounced. Then came the return journey to the Tower, the edge of the headsman's axe turned towards the prisoners.

But it was still by no means certain when, or even if, the executions would take place. Already another fate was being reserved for Thomas Cranmer, while the general opinion remained that Lady Jane and the rest of the young Dudleys would be spared. 'It is believed that Jane will not die', reported Renard on the day after the trial; and, again, three days later: 'As for Jane, I am told her life is safe.'

7

The Ende of the Lady Jane Duddeley

Great pity was it for the casting away of that fair lady, whom nature had not only so beautified but God also had endowed with singular gifts and graces.

The social position of the Suffolk Greys in the late autumn of 1553 must surely have been uniquely unusual. While her eldest daughter and son-in-law remained in the Tower, convicted traitors lying under sentence of death, albeit suspended sentence, the Duchess of Suffolk was to be found preening herself at court, apparently in high favour. On at least one occasion that winter the Queen had chosen to give her cousin Frances precedence over her half-sister Elizabeth, with whom she was on increasingly bad terms. In his eagerness to cut his connections with the Greys, the Earl of Pembroke had repudiated his son's marriage with the Lady Catherine and packed her off back to her parents; and Catherine – who was growing into a very pretty girl, the only one of the sisters to show promise of inheriting their Tudor grandmother's wilful beauty – was now at court with her mother, she and plain little Mary Grey having been admitted to the privileged ranks of the Queen's maids of honour. Even the Duke of Suffolk, reported Simon Renard on 17 November, had 'made his confession as to religion' and as a result had been let off paying a fine of £20,000 and reinstated in polite society by means of a general pardon. Although Renard continued to regard the whole Grey family with the deepest suspicion – almost as much as he did the sly and heretical Princess Elizabeth – it is hardly surprising that in the circumstances Lady Jane's trial should have been regarded as little more than a formality and her release expected to be no more than a matter of time.

But even before Jane stood in the Guildhall to hear verdict and sentence pronounced on her, the chain of events which would lead to her death had begun its inexorable progression. 'In the beginning of November was the first notice among the people touching the marriage of the Queen to the King of Spain', noted the *Chronicle of Queen Jane*, and as it became generally known that Mary intended to marry her cousin Philip, son and heir of the Emperor Charles V, rumbles of disapproval, ominous as distant thunder, were immediately audible. Some people, indeed, were moved to wonder if the late Duke of Northumberland was going to be proved right after all, for Philip was not merely a foreigner and a Catholic, he represented the most formidable Catholic power bloc in Europe. The various Protestant pressure groups reacted by intensifying their anti-Catholic propaganda campaign; both Houses of Parliament joined in sending a deputation to the Queen begging her to marry an Englishman and there were serious misgivings within the Privy Council itself.

No responsible person, of course, questioned that the Queen should marry. The idea of a single woman attempting to govern a nation so notoriously unruly as the English was not to be thought of. Obviously she must have a husband to support and guide her and undertake, as Renard delicately put it, 'those duties which were not the province of ladies' but, in the opinion of the great majority of her subjects, her wisest choice of consort would have been Edward Courtenay, the last sprig of the white Plantagenet rose. Courtenay, now in his mid-twenties, had high birth, good looks, good manners and plenty of personal charm to recommend him: 'le plus beau et plus agréable gentilhomme d'Angleterre', commented Antoine de Noailles approvingly. Mary had released him from the Tower and was quite prepared to be kind to him – his only crime, after all, lay in being the great-grandson of King Edward IV, and his parents had been among Queen Catherine of Aragon's most active supporters – but she made it perfectly clear that she had no intention of marrying him, or any other Englishman for that matter. Tragically, nothing in Mary's experience had ever given her cause to love or trust her own countrymen. Ever since her unhappy teens she had been forced to turn to her mother's kin for advice and friendship and now the fact that Philip of Spain, a twenty-six-year-old widower, happened to be the most brilliant match in Europe undoubtedly weighed far less with her than the fact that he was also the grandson of her mother's sister.

She had not reached her decision lightly. It had taken Simon Renard three months of patient and tactful persuasion, three months of slipping in and out of back entrys and up the privy stairs for quiet late-evening talks to reassure the nervous Queen and overcome her maidenly shrinking, her self-doubts and fears that Philip was too young for her – or she too old for him – that in her ignorance of 'that which was called love' she would not be able to satisfy him; for, as she shyly confessed, she had never harboured thoughts of voluptuousness, had never even considered marriage until God had been pleased to raise her to the throne. Although one of the reasons publicly advanced in favour of the Queen's marriage was to secure an heir to safeguard the succession, few people seriously believed that Mary, at her age and with her medical history, would ever be able to bear a child. Mary herself was not so sure. God had already worked one miracle for her. Might he not be planning to work another, to give her a son – a future Catholic King of England? For, with Philip at her side and all the might of the Holy Roman Empire behind her, surely nothing could prevent her from carrying out God's manifest purpose of leading her country back into the arms of the true Church? When, therefore, at the end of October 1553, after weeks of heart-searching and prayer, the Queen finally pledged her word to Renard in the presence of the Holy Sacrament that she would marry Philip and love him perfectly, it was done with desperate sincerity and in the conviction that her answer had been divinely inspired.

The only Englishman who might have been able to get Mary to see the sort of trouble she was storing up for herself was Stephen Gardiner, now her Lord Chancellor, but, again unhappily, little trust or ease of communication existed between them. Mary could not forget the part the Bishop of Winchester had once played in helping her father to divorce her mother and Gardiner, faced with a stubborn, emotional woman who had already given her confidence elsewhere, seems to have lacked both nerve and heart for doing battle. He could argue cogently enough with Renard, but to Mary could only object rather lamely that the people would never stomach a foreigner who would make promises he would not keep. The Queen retorted that her mind was made up, and if her Chancellor put the will of the people before her wishes, then he was not keeping *his* promises. Stephen Gardiner, with his long and bitter experience of Tudor temperament, retreated saying the matter was too dangerous to meddle with and he was, in any case, handicapped by his known partiality for Courtenay, to whom he had become much attached while they were in the Tower together. As Mary waspishly remarked, was it reasonable to expect her to marry someone just because the Bishop had made friends with him in prison? She took an even higher tone with the Speaker of the House of Commons. Her marriage was entirely her own affair and Parliament had no business to interfere in her private life. Besides, she added in a burst of petulance, if they tried to force her to take a husband who would not be to her liking, they would cause her death: she would not live three months and would have no children and then perhaps they would be sorry!

Across the Channel the French were taking a thoroughly gloomy view of the situation. Faced with the prospect of seeing his good sister the Queen of England married to his greatest enemy, King Henri II took little comfort from Mary's assurances that she meant to continue to live in peace and amity with her neighbours no matter whom she married. As he observed to the English ambassador Nicholas Wotton in December: 'It is to be considered that a husband may do much with his wife; and it shall be very hard for any wife to refuse her husband any thing that he shall earnestly require of her.' Wotton had been about in the world, the King went on, and knew how subtle and crafty the Spaniards were. Indeed, the danger that England would be dragged into war with France was one of the most serious and, as it turned out, well-founded objections to the Spanish marriage.

In drawing up his son's marriage treaty, Charles V was leaning over backwards in his efforts to take account of the delicate susceptibilities of the English – an alliance which would give him command of the vital sea route between Spain and the Netherlands was worth any amount of diplomacy. But the English were currently in the grip of one of their periodic attacks of xenophobia, and many otherwise quite level-headed people preferred to listen to the scaremongering of such interested parties as the French ambassador and the left-wing Protestants, who were busy spreading rumours that a horde of Spaniards, all armed to the teeth, was poised to invade their shores; that England was about to become a province of the Empire with the Pope's authority reimposed by force.

As the year drew to its close public alarm and suspicion, plus widespread dissatisfaction over the government's handling of affairs in general, was reaching a point where Antoine de Noailles at the French embassy felt the time had come to attempt further destabilization, especially as the means lay so conveniently ready to hand. The Queen might have chosen to reject Edward Courtenay, but there was always Elizabeth, 'and from what I hear', wrote de Noailles on 14 December,

it only requires that my Lord Courtenay should marry her, and that they should go together to the counties of Devonshire and Cornwall. Here it can easily be believed that they would find many adherents, and they could then make a strong claim to the crown, and the Emperor and the Prince of Spain would find it difficult to suppress this rising.

Certainly Elizabeth and Courtenay, who had recently been created Earl of Devon, should have made a powerful combination. Indeed, the romantic appeal of this handsome, well-matched young couple, both of the English blood royal, ought to have been irresistible, but for one serious snag. 'The misfortune', admitted de Noailles, 'is that the said Courtenay is of such a fearful and timid disposition that he dare not make the venture.' It was exasperating when so many influential people would have been ready and willing to help, but there was no denying the fact that, for all his patrician breeding and winning ways, Courtenay had turned out to be a poor creature, with a vicious streak beneath the charm. He was plainly untrustworthy and would doubtless go to pieces in a crisis. However, de Noailles, who had to work with the material available, continued to hope that, carefully handled, he would make a useful tool. As for Elizabeth, the ambassador seems to have taken her co-operation for granted. Whether he had any grounds, other than his own and other people's wishful thinking, for making this assumption it is impossible to say; but if the Princess ever did seriously contemplate raising a rebellion against her sister, the chicken-hearted Courtenay was surely the last person with whom she would willingly have joined forces.

Nevertheless, detailed plans for resisting the threatened Spanish 'invasion' were now being drawn up in several quarters and were still under discussion when, on 2 January 1554, the Imperial envoys, led by Count Egmont, arrived 'for the knitting up of the marriage' between the Queen and the Prince of Spain. Egmont and his colleagues landed at Tower Wharf to a salute of guns from the Tower batteries, and on Tower Hill a reception committee, headed by Courtenay, was waiting to conduct them ceremoniously through the city. But they got no welcome from the watching crowds, for 'the people, nothing rejoicing, held down their heads sorrowfully'. The day before, the embassy servants had been pelted with snowballs, but at least nothing was actually thrown at the distinguished visitors themselves.

The treaty signed on 12 January should have been generous enough in its provisions and safeguards to satisfy the most exacting Englishman, but unfortunately the rising tide of panic and prejudice sweeping the country could no longer be stemmed by reason. The mindless rallying-cry: 'We will have no foreigner for our King', had temporarily driven out common sense, and within a week word reached London that Sir Peter Carew was up in Devonshire 'resisting of the King of Spain's coming'. Almost simultaneously news came in that Sir Thomas Wyatt, son of the poet, was up in Kent 'for the said quarrel in resisting the said King of Spain'; that Sir James Crofts had departed for Wales, 'as it is thought to raise his power there'; and that the Duke of Suffolk and his brothers had mysteriously vanished from Sheen.

The fourfold rising had originally been timed for March – to coincide with the expected date of Philip's arrival – but that 'young fool of a Lord Courtenay', always the weak link, had lost what little nerve he possessed and blabbed to Gardiner; either that, or the Lord Chancellor, who was already suspicious, had wormed a confession out of his protégé. At any rate, he told all he knew about 'the enterprise of Peter Carew and his companions'. The other conspirators, not knowing to what extent their plans had been betrayed and too deeply committed to draw back, were thus scrambled into premature action.

The movement in the West Country had always depended heavily for success on Courtenay's presence, on the prestige of his name and strong family connections with the area. Without him it died at birth and Peter Carew was obliged to leave hurriedly for France, while James Crofts never even got as far as Wales. But in Kent things were different. By 26 January, Thomas Wyatt had taken possession of Rochester and the crews of the royal ships lying in the Medway had gone over to him with their guns and ammunition.

A hastily mustered force, consisting of men of the Queen's guard and the city militia under the command of that reliable old war horse the Duke of Norfolk, was despatched to counter the threat; but the Londoners and a good proportion of the guard promptly defected to the rebels amid rousing cries of 'We are all Englishmen!' In the words of one Alexander Brett, they preferred to spend their blood in the quarrel of 'this worthy captain Master Wyatt' and prevent at all costs the approach of the proud Spaniards who, as every right-thinking Englishman knew, would treat them like slaves, despoil them of their goods and lands, ravish their wives before their faces and deflower their daughters in their presence.

Thus encouraged, Wyatt pressed on towards the capital and on 30 January he was camped around Blackheath and Greenwich. London was in an uproar of alarm and confusion and for a couple of tensely anxious days the loyalty of the citizens hung in the balance. It was Mary herself who really saved the situation. Reacting like a true Tudor she ignored advice to seek her own safety and marched into the city to make a fighting speech in the crowded Guildhall that not even Elizabeth could have bettered. Her audience rose to her, and when Wyatt reached Southwark on 3 February he found the bridge closed and defended against him.

It was a long time since London had last had an army at its gates and 'much noise and tumult was everywhere' as shops were shuttered, market stalls hastily dismantled and weapons unearthed from store. Children gazed wide-eyed at the Lord Mayor and his aldermen riding about the streets in unaccustomed battle array, 'aged men were astonished' and the women wept for fear. The queen had refused to allow the Tower guns to be turned on the rebels in case the innocent inhabitants of Southwark might be harmed, and after three days' uneasy stalemate Wyatt withdrew his men from the bridge foot, marching them up-river to Kingston, where they crossed to the northern bank and turned eastward again. But the steam had gone out of them now. They were tired and hungry and too much time had been wasted. Still they came trudging on through the western suburbs, reaching Knightsbridge by eleven o'clock on the morning of Ash Wednesday 7 February. There followed some rather indecisive skirmishing with the royal forces, commanded by the Earl of Pembroke, round St James's and Charing Cross and some panic at Whitehall when, in the general turmoil, a cry of treason was raised within the palace as a rumour spread that Pembroke had gone over to the enemy. 'There', remarked one observer, 'should ye have seen running and crying of ladies and gentlewomen, shutting of doors, and such a screeching and noise as it was wonderful to hear.' But although her very presence chamber was full of armed men and the gunfire from Charing Cross clearly audible, the Queen stood fast, determined that 'she would tarry to see the uttermost'. She asked for the Earl of Pembroke and was told he was in the field. 'Well then,' answered Mary, 'fall to prayer, and I warrant you we shall hear better news anon; for my lord will not deceive me I know well.'

On this occasion at least, her confidence was not misplaced. Wyatt and a handful of followers got through Temple Bar and on down Fleet Street, but found Ludgate barred and strongly held by Lord William Howard, the Lord Admiral. It was the end for Wyatt. He himself had 'kept touch', as he said, but when it came to the point his friends in the city had failed him. He sat for a while in the rain on a bench outside the Belle Sauvage inn and then, realizing it was hopeless, turned back towards Charing Cross. Fighting flared again briefly as Pembroke's forces came up and the men round Wyatt prepared to sell their lives dearly, but the bloodshed was stopped by Norroy herald who approached Wyatt and begged him to give himself up. Wyatt, soaked, exhausted and confused, hesitated for a moment and then yielded.

The rebellion was over, but the Queen's troubles were only just beginning, for either she must bow to the will of the people violently expressed and abandon her marriage or she must stand firm. Mary, deeply hurt, angry and bewildered, knew that she must stand firm and this meant she could no longer afford the luxury of showing mercy. Inevitably the first victim of the government's new hard-line policy was the Nine Days Queen. Jane Grey might have been innocent of any complicity in Northumberland's treason; innocent she undoubtedly was of complicity in the Wyatt rebellion – but this did not alter the fact that her continued existence had now come to represent an unacceptable danger to the state. Her own father's recent behaviour alone made that abundantly clear.

Henry Grey, Duke of Suffolk, who owed his life and liberty entirely to Mary's generosity, had repaid her by attempting to raise the midland shires against her and had been deeply involved with Wyatt. Summoned to court on 25 January, he told the messenger that he was on the point of hastening to the Queen's side. 'Marry, I was coming to her grace. Ye may see I am booted and spurred ready to ride; and I will but break my fast and go.' Instead he rode northwards and was next heard of at Stony Stratford. He subsequently turned up in the towns of Leicester and Melton Mowbray, issuing proclamations against the Spanish marriage and to 'avoid strangers out of the realm', but he gathered little or no support. Coventry barred its gates against him and by this time the Earl of Huntingdon was in hot pursuit. Increasingly isolated and finding himself 'destitute of all such aid as he looked for among his friends in the two shires of Leicester and Warwick', the Duke fled to his nearby manor of Astley, where he and his brother John 'bestowed themselves in secret places' within the park. The story goes that they were betrayed by a keeper named Underwood and that the Duke was found concealed in the trunk of a hollow tree and Lord John buried under a pile of hay. Some accounts add the picturesque detail that the Duke's hiding place was sniffed out by a dog, whose barking led the hunters to their quarry.

The assertion that Suffolk had re-proclaimed his daughter during this unprofitable excursion round the shires appears to be inaccurate – indeed it is explicitly denied by the Chronicles of Stowe and Holinshed. But either way it hardly matters. What did matter was that Jane *had* once been publicly proclaimed; that she had been nominated as heir by the late King Edward, who was now equipped with a fully grown Protestant halo, and that she had actually worn the crown. What was more likely, in the present highly volatile political situation, than that she might again be used as the figurehead of a Protestant plot? Few people urged this view more strongly than men like Arundel, Winchester and Pembroke, so recently prominent Protestant plotters themselves and who – with the prospect of the

imminent arrival of a strong-minded Spanish consort before them –
were more than ever determined to see any inconvenient reminders
of their past indiscretions permanently obliterated. Mary would
have saved Jane if it had been within her power to do so, but neither
Mary, for all her obstinate, conscientious courage, nor Jane with her
formidable intellectual capacity and passionate intensity of conviction, was a match for the desperate, ruthless mafiosi which surrounded them. Both, in their different ways, were the helpless prisoners of their circumstances.

Guildford Dudley was to die with his wife, and their execution
date was originally fixed for Friday 9 February. But although the
Queen had been unable to save her cousin's life, she was determined
to make a last-minute effort to save her soul and sent Dr Feckenham,
the new Dean of St Paul's, over to the Tower with a few days' grace to
see what he could do with this especially obdurate heretic.

In his late thirties, comfortably stout and pink-faced, John Feckenham had a reputation for persuasiveness. A kind-hearted man,
able and sensible, he was also unusually liberal in his outlook for a
cleric in that embattled age. Jane received him politely, telling him
he was welcome if his coming was to give Christian exhortation, and
prepared to engage in the stimulating cut and thrust of theological
debate for the last time.

She defended the Protestant doctrine of justification by faith
alone, parrying Feckenham's 'St Paul saith, "If I have all faith without love, it is nothing" ' with a sharp:

'True it is; for how can I love him whom I trust not, or how can I
trust him whom I love not? Faith and love go both together, and yet
love is comprehended in faith.' It was perfectly acceptable for a
Christian to do good works, 'yet may we not say that they profit to
our salvation. For when we have done all, yet we be unprofitable servants, and faith only in Christ's blood saveth us.'

The discussion then touched on the correct scriptural number of
the sacraments, before coming to what was always the crux of any
argument between the two creeds, the true nature of the eucharist.
Jane's position was predictably unambiguous:

'The sacrament of the Lord's Supper . . . is a sure seal and testimony that I am, by the blood of Christ, which he shed for me on the
cross, made partaker of the everlasting kingdom.'

And when she was asked: 'What do you receive in that sacrament?
Do you not receive the very body and blood of Christ?' her response
came prompt and confident:

'No surely, I do not so believe. I think that at the supper I neither
receive flesh nor blood, but bread and wine; which bread when it is

LA ROYNE MARIE

(ASHMOLEAN MUSEUM, OXFORD)

*Mary Tudor as Queen of France, probably drawn in
1515, when she was just twenty years old*

*Cloth of frieze is matched with cloth of gold – the wedding
portrait of Charles Brandon, Duke of Suffolk, and Mary
Tudor, Queen of France, painted to mark the occasion of their
public marriage at Greenwich Palace in May 1515*

Henry VIII, ten years after his accession when he was still being described as 'much handsomer than any other sovereign in Christendom'

*Charles Brandon, Duke of Suffolk. Like his friend
the King, Suffolk tended to put on weight as he grew
older. Here he is probably already in his fifties*

*My Lady of Suffolk.
Catherine Willoughby, a
baroness in her own right, was
the Duke's ward and fourteen
years old to his forty-eight or
nine when they were married in
September 1533. A 'valiant
spirit', intelligent, witty and
devoutly religious, she strove
all her life to promote the cause
of Protestantism in England*

*Henry and Charles Brandon, the Duke's sons by
Catherine Willoughby. Exceptionally gifted,
handsome and attractive children, they died
tragically in their teens within hours of one another,
of the dreaded sweating sickness*

Of person rare strong limbes & manly shape,
of nature framed to serue on sea & lande
of Frindship firm in good state & ill hope
in peace heade and in warr skill great bould hande
on horse on fote in perill or in playe
none could excel though many did assaye
A subiecte true to Kinge a seruant greate
frind to Gods truth enimye to romes deceate
sumptuose abroad for honor of the lande
temperate at home yet keepts great state & sig
and gaue more mouthes more meate
then some aduanst one higher steps to stand
yet against nature reson & iust lawes
his bloud twase spilt iustlesse wout iust cause

*Thomas, Baron Seymour of Sudeley, younger brother of the
Lord Protector, and Lord High Admiral of England.
Fiercely ambitious, the Admiral 'bought' Lady Jane Grey
from her parents for the sum of two thousand pounds, hoping
to use her to further his own political career*

KATHARINE PARRE

Catherine Parr: Henry VIII's sixth and last wife, who
'always got on pleasantly with the King and had no caprices'.
A committed Protestant and influential patron of the New
Learning, she befriended both Jane Grey and the young
Elizabeth Tudor

Roger Ascham, tutor to the young Elizabeth, scholar, humanist and devoted admirer of Jane Grey. He long remembered his conversation with her at Bradgate in the summer of 1550 and recorded it in The Scholemaster, *his classic treatise on education*

Portrait of a Tudor lady, usually identified as Lady Jane Grey

Bradgate Manor in Leicestershire,  *the red-brick, stone-turreted mansion on the fringes of Charnwood Forest, where Jane Grey and her sisters were born and spent their early childhood*

The Old Palace at Chelsea, which stood on the banks of the River Thames on the site of the present Cheyne Walk. Built by Henry VIII in the late 1530s, it formed part of Queen Catherine Parr's jointure, and she went to live there when the King died, taking the Lady Elizabeth and Lady Jane Grey with her

Edward VI was about ten years old when this portrait was painted. As a child of nine he had been the first King of England to be crowned as Supreme Head of the Church, and the European reformers earnestly hoped that he would marry his cousin, the 'noble virgin' Jane Grey. 'How happy would be the unions,' they exclaimed, 'and how beneficial to the church.'

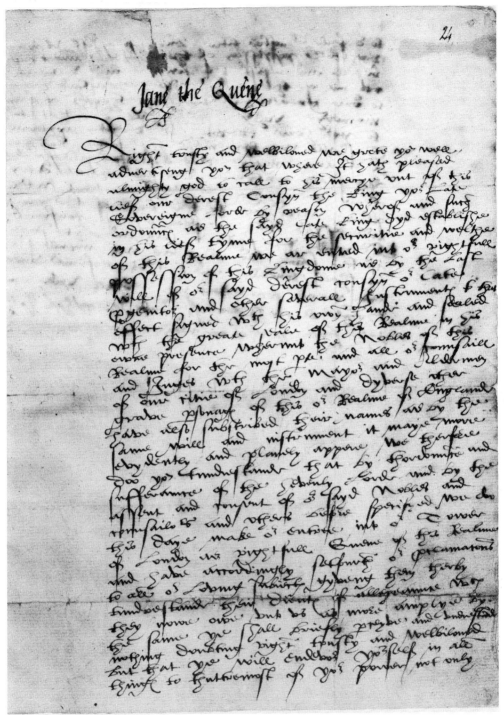

One of the Letters Patent issued over the sign manual of Queen Jane, across the back of which Mr Secretary Cecil later wrote: 'Jana non Regina'

The great fortress prison of the Tower of London as it appeared in the mid-sixteenth century, and showing the royal apartments, which stood between the White Tower and the river

John Dudley, Duke of Northumberland: the strong man who seized power in the 1549 October coup and master-minded the 1553 July coup which led to the nine-day reign of his daughter-in-law, Jane the Quene

The elaborately carved relief on a wall in the Beauchamp Tower, where the Duke of Northumberland's sons were imprisoned after the failure of the 1553 coup. The work of the eldest surviving brother, John, it shows the Dudley badge of the bear and ragged staff

Jane's prayer book, which she carried to the scaffold, and in which she wrote a message to her father, reassuring him that, by losing this mortal life, she and Guildford Dudley would have won an immortal life

Sir Thomas Wyatt, son of the poet Thomas Wyatt and himself a soldier, diplomat and courtier, who led the Kentish rebellion in 1554 'against the coming in of the Prince of Spain' and very nearly succeeded in his objective

This portrait has for many years been described as Lady Frances Brandon and her second husband Adrian Stokes, though this attribution is now in some doubt. The Lady Frances, elder daughter of Mary Tudor and Charles Brandon, Marchioness of Dorset and later Duchess of Suffolk, was the mother of Jane Grey. Adrian Stokes, who is said to have been her Master of the Horse, was some sixteen years her junior

Queen Mary Tudor, the daughter of Henry VIII's first marriage, who once described herself as 'the most unhappy lady in Christendom' but whose policy of religious persecution against the Protestant minority earned her the nickname of 'Bloody Mary'

Queen Elizabeth I. Although never a beauty in the accepted sense, she was an attractive woman, graceful, elegant, stylish and supremely self-confident. This portrait by an unknown artist shows her in her prime, probably in her late twenties or early thirties

broken, and the wine when it is drunken, put me in remembrance how that for my sins the body of Christ was broken, and his blood shed on the cross.'

'But', protested Feckenham, 'doth not Christ speak these words: "Take eat, this is my body?" Require you any plainer words? Doth he not say it is his body?'

'And so he saith, "I am the vine, I am the door",' retorted Jane. 'Doth not St Paul say, "He calleth things that are not, as though they were"?' Surely anyone could recognize figurative speech for what it was. And now she went over to the attack: 'And I pray you, answer me this one question: Where was Christ when he said, "Take eat, this is my body"? Was he not at the table when he said so? He was at that time alive and suffered not till the next day. What took he but bread? What brake he but bread? And what gave he but bread?'

When Feckenham objected that she was grounding her faith 'upon such authors as say and unsay, both with a breath, and not upon the church', again the reply came with the authentic ring of total, terrifying conviction:

'I ground my faith upon God's word, and not upon the church. . . . The faith of the church must be tried by God's word, and not God's word by the church; neither yet my faith.'

Feckenham was not yet ready to admit defeat in the battle to secure this so desirable convert and continued the argument with 'many strong and logical persuasions'; but faith, wrote Jane, had armed her resolution against words and to forsake that faith for love of life, as her old dread Northumberland had done, would still have been the ultimate shame for this eager, vital sixteen-year-old.

The account of the confrontation with Feckenham, which has come down to us in the robustly Protestant pages of John Foxe, naturally gives Jane the last word and the victory; but Jane herself, who accepted Feckenham's offer to accompany her to the scaffold, parted from him with some regret, since they plainly could not look forward to resuming their discussions in the hereafter. Unless, of course, he repented and turned to God. She would, she told him, 'pray God in the bowels of his mercy to send you his Holy Spirit; for he hath given you his great gift of utterance, if it pleased him also to open the eyes of your heart'. She seems, in fact, to have been rather disturbed by the realization that she had come dangerously close to liking a Catholic priest; that she had found him sympathetic, intelligent and cultivated – rather more so than a good many of the Protestants she had known. In the circumstances it was perhaps just as well that she had so little time to brood on the worrying implications of this discovery, which seem to be hinted at in the prayer she is said to have composed shortly before her execution:

> O merciful God ... be thou now unto me a strong tower of
> defence. . . . Suffer me not to be tempted above my power, but either
> be thou a deliverer unto me out of this great misery, of else give me
> grace patiently to bear thy heavy hand and sharp correction. . . . Arm
> me, I beseech thee, with thy armour, that I may stand fast . . . above
> all things, taking to me the shield of faith, wherewith I may be able to
> quench all the fiery darts of the wicked.

The sharp correction was now no longer to be delayed and those
last days were taken up with the macabre preparations which had to
be made by all high-born victims of judicial execution. The Lady
Jane must choose a suitable dress for her final public appearance and
nominate two members of her little household to witness her death
and afterwards 'decently dispose' of her body. The speech which she
would make from the scaffold must be polished and copied out for
subsequent circulation and publication. There were farewell letters
to be written, too, and farewell presents to be chosen. Her sister
Catherine got her Greek testament – 'it will teach you to live and
learn you to die' – plus a long and windy letter of spiritual exhortation, wasted on feather-headed Catherine. To her father, who had
been brought back to the Tower on Saturday 10 February, Jane sent
a message of comfort, though her outraged sense of justice had also
impelled her to remind him that her death was being hastened by one
'by whom my life should rather have been lengthened'. There was no
letter or message for her mother and none for her husband.

The story is told that Guildford had expressed an earnest wish to
see Jane once more before he died. This was repeated to the Queen,
who sent word that if it would be of any consolation to them the
young couple might be allowed to meet to say goodbye, but Jane
refused the proffered indulgence, saying it would only be upsetting
and disturb their 'holy tranquillity' – better to wait until they met
again 'in a better place'. It's possible that she may have hoped she
would like him better there, but the story has the same odour of
sanctimonious sentimentality which hangs over most of the anec-
dotes which have gathered around Jane, and there seems to be no
real evidence that she ever showed the slightest interest in Guildford
at any time during their imprisonment, or he in her. Much has been
made of the fact that the name 'Jane' was found carved on a wall of
the prison quarters shared by the Dudley brothers, but there is no
proof that this was a testimony to anything other than boredom; no
proof that it was even Guildford's work or referred to Jane Grey – the
Duchess of Northumberland was also called Jane.

However, when the unlucky Guildford was brought out of the
Beauchamp Tower at ten o'clock on the morning of Monday 12 February on his way to the execution ground on Tower Hill, Jane had
stationed herself at her window to see his procession leave. She
waited obstinately for its return, and presently the cart with the
decapitated carcase of that tall, strong boy who had wanted her to
make him a king lying on the bloodstained straw, the head wrapped
roughly in a cloth, rattled past below her on its way to St Peter's. The
sight moved her perhaps more than she had expected, and those
standing by heard her murmur Guildford's name and something
about 'the bitterness of death'.

Guildford Dudley had died like a gentleman, quietly and without
fuss, and now it was Jane's turn. Her execution, as befitted a princess
of the blood royal, was to take place privately on Tower Green – from
Partridge's house she would have had an excellent view of her scaffold being erected 'over against the White Tower' – and as soon as
the officials were ready she came out leaning on the arm of the
Lieutenant, Sir John Brydges. Her two attendants, Mrs Ellen and
Elizabeth Tylney, were in tears, but Jane herself, wearing the same
black gown she had worn to her trial, appeared dry-eyed and perfectly composed, her little prayer book open in her free hand. She
climbed the steps of the scaffold and then turned, ready to address
the invited audience which had gathered to see justice done.

Jane did not waste words. She admitted again that she had done
wrong in accepting the crown. 'The fact, indeed, against the queen's
highness was unlawful, and the consenting thereunto by me; but
touching the procurement and desire thereof by me or on my behalf,
I do wash my hands in innocency, before God and the face of you,
good Christian people this day.' And, says the eyewitness account,
'she wrung her hands, in which she had her book'. She asked all those
present to bear witness that she died a good Christian woman and
that she looked to be saved 'by none other mean, but only by the
mercy of God in the merits of the blood of his only son Jesus
Christ. . . . And now, good people,' she ended, 'while I am alive, I
pray you to assist me with your prayers.' Even in that last dreadful
moment she could find the strength to remain true to her stern Protestant faith and steadfastly reject the age-old comfort of prayers for
the dead. Kneeling, she turned to John Feckenham saying: 'Shall I
say this psalm?' and then repeated the fifty-first psalm, the Miserere,
in English 'in most devout manner' to the end, Feckenham beside
her following her in Latin.

Now there were just the final formalities to be gone through. She
got to her feet, handed her gloves and handkerchief to Mrs Tylney

and her prayer book to John Brydges's brother Thomas, and began to untie the fastenings of her gown. As the executioner, that nightmare masked figure, stepped forward, Jane, not understanding perhaps that his victim's outer garments were the hangman's traditional perquisite, shrank back and 'desired him to leave her alone'. Nurse Ellen and Elizabeth Tylney helped her to undress and gave her 'a fair handkercher to knit about her eyes'. Now the hangman was kneeling for the ritual asking and receiving of forgiveness. He told her to stand upon the straw and in so doing she saw the block for the first time. There was nothing left to do but make an end. Whispering, 'I pray you despatch me quickly', she tied the blindfold over her eyes. The world vanished and she was alone, groping in the darkness, crying shockingly: 'What shall I do? Where is it?' Someone stepped forward to guide her and 'she laid her down upon the block and stretched forth her body and said, Lord into thy hands I commend my spirit'. The axe swung and blood spouted obscenely over the scaffold, soaking the straw and spattering the standers-by.

The Tower officials, their work done, began to disperse. Perhaps John Brydges was already reading the message Jane had written for him on the flyleaf of her prayer book:

> Forasmuch as you have desired so simple a woman to write in so worthy a book, good Master Lieutenant, therefore shall I as a friend desire you, and as a Christian require you, to call upon God, to incline your heart to his laws and not to take the word of truth utterly out of your mouth. Live still to die, that by death you may purchase eternal life. . . . For, as the preacher sayeth, there is a time to be born and a time to die; and the day of death is better than the day of our birth. Yours, as the Lord knoweth as a friend, Jane Duddeley.

Some time later that day the butchered corpse of King Henry VIII's great-niece was thrust unceremoniously under the stones of St Peter-ad-Vincula to lie between the bones of two headless Queens: Anne Boleyn and Catherine Howard. Another instalment of the debt incurred in the chapel at Cluny forty years before had been repaid.

The judicial murder of Jane Grey – for no one, even at the time, ever pretended it was anything else – must surely count as one of the most coldly horrifying episodes in English history, but it caused no great stir at the time, even among the aggressively Protestant Londoners. Public opinion, which played such a significant part in saving the life of her cousin Elizabeth, was not mobilized to help Jane, whose name, so far as it was remembered at all, remained too closely associated with the Dudleys and their failed coup to rouse much sympathy. There is a tradition that the oak trees in Bradgate Park were pollarded as a gesture of mourning and defiance when news of Lady Jane's beheading reached Leicestershire, and a story that the judge who had sentenced her died in a raving delirium, crying, 'Take the Lady Jane from me! Take away the Lady Jane!'

Roger Ascham remembered her, of course. So did John Aylmer, who rose to become Bishop of London under Queen Elizabeth, and so perhaps did John Feckenham, who spent most of the rest of his long life in prison for his religious beliefs, dying in the concentration camp for Catholic priests at Wisbech in Cambridgeshire in 1585, almost the last survivor of his generation. John Foxe included Jane among his gallery of Protestant martyrs, and a somewhat per-functory regret for the 'casting away' of a fair lady whom both God and nature had endowed with singular gifts and graces is expressed in the contemporary histories. In general, though, for reasons both personal and political, it became increasingly tactless to mention the Suffolk family in polite Elizabethan circles. The eighteenth and nineteenth centuries resurrected, canonized and dehumanized Jane Grey, so that the cool, sceptical early twentieth century found her totally incomprehensible. The later twentieth century should have no such difficulty, being rather better acquainted with the effects of ideological commitment on personality, for it is only in terms of total commitment to an ideology that Jane can be understood. Only thus is it possible to recognize the loving, lively, gifted child, consistently starved of affection, growing into a forceful, passionate young woman sublimating all her overflowing energies and urges in devo-tion to an idea, to an ideal. Jane, in fact, had all the makings of a true fanatic. In another age she would have been the perfect prototype of the partisan, the resistance or freedom fighter, the urban guerrilla, perfectly prepared to sacrifice her own or anyone else's life in the furtherance of some cause, be it religious or political.

On the day that Jane and Guildford Dudley died, gallows were being erected all over London, in the suburbs of Bermondsey and Southwark, at Leadenhall, in Cheapside and Fleet Street and west-ward to Charing Cross and Hyde Park Corner, and soon all the city gates were decorated with severed heads and dismembered corpses – an intentionally grim reminder of the consequences of unsuccessful rebellion. The extermination of the House of Suffolk was also pro-ceeding to what Simon Renard still regarded as its long overdue con-clusion. On Saturday 17 February, Henry, Duke of Suffolk, was taken by river from the Tower to Westminster for his trial, who 'at his going out went out very stoutly and cheerfully enough' but returned 'with a countenance very heavy and pensive, desiring all men to pray for him'.

Suffolk, whose only justification for his erratic behaviour apparently was that he had felt himself slighted by the Council since the Northumberland affair, had told his judges that he thought it 'no treason for a peer of the realm as he was to raise his power and make proclamation only to avoid strangers out of the realm'. This might have been a good point, but he spoilt it by going on to boast that he had resisted the Queen's Lieutenant in the person of the Earl of Huntingdon and then rather unsportingly tried to blame his brother Thomas for having persuaded him to seek the safety of Leicestershire, telling him that 'it was to be feared he should be put again in the Tower', but 'being in his own country and amongst friends and tenants, who durst fetch him?' Neither of these lines of defence impressed the court, presided over by the Earl of Arundel, and the Duke was duly convicted and condemned. 'A man of high nobility by birth . . . ' pronounced Holinshed's *Chronicle*, 'to his friends gentle and courteous, more easy indeed to be led than was thought expedient, of stomach nevertheless stout and hardy, hasty and soon kindled, but pacified straight again . . . upright and plain in his private dealing'. But in public dealing shifty and deceitful, with an unerring instinct for picking the losing side. A weak man, irascible, unstable and possessing the soul of a petty crook, Henry Grey paid the usual forfeit to the executioner on Tower Hill on Friday 23 February. Like his daughter, he was attended on the scaffold by a Catholic priest, but he died in the Protestant faith, believing, he assured the watching crowd, 'to be saved by none other but only by almighty God, through the passion of his son Jesus Christ'.

Lord Thomas Grey, who had been picked up at Oswestry near the Welsh border as he tried to make his way to the coast, was executed towards the end of April and was among the last of the Wyatt conspirators to suffer. By this time the Queen was beginning to issue pardons to convicted rebels and London juries were beginning to return not-guilty verdicts. John Grey, although tried and 'cast' as a traitor, was later pardoned and released, as were the surviving Dudley brothers. Edward Courtenay and the Princess Elizabeth also escaped with their lives – much to the annoyance of Simon Renard, who did not hesitate to express his opinion that the Queen had wasted a heaven-sent opportunity to rid herself of these two so obviously dangerous enemies of the state. By May the prisons were emptying. Courtenay was consigned to a period of house arrest at Fotheringay Castle, from whence he would presently be sent to travel abroad and find his death from fever in Italy. Elizabeth, after her brief but well-publicized imprisonment in the Tower, was also despatched to languish in preventive detention in a remote country house – the old royal hunting lodge at Woodstock in Oxfordshire – and Mary left for Richmond Palace to prepare for her wedding, which was expected to take place at Winchester some time before the end of June. Gradually the rotting corpses and other depressing relics of the winter of discontent were tidied out of sight. It looked like the end of a chapter.

The dukedom of Suffolk was now once more extinct, but the widowed Duchess consoled herself with even greater rapidity than once her father had done. Three weeks or so after her husband's execution she married again – to young Master Adrian Stokes, who is variously described as her steward, equerry or master of the horse. There seems to be little or no other information about Adrian Stokes, except that he was fifteen years younger than his bride, red-haired and with a flashy taste in dress. All the eighteenth- and nineteenth-century chroniclers were scathing about the match, both because of its unseemly haste and the social class of the bridegroom. Obviously the Duchess had married beneath her; but it does not follow that Stokes was some illiterate peasant – on the contrary, there is evidence to suggest that he was an educated man. He was presumably one of those aspiring gentlemen servants who swarmed in every great household: eager, resourceful young men drawn from the ranks of the rising professional middle classes and looking for an opening, an opportunity to carve out a career in the service of an influential patron. In a society which saw nothing in the least demeaning in the concept of personal service, this was a perfectly respectable and well-recognized, if chancy, method of getting one's start in life.

Frances Grey was following a family precedent by marrying into a lower social stratum, nor was she the only former Duchess of Suffolk to have chosen a second husband from among the ranks of her household staff, for in January 1553, after nearly eight years of widowhood, Catherine Brandon had married her gentleman usher, Richard Bertie. Some accounts make Bertie the son of a stonemason. More plausibly, his father, Thomas, had been the governor or 'captain' of Hurst Castle, the fortress built by Henry VIII to guard the entrance to the Solent. Richard was born in Southampton in 1517, making him about two years older than his wife. Educated at Oxford, at Corpus Christi, he was an accomplished cultivated gentleman, speaking fluent French and Italian and reputed to be 'bold in discourse and quick at repartee'. He had served for a while in the household of the Lord Chancellor Wriothesley and is said to have been trained as a lawyer. He was also, like Catherine, a committed member of the reformed Church and their marriage, based on shared interests and mutual respect and affection, to have been a total success.

The Berties had played no part in the stirring events of 1553. Catherine, who continued to be known as 'my lady of Suffolk', much as her predecessor Mary Tudor had continued to be known as the French Queen after *her* second marriage, was pregnant and gave birth to a daughter, christened Susan, early in 1554. The couple remained living very quietly on Catherine's Lincolnshire estates, no doubt hoping to avoid attracting official attention; for they both knew that the change of administration in London boded them no good – especially bearing in mind that Stephen Gardiner had a long score to settle with Catherine Bertie. In spite of this Catherine had been sending gifts of money to the imprisoned Protestant bishops Ridley and Latimer (Hugh Latimer was a particularly old and valued friend), and she did not expect to be left in peace indefinitely. Sure enough, in Lent 1554 a peremptory summons reached Grimsthorpe via the Sheriff of Lincoln ordering Richard Bertie up to London to appear before the Lord Chancellor who, says John Foxe, had picked the holy time of Lent to devise a holy practice of revenge against the Lady Catherine, 'first touching her in the person of her husband'.

According to the reports printed by Holinshed and Foxe, Gardiner opened the attack by demanding the immediate repayment of the four thousand pounds still owed to the crown by Catherine's former husband, the late Duke Charles. Bertie, however, refused to be rattled. He was able to show that the debt was 'estalled' – that is, being paid by instalments – as agreed by Henry VIII, and that the payments were fully up to date. Gardiner then shifted his ground. He had heard bad reports of Bertie's religious opinions, he said, but knowing something of his background and education, he was prepared to give him the benefit of the doubt. But:

> 'If I may ask the question of my lady your wife, is she now as ready to set up the mass, as she was lately to pull it down, when she caused in her progress a dog in a rochet to be carried and called by my name? Or doth she think her lambs now safe enough, which said to me, when I veilled [doffed] my bonnet to her out of my chamber window in the Tower, that it was merry with the lambs, now the wolf was shut up?

And Stephen Gardiner, it seemed, had other, even older grievances against my lady of Suffolk which still rankled. There had been an occasion once when Duke Charles had held a dinner party, inviting every lady present to sit beside 'him whom she loved best' and Catherine had taken the bishop by the hand, saying that as she could not sit down with her lord, whom she loved best, 'she had chosen him whom she loved worst'.

Stolidly, Richard Bertie defended his tactless wife. If her words had sounded bitter, he was sure they had never been intended personally. Of the device of the dog, certainly in poor taste, 'she was neither the author nor the allower'. But when it came to setting up the mass again, this was something which she learned inwardly to abhor by the strong persuasions of many excellent and respected divines, as well as the universal consent and order of six whole years. If she were now to allow it outwardly, she would show herself to Christ a false Christian and to her Prince a masking subject. Surely Gardiner realized that a false or forced confession of religion meant nothing, and that one convert turned by judgement and persuasion was worth more than a thousand merely paying lip-service?

Would it be possible to persuade Catherine? asked Gardiner.

Oh yes, said Bertie, 'with the truth: for she is reasonable enough'.

It would be a marvellous grief to the Prince of Spain and his company, sighed the Chancellor, in an allusion to Catherine's Spanish mother, 'when they shall find but two noble personages of the Spanish race within this land, the Queen and my lady your wife; and one of them gone from the faith'.

Richard Bertie could only reply that he trusted 'they should find no fruits of infidelity in her' and there, for the moment, the matter rested. But neither of the Berties believed they had heard the last of it.

Already a number of prominent religious dissidents were being driven to seek refuge abroad in Protestant Germany and Switzerland, in Strasbourg and Frankfurt, Basle, Zürich and the fountainhead of Calvinism, Geneva itself, and now the Duchess and her husband – warned by their friends, says Foxe, that Gardiner meant to call her to an account of her faith 'whereby extremity might follow' – began to devise ways and means how, by the queen's licence, they too might 'pass the seas'. Richard Bertie waited on the Chancellor again and mentioned that there were some substantial sums of money due to the old Duke of Suffolk from overseas, principally from the Emperor Charles V. So far, all attempts to extract these moneys had failed, but now, with the Queen's marriage not yet finalized, was surely the best time to apply pressure in Brussels. As one of her late husband's executors, his wife had authorized him to act for her in this matter and he therefore sought the Chancellor's help in applying for a passport. He got it without difficulty and early in June, again according to Foxe, sailed from Dover to make arrangements for his family to follow him.

As it turned out, it was six months before he was able to send for them, and for Catherine, that vigorous outspoken energetic soul who had once written to William Cecil 'from Grimsthorpe . . . at six o'clock in the morning and like a sluggard in my bed', this waiting period must have been especially trying. She had moved with the baby Susan from Lincolnshire to her London house in the Barbican and with the city full of government spies she was, for the first time in her life, having to guard her tongue. When at last Bertie's summons reached her, some time during the Christmas holidays, she faced another new experience. My lady of Suffolk had always been accustomed to travel with a retinue of servants and the rest of the paraphernalia of coaches, baggage wagons and outriders which normally surrounded any important personage on the move; now she and her infant daughter must set out on their long and perilous journey with only a bare minimum of luggage and the escort of no more than a handful of servants, and those the meanest, for, says John Foxe, 'she doubted the best would not adventure that fortune with her'. In the end she took four men, 'one a Greek born which was a rider of horses, another a joiner, the third a brewer, the fourth a fool, one of the kitchen', plus one gentlewoman and a laundress.

This oddly assorted little party stole out of the Barbican between four and five o'clock on the pitch dark foggy morning of 1 January 1555, but just as they reached the street, the watchman, described by Foxe as 'a herald' and who may have been one of Gardiner's men, heard a noise in the house and came out with a torch to investigate. In their haste the fugitives dropped a pot of milk and the trunk containing the baby's clothes in the gatehouse, and the watchman, thus fortunately diverted, paused to examine his surprising finds, giving Catherine and her women just enough time to slip into the gateway of the nearby Charterhouse. The men hurried off in the opposite direction, so that when their pursuer emerged, he found the street empty and 'nobody stirring'. As soon as the coast seemed to be clear, Catherine set out again, making for the Lion Quay between Billingsgate and London Bridge. Neither she nor her companions were at all sure of the way and the three women groped through the murk past Finsbury Fields, my lady of Suffolk clutching her baby and appearing 'like a mean merchant's wife . . . walking the streets unknown'. But at Moorgate they suddenly met up with the rest of the party again and at Lion Quay came to the barge which had been hired to take them down-river to the Essex port of Leigh, although the boatmen showed every sign of reluctance to 'launch out' on so misty a morning and had to be persuaded – no doubt with more gold coins.

When they reached Leigh, Robert Cranwell, an old and trusted friend of Richard Bertie's, was waiting to meet them. Catherine's flight was known by this time, of course, but she had to wait for the wind and tide before embarking on the sea crossing and Cranwell chose to pass her off as 'Mistress White', the married daughter of an acquaintance of his living in Leigh. After a night spent nervously at an inn, Mistress White and her two female attendants (the men seem to have fallen by the wayside) were at last able to go aboard a ship for Flanders, but their troubles were not yet over. Twice the wind veered, driving them back on to the English coast, and the second time this happened they found themselves almost back where they had started. The master of the little vessel was obliged to send one of the crew ashore to buy fresh provisions and by now certain inquisitive persons were asking questions about the identity of the lady passengers. Again the ship set sail and this time she made the coast of Brabant where husband and wife were reunited – although one account has it that Bertie had been in hiding in England and had joined Catherine at Leigh.

Notwithstanding all this melodrama, the prosaic truth is that Catherine of Suffolk had never been in any very serious danger of arrest, it being government, or rather Stephen Gardiner's, policy to encourage hard-line Protestants – especially the leaders of Protestant opinion – to take themselves and their awkward consciences overseas. The Chancellor, in fact, was known to boast that if such individuals looked like being reluctant to go, he would summon them to his presence and this seldom failed to have the desired effect. In the case of the Berties, Gardiner had no doubt derived a certain amount of simple pleasure from putting the frighteners on, but he would have been seriously embarrassed if they had decided to call his bluff. Some examples were about to be made, but it would have done the Catholic cause no good to have made a martyr out of my lady of Suffolk.

8

The Knot of Secret Might

*So trust uniteth faithful minds with knot of
secret might,
Whose force to break (but greedy Death) no wight
possesseth power.*

The dreaded Prince of Spain had finally arrived in England towards
the end of July 1554 to be greeted not by riots and insult and hostile
crowds but, in far more typical fashion, by a persistent soaking
downpour of fine summer rain. In fact, the crowds of sightseers who
flocked to catch a glimpse of him as he came ashore at Southampton
and trampled over one another in the streets of Winchester were
more curious than unfriendly, and perhaps even a little disappointed
when the bloodstained monster of the Protestant propaganda
machine was revealed as a slim, dapper young man, rather below
average height, whose blue eyes, fair hair and beard made him look,
it was thought, more like a Fleming than a Spaniard.

The royal wedding took place in Winchester Cathedral on Wednesday 25 July with all the solemn ritual, all the pomp and splendour
proper to the marriage of a queen regnant, the flickering tapers glint-
ing on the cloth of gold mantles worn by the bridal couple, on the velvet and satin and jewels adorning the wedding guests and the vestments of the officiating clergy – six bishops coped and mitred and
led, naturally enough, by Stephen Gardiner doing the honours in his
own cathedral church.

It is not recorded whether the Queen's cousin Frances and the
ladies Catherine and Mary Grey were among the 'great company of
ladies and gentlewomen richly apparelled' who supported her at the
ceremony and were later present at the sumptuous wedding breakfast served on gold plate in the great hall of the Bishop's palace, but
it seems more than likely that they were. Mary never showed any
sign of bearing a grudge against the surviving members of the House

of Suffolk. Even Frances's second marriage had not apparently affected her status, and the Queen quite went out of her way to be kind to the two girls who both retained their places among the maids of honour.

After a short honeymoon at Winchester the court set out on the return journey to London, travelling by way of Basing, Reading and Windsor, where Philip was installed as a Knight of the Garter. 'Their majesties are the happiest couple in the world and more in love than words can say', gushed one member of the Prince's suite in a letter home. Certainly Mary, poor soul, was already hopelessly, helplessly in love while Philip was unfailingly polite – attentive, said another Spaniard with perhaps unconscious cruelty, attentive as a son. The Queen was, of course, a dear good creature, a perfect saint in fact, but she looked older than anyone had expected, dressed badly and could not, by any stretch of the imagination, be described as beautiful. It was as well, wrote Philip's best friend, Ruy Gomez, that the Prince had always known that the English marriage was intended for political and not fleshly considerations, as this pathetic flabby little virgin would obviously be no good in bed.

The household reached Richmond on 11 August and a week later Mary brought her husband to London, now swept clean of gibbets and blackened heads and decorated instead with pageants and shows and new paint. The citizens, well primed with free drink, were in benevolent mood, although there was inevitably a fair amount of jealousy and bad feeling between the two nations. The Spaniards complained that they were being palmed off with inferior accommodation and charged about twenty-five times the proper prices in shops and inns; while the English grumbled that the city was being overrun with foreigners and the Queen appeared to care nothing for her own subjects but only for Spaniards and bishops. All the same, and considering the events of the previous winter, on the surface things were going reasonably well.

Philip was determined they should continue to do so. The whole point of this marriage – and the only reason why he had agreed to it – was to bring England permanently into the imperial Hapsburg orbit, and that meant avoiding all unnecessary friction. Mary, lost in her fool's paradise of love, was only too happy to leave everything in his hands, to trust prudent, pious, Catholic Philip to be wise for both of them, and on 12 November they went together to open the third Parliament of the reign: a Parliament which, if all went well, would complete the work of dismantling the English Reformation.

Two weeks later Cardinal Pole, the first papal legate to set foot on English soil since the days of Henry VIII's divorce, landed at Dover, bringing with him papal absolution for the schismatic islanders. On 30 November the three estates of the realm knelt together in the Great Chamber of the Court at Westminster to receive that absolution, pronounced by the lord Bishop of Winchester, and England was once again a member of the Roman Catholic communion.

Negotiations leading up to this historic moment had been going on for many months and had been principally concerned with safeguarding the property rights of all holders of former church lands. Once this had been accomplished to the satisfaction of the property owners in question, the Commons, which had been carefully chosen from 'the wise, grave and Catholic sort', was graciously prepared to accept the Pope's forgiveness and to proceed with the repeal of all the religious and ecclesiastical legislation passed under Henry VIII, to abrogate the royal supremacy and restore the mediaeval laws and penalties relating to heresy.

Serious heresy hunting began in February 1555 and was to continue spasmodically for the next three and a half years, during which time some three hundred persons, including sixty women, were burnt alive. As religious persecutions went, the campaign which has left such an indelible stain on Queen Mary Tudor's memory and earned her her unenviable nickname was not an especially ruthless one; it affected only a small minority of the population, being largely confined to London and the south-east, but it nevertheless cast a deepening shadow of gloom and disgust over the whole country. One of its least attractive features lay in the fact that, apart from Thomas Cranmer and a handful of other clerics, among them John Hooper, Nicholas Ridley and my lady of Suffolk's old friend and mentor Hugh Latimer, the victims were drawn almost exclusively from the working class – poor widows, journeymen and apprentices, agricultural labourers, weavers and clothworkers whose readiness to bear witness to their faith by dying an agonizing death in the local market place made an unforgettable impression on their less resolute neighbours. In the inspired words of Bishop Latimer as he and Ridley stood bound to the stake in the dry ditch outside the walls of Oxford, the fires which consumed the Protestant martyrs did indeed light such a candle, by God's grace, in England as never was put out.

In the spring and summer of 1555, however, all the attention of the more politically minded was concentrated on the Queen's supposed pregnancy. Mary had announced that she was with child the previous autumn and at the beginning of April she moved out to Hampton Court to 'take her chamber' preparatory to lying in. 'Everything in this kingdom depends on the Queen's safe deliverance', wrote Simon Renard; and if, against all the odds, Mary did now succeed in producing a healthy, half-Hapsburg offspring of either sex, then of course the Hapsburgs would have absorbed England as efficiently and cheaply as in past generations they had absorbed the kingdoms of Spain and the rich Burgundian inheritance of the Netherlands, and the English political landscape would be transformed for generations to come.

Early in the morning of 30 April word reached London that the Queen had indeed been delivered of a male child 'with little pain and no danger'. Despite the lack of any official confirmation, this rumour was generally believed. Church bells were rung, bonfires lit in the streets and free wine provided for all comers. Whatever its long-term implications, the birth of a prince was automatically an occasion for rejoicing. But rejoicing turned out to be premature, as were the accompanying prophecies of doom. On 24 June, Renard reported that the royal doctors had proved to be two months out in their calculations and the Queen did not expect to be confined for another week or ten days. July came in and still the empty cradle waited, but Mary stubbornly refused to give up hope. The doctors and midwives were still talking about miscalculation and hinting that the Queen might not be delivered until August, or even September, but by now only the hapless Queen believed them. At the beginning of August the court moved away to the small summer palace of Oatlands and, as the Venetian ambassador put it, the royal pregnancy seemed to have ended in wind. In fact, the amenorrhoea and digestive troubles which had afflicted Mary ever since her teens had combined with what was probably incipient cancer of the womb and a desperate longing to bear Philip's child to create that tragic self-deception which, according to the omniscient Venetians, even produced 'swelling of the paps and their emission of milk'.

At the end of August the Queen's misery and humiliation were compounded by the departure of her husband. Philip had spent over a year in a country he disliked, being affable to people he despised and distrusted, affectionate towards a demanding, physically unattractive and unfruitful wife. He felt he had done as much to promote the English alliance as could reasonably be expected, but before he left for more congenial surroundings he took certain steps intended to guard the future. He had already insisted on the release and rehabilitation of the Lady Elizabeth and now he told the Queen that he particularly wanted the Princess to be treated with all due consideration and respect. The embarrassing events of the summer had made it clear that, barring accidents, Elizabeth would in due course succeed her sister on the English throne and, despite her illegitimacy and her more than doubtful religious orthodoxy, from the Spanish

Hapsburg point of view she remained an infinitely preferable alternative to the half-French Queen of Scots, who was fast approaching marriageable age and marriage to the French Dauphin.

Elizabeth Tudor, on the other hand, although nearly twenty-two, was still unbetrothed and apparently fancy free, and once he had reluctantly come to terms with the fact that it was not going to be possible to cut off Elizabeth's head, Simon Renard began to urge his masters to do something practical about attaching the English heiress to their interests – something like arranging a suitable marriage for her. Several more or less credible candidates were suggested, but for some time the favourite was Philibert Emmanuel, the dispossessed Duke of Savoy.

Elizabeth, though, was uncooperative, saying repeatedly that she didn't want to marry anyone and would rather die than marry the Duke of Savoy, a Hapsburg poor relation and a professional soldier popularly reputed to be in the habit of going to bed in his armour. Mary, too, was being difficult, resisting every effort to persuade her to recognize her sister as the heir presumptive. It was, of course, an open secret that the Queen's 'evil disposition' towards Elizabeth was rooted in the sour soil of old grievances. 'She still resents the injuries inflicted on Queen Catherine, her lady mother, by the machinations of Anne Boleyn, mother of Elizabeth', Renard had written, with a touch of exasperation, back in the winter of 1553. Now Mary was saying that she could not even be certain that Elizabeth was King Henry's bastard, that her mother had been an infamous woman and she would not hear of favouring her.

Philip, who was not interested in the ancient feuds of the Tudor family and wanted to put an end to any remaining uncertainty over the English succession, was not unnaturally irritated by this double display of feminine unreasonableness, but Mary, although miserable in the knowledge that she was alienating whatever kindness her husband might still feel for her, could not be blackmailed. Old wrongs cast long shadows and for the sad, sick woman, now facing the ruin of all her hopes, the bitter past was as real as, perhaps more real than, the bitter present. Once she had acknowledged Elizabeth's right to succeed her, she would have acknowledged that Anne Boleyn and her daughter had won, and not even for Philip, not even for the Catholic Church, could Catherine of Aragon's daughter bring herself to admit that ultimate defeat. As for Elizabeth, she continued calmly to express her determined preference for a spinster's life, telling the governor of her household, Sir Thomas Pope, that she would not change it: 'no, though I were offered the greatest prince in all Europe'.

Philip was particularly busy just then, preparing for another bout of hostilities with France and taking over the reins of government from his father – the old Emperor having decided to abdicate and end his days in a monastery. So once again the matter of Elizabeth's future and with it the future of the English alliance had to be put on the back burner. But Spain was not the only country with an interest in the affairs of the island kingdom, and in the spring of 1557 the retiring Venetian ambassador in London prepared a detailed resumé of the English political situation for the information of the Venetian senate, with special reference to the highly complicated question of the succession.

The first and principal competitor, explained Giovanni Michiel, was, of course, the Queen's sister, my lady Elizabeth, who had been named as heir in the will of her father King Henry, 'the will being confirmed by Act of Parliament, which signifies by the will of the whole kingdom'. It was, however, objected that 'kings cannot dispose of the succession of their kingdoms to the prejudice of succeeding generations, otherwise than it is ordained by God and by nature' and that Elizabeth, being a bastard, should not take precedence over the legitimate heirs.

If Elizabeth were thus excluded, the second competitor was Mary Queen of Scots, granddaughter of King Henry's elder sister Margaret 'who was married in Scotland'. The obstacle here was the existence of a 'municipal law' which prohibited any person born out of England from inheriting anything within the realm. But the supporters of the Queen of Scots raised the same objection to this law as they did to the King's will, 'namely, that a municipal law, even were it a true one . . . cannot in the case of succession be opposed to the law of nature'. In other words, an heir could never be deprived of his or her God-given natural rights, 'except by force, or when the heir is acknowledged to be a rebel and traitor, and after condemnation as such'. The claim of the Queen of Scotland, added Michiel thoughtfully, 'would be yet more strengthened in case of need by the might and power of the King of France, she being at his Court as the destined wife of Monseigneur the Dauphin'.

The third claimants were the heirs of Henry VIII's younger sister Mary, 'who was first married to King Louis XII and took for her second husband Charles Brandon, Duke of Suffolk'. These claimants, Michiel continued, besides possessing natural rights as the granddaughters of the first Mary Tudor, born of her elder daughter Frances, had also been confirmed as heirs by the will of the said Henry VIII and on the death of Queen Mary they, following the example of their sister Jane Grey, could be expected to attempt to lay claim to the succession in preference even to my lady Elizabeth.

The ambassador concluded his report with a reference to the 'fourth claim', which proceeded from Eleanor Brandon now deceased, the younger sister of Frances, who had married the Earl of Cumberland and left a daughter named Margaret, the wife of Lord Strange, eldest son of the Earl of Derby and one of the chief noblemen of the kingdom. Since the senior branch of the Suffolk line, represented by Frances and her surviving children, was now 're-proached' with treason and might thus be considered as disqualified, Lady Margaret Strange was 'nearest of all to the blood royal and to her the succession belongs'. (This opinion, incidentally, was shared by Margaret Strange, if by no one else.) Giovanni Michiel obviously thought it regrettable that all these claimants should be so exclusively female, the recent death in Padua of Edward Courtenay having removed all but the most distant male competitors, and as a result the English had 'utterly lost the hope of ever having a king of the blood royal, unless in a very remote degree'.

Michiel had mentioned that Frances Brandon's daughters were living with her, but Catherine was now spending a good deal of time with the Seymour family for, since making her début at court, she had become very friendly with Lady Jane Seymour, daughter of the late Protector Somerset and another of Queen Mary's maids of honour. Jane Seymour, who had once been regarded as a possible rival to Jane Grey in the English royal marriage stakes, was delicate – she was probably already consumptive – and the Queen, aware of the close and long-standing ties between their families, appears to have encouraged Catherine to accompany her friend on the frequent occasions when Jane had to be sent home on sick leave.

Home for the Seymours was currently at Hanworth, the Middlesex manor which had once formed part of Queen Catherine Parr's dower lands and had subsequently passed into the possession of the widowed Duchess of Somerset, who was living there with her second husband, Francis Newdigate. (Anne, Duchess of Somerset, made up the trio of ex-Duchesses who had married members of their household staff, Newdigate having formerly served as the Lord Protector's steward.) Also living at Hanworth was her eldest son, a good-looking, dark-eyed boy now in his late teens, and in the circumstances it is hardly surprising that Edward Seymour and Catherine Grey should have formed a romantic attachment. They had known one another from infancy, of course. Edward, born in 1539, had, like the Dudley boys, been brought up and educated to take his place among the highest in the land and had once been tentatively betrothed to Jane Grey. Duchess Frances still called him 'son'.

Nor was class and family background all the two young people shared. Both had traumatic first-hand experience of the destructive forces released by ill-advised personal ambition. Both had lost fathers to the headsman's axe and, as a result, both had become contaminated with the social blight of treason. True, Edward had been 'restored in blood' – that is, the civil rights forfeited by the attainder of the Lord Protector had been restored to his son – but the greater part of the Seymour family wealth was still expropriated and the family title remained in abeyance. For her part, Catherine had suffered the humiliation of public repudiation by the Herberts and no other plans had yet been made for her future, although she was now past the normal age for betrothal and marriage. Proximity to the throne, which made her a tempting proposition, also made her a potentially very dangerous one: the example of Guildford Dudley was not, after all, calculated to reassure caring parents with eligible sons to dispose of.

Certainly this aspect of the situation developing under her roof was exercising the Duchess of Somerset when she taxed her son about his intentions towards Catherine Grey. He, however, replied coolly that 'young folks meaning well may well accompany', adding that he saw no reason why he should not continue to see Lady Catherine, both at Hanworth and at court, their friendship 'not having been forbidden by the Queen's commandment'. On another occasion he is said to have remarked that as Lady Catherine had been sent to live with his mother at Hanworth by the Queen, knowing he was there, 'her majesty's feelings in this matter cannot be doubted'.

But although the match was being discussed in private between the families with the Queen's consent apparently taken for granted, nothing further was done and no effort made to obtain a formal royal blessing. The reason for this inertia, it must be assumed, was all part of the prevailing state of suspended animation on the English political scene. After the first eighteen months or so it had become generally, if tacitly, accepted that the period of Mary's rule would be no more than an interlude – hopefully short and certainly regrettable – and while the more obstinate members of the proletariat were providing their religion with its martyrology, the 'better sort' of Protestants, including, of course, aspiring young men like Edward Seymour, went to mass, kept their heads down and waited for better times.

These arrived in mid-November 1558, at six a.m. on Thursday the seventeenth to be precise. There was little pretence of public mourning. As news of Mary Tudor's death spread through the city the church bells rang out, and by afternoon the winter dusk was illuminated by the usual bonfires as the Londoners set out tables in the streets and prepared to 'eat and drink and make merry for the new Queen Elizabeth'.

When it came to the point there had been no question about the succession and the transition to the new reign was stage-managed with remarkable smoothness, thanks in part at least to the statesmanlike behaviour of the Archbishop of York, Nicholas Heath, who had been appointed Lord Chancellor after Stephen Gardiner's death. Parliament was currently in session and, on the morning of 17 November, Heath summoned the Speaker and 'the knights and burgesses of the nether house' to come immediately to the Lords. After making the announcement of Mary's death, he went on to thank the providence of Almighty God in leaving

> a true, lawful and right inheritrice to the crown of this realm, which is the Lady Elizabeth, of whose lawful right and title we need not to doubt. Wherefore the lords of this house have determined . . . to pass from hence into the palace, and there to proclaim the said Lady Elizabeth Queen of this realm without further tract of time.

There were no dissenting voices and Nicholas Heath, by his prompt action, had not only ensured Elizabeth's public recognition by both Houses of Parliament before they were automatically dissolved by the demise of the reigning monarch; but, as himself a leading Catholic, had secured the loyalty of any doubtful members of his party for the new sovereign.

The new sovereign made her state entry into London some ten days later, riding through streets gay with banners and streamers and lined with cheering crowds. The trumpets sounded, the city musicians blew and thumped enthusiastically on their various instruments, church bells pealed and the Tower guns thundered a salute such as 'never was heard afore' in greeting to the last of King Henry VIII's children as she came to claim her right.

At the time of her accession Elizabeth Tudor had just passed her twenty-fifth birthday. Giovanni Michiel thought her 'comely' rather than handsome, but had remarked on her fine eyes and the beautiful hands which she was always careful to display – those incredibly long beringed white fingers prominently featured in so many portraits. Her hair was more red than yellow and curled naturally, at least when she was in her twenties. She had the ultra-pale skin which often goes with red hair and which she accentuated with cosmetics (the commentator who described her complexion as 'olivastra' or sallow must have seen her in a bad light or on a bad day), and although her spare, wiry figure and high-nosed profile may not have measured up to the accepted standard of feminine beauty, Elizabeth in her prime was undoubtedly an attractive woman, graceful, stylish and supremely self-confident. Michiel had noted, with a faint air of disapproval, that while she knew she was born of 'such a mother', she did not consider herself as being of inferior degree to Queen Mary. She did not, it seems, even consider herself to be a bastard, since her parents' marriage had had the blessing of the Archbishop of Canterbury. 'She prides herself on her father and glories in him', the Venetian envoy had written in his 1557 report, 'everybody saying that she also resembles him more than the Queen does'; and remembering Mary's freely expressed reservations about her parentage, this must surely have given Elizabeth some very human satisfaction.

No one at any time had any doubts about her mental capacities. 'Her mind has no womanly weakness, her perseverance is equal to that of a man and her memory long keeps what it quickly picks up,' Roger Ascham had said of her when she was sixteen, and more recently he told John Sturm in Strasbourg that he had been reading the orations of Aeschines and Demosthenes on the crown with his former pupil, and the Lady Elizabeth 'at first sight understands everything . . . in a way to strike you with astonishment'.

But if the Lady Elizabeth had already more than proved the quality of her intellect and understanding, she was now to prove herself also as a born ruler and a woman of astonishingly mature political sense. In circumstances where Mary, so well meaning, so anxious to do her duty, to do what she believed to be right, had floundered helplessly, Elizabeth, tough, subtle and shrewd, was immediately at home, moving with sure-footed, almost nonchalant composure. Within a matter of weeks the Spanish ambassador was reporting that the new Queen of England seemed 'incomparably more feared than her sister, and gives her orders and has her way as absolutely as her father did'.

Nevertheless, after their recent unfortunate experience of petticoat government, by no means all her subjects were convinced that the country would be any better off in the long run under a woman head of state. The bogey of a disputed and uncertain succession continued to cast its shadow over the political landscape and there's little doubt that in the opinion of the great majority of Englishmen the most valuable service their new Queen could render them would have been to marry and bear sturdy red-headed English sons to guard their own and their children's future. In January 1559, therefore, a deputation of M.P.s and Privy Councillors, headed by the Speaker of the House of Commons, waited on the Queen to deliver an earnest petition that she would choose some man to be her husband, so that she might by marriage bring forth children and thus ensure her own immortality – this being 'the single, the only, the all-comprehending prayer of all Englishmen'.

The petitioners got little satisfaction from their sovereign, who reminded them sharply that she had already joined herself in marriage to a husband, 'namely, the kingdom of England', and taking the coronation ring from her finger flourished 'the pledge of this my wedlock' (which she marvelled they could have forgotten) under their surprised noses. As for children: 'Do not', snapped Elizabeth Tudor, 'upbraid me with miserable lack of children; for every one of you, and as many as are Englishmen, are children and kinsmen to me.' The Queen did then relent sufficiently to promise that if she were ever to consider taking a more conventional husband, they could be sure it would be someone who could be trusted to be as careful of the commonwealth as she was. But if she continued in the course of life she had begun – and still much preferred – she had no doubt that, in the fullness of time, God would provide a suitable successor. She herself would be more than content to have engraved on her tombstone: Here lieth Elizabeth which reigned a virgin and died a virgin.

This was only the first of many similar encounters between an increasingly importunate Parliament and a stubbornly virgin queen – only the first of many similar 'answers answerless'. The reasons for Elizabeth's determination to stay single have been exhaustively discussed over the centuries since her death but, other speculation set aside, it seems that by her early twenties she had already faced and accepted the fact that in her male-dominated world marriage and a career as a reigning monarch could not be combined, and for Elizabeth her career came first. This did not mean that she was not fully alive to the immense advantages attached to being 'the best match in her parish', and she exploited them for all they were worth over the next twenty years, giving her numerous European suitors just enough encouragement to keep them hopeful for just as long as it happened to suit her purpose.

But much as she always appeared to delight in the ritual dance of courtship, there was one proposal she did reject out of hand: the one which came from, of all people, her former brother-in-law. Philip of Spain might be willing to sacrifice himself a second time for the sake of the English alliance and the Catholic religion; Elizabeth was quite definitely not going to repeat her sister's mistakes. She was, though, very interested in Philip's friendship and allowed him to suggest his Austrian cousins, the Arch-Dukes Ferdinand and Charles von

Hapsburg, as possible substitutes. Ferdinand's uncompromising Catholicism soon put him out of the running, for by Easter 1559 England had once more become a Protestant country with its own national Church, but the more amenable Charles long remained a useful stand-by, to be brought out and solemnly reconsidered whenever the marriage question was being pressed.

The marriage question was repeatedly pressed and with mounting urgency, for the problem of the succession would not go away. When Elizabeth came to the throne England and Spain were still technically at war with France, although active hostilities had ceased and peace talks were in progress. The two great powers, having fought one another to a standstill over the past fifty years, were now both on the verge of bankruptcy and anxious to reach a settlement. But for England the negotiations were complicated by the fact that the French King was currently 'bestriding the realm', with one foot in Calais (that last outpost of England's once great continental empire having fallen in the late war) and the other in Scotland, as well as by his deliberate parade of 'the Scottish Queen's feigned title to the crown of England'. According to Lord Cobham, reporting from Brussels in December 1558, the French were not hesitating to say that Elizabeth was not lawful Queen of England, and a few weeks later Sir Edward Carne was writing from Rome that 'the ambassador of the French laboreth the Pope to declare the Queen illegitimate and the Scottish Queen successor to Queen Mary'.

For England's envoys abroad this was a touchy subject. In the eyes of Rome and the rest of orthodox Catholic Europe, Elizabeth Tudor *was* illegitimate, and therefore the Scottish Queen could indeed be held to possess some claim to be regarded as Queen Mary's successor. Queen Elizabeth, understandably, would admit no discussion of the matter. Unlike her sister she did not even bother to have herself officially relegitimated by Parliament. Advised by the eminent lawyer Nicholas Bacon, she took her stand on the 1544 Act of Succession and on the principle that 'the crown once worn quite taketh away all defects whatsoever'.

But the King of France, equally understandably, was determined to extract all the available diplomatic mileage out of his new daughter-in-law's family connections (Mary Stewart had married the Dauphin in the spring of 1558) and he had her proclaimed Queen of England on Mary Tudor's death. She and her husband began to quarter the English royal arms with those of France, and the sixteen-year-old Queen Dauphiness was styled Queen of England and Scotland in official documents, so that when the question of the restitution of Calais came up at the negotiating table, the French commissioners wondered aloud to whom Calais should be restored, for was not the Queen of Scotland rightful Queen of England?

While no one seriously expected King Henri to make any attempt to prosecute Mary Stewart's claim by force of arms – not yet, anyway – these developments had the effect of alarming and irritating the English, and prompted Nicholas Wootton, a member of the English negotiating team, to reflect gloomily on his country's present military weakness, on French perfidy and the 'commodity they now have to invade us by land on Scotland-side'. Spain was also prompted to look for possible ways and means of checking France's undesirable cross-Channel pretensions, and in March 1559 the Spanish ambassador in London brought up the subject of Lady Catherine Grey.

The accession of Elizabeth had made little outward or visible difference to the status of either Catherine or Mary Grey, who retained their places at court, but, like it or not, Catherine had now become a figure of some international significance. At eighteen years old she had developed, if not into a beauty, at least into an above average looking girl, petite and slender, with the royal family's reddish auburn hair colouring and an appealing air of feminine fragility. She had grown up in the shadow of her formidable elder sister but displayed none of Jane's powerful intellect, abrasive personality and heroic religiosity. On the contrary, it was Catherine's misfortune to be a very ordinary young woman trapped by accident of birth in a quite extraordinary situation. Not particularly bright, it soon became all too clear that she lacked even the elementary qualities of tact and discretion which might have helped her to survive in the political jungle, and matters were not improved by the ill-will which had always existed between the Suffolk family and Elizabeth. This no doubt had its origins in the friendship which had once existed between the first Mary Tudor and Queen Catherine of Aragon, united in their loathing of Anne Boleyn; in the friendship which had continued between Mary's daughter and Catherine's daughter, united in regarding Anne's daughter as a social outsider. The fact that Queen Mary had been obliged to sanction the executions of her cousin Frances's husband and daughter had in no way affected their personal relations. These things happened in the best of families – indeed they happened most often in the best of families – and were accepted by the survivors with well-bred stoicism. Mary had always tried to be kind to Catherine, and Catherine would have been brought up to share the received opinion of Elizabeth, on whom her future now depended and whom she seems to have approached with an unhealthy mixture of fear and resentment. For her part, Elizabeth despised her Grey cousins quite impartially and did not bother to hide it.

The fact that the Queen and her resident heiress were on bad terms was, of course, quickly noted with interest by the diplomatic corps. King Philip's ambassador, the magnificent Don Gomez Suarez de Figueroa, Count de Feria, who had been cultivating Lady Catherine's acquaintance, informed his master that she had told him in confidence that Elizabeth did not wish her to succeed. She was dissatisfied and offended at this 'and at the Queen's only making her one of the ladies of the presence, whereas she was in the privy chamber of the late Queen, who showed her much favour. . . . I try to keep Lady Catherine very friendly', continued de Feria, 'and she has promised me not to change her religion, nor to marry without my consent.'

The count was not the most discerning judge of character, especially not of the English whom he detested, and he apparently had no suspicion that the demure Lady Catherine might be hatching plans of her own not yet divulged to anyone outside her immediate family circle. It was, in fact, in March 1559, just about the time de Feria was writing, that Edward Seymour (now restored to his former title of Earl of Hertford) visited the Duchess of Suffolk at Sheen and formally asked for and obtained her consent to his and Catherine's marriage. A family conference was then held to discuss the best way of broaching the matter to the queen and it was agreed that, while Hertford should 'make suit' to those members of the Council most likely to be willing to use their influence on his behalf, the duchess – or Lady Frances, as she was always known within the family – should write a letter to Elizabeth 'for her majesty's favour and good will'. Adrian Stokes was entrusted with the task of making a rough draft for his wife to copy, but unfortunately Lady Frances became seriously ill almost at once and it was felt wiser to postpone the sending of such an important letter until she was well enough to follow it up with a personal visit to court.

Meanwhile, other and more sinister plans were being made for Lady Catherine's future. At the beginning of August an interesting piece of information was passed to Sir Thomas Challoner, English ambassador to Spain based in the Low Countries, from one Robert Huggyns or Hoggins, an Englishman in the service of the King of Spain. According to Hoggins, an element at the court in Brussels, 'fearing the French king's pretended titles for the Scottish Queen, sought means to solicit and get into their hands my Lady Catherine Grey'. The idea was to marry her off to either Philip's imbecile son, Don Carlos, or 'some other person of less degree if less depended on her', and then keep her to be used as a counter-claimant to Mary Queen of Scots should occasion arise.

In a follow-up report written in October, Hoggins disclosed that the kidnap plot had been 'three or four times talked of' and would have been put into operation had not the King of France been killed in a freakish tiltyard accident during the summer. His successor, the Queen of Scots' youthful and sickly husband François II, was regarded as a nonentity – 'the King here [Philip] does not so much fear the French King that now is as he did his father' – and consequently Spanish interest in Catherine Grey had waned, for the moment at least. But her 'discontented mind' was common knowledge in government circles abroad and 'it was hence thought that she could be enticed away if some trusty body spoke with her'.

It was also being said that Lady Catherine's mother and stepfather did not love her and that in particular her uncle, John Grey, 'would in no wise abide to hear of her' so that she lived as it were 'in great despair'. This sounds like a scrap of servants' gossip following a family row: Catherine may well have been growing restive over the delay in arranging her betrothal. More serious was the rumour that she was also in the Queen's great displeasure 'who could not well abide the sight of her'. According to the Duke of Saxony's envoy, Catherine had spoken some 'very arrogant and unseemly words in the hearing of the Queen and others standing by'. What these words were is unfortunately not recorded, but no one was ever rude to Elizabeth Tudor without living to regret it, and for Catherine to have picked this moment of all others still further to antagonize her alarming cousin was not far short of suicidal – more especially as her mother died that November without having made any approach to the Queen on her behalf.

The other Duchess of Suffolk, Catherine Bertie, and her husband had returned to England in August, after an adventurous three and a half years of exile which had taken them from the Rhineland as far afield as Lithuania, then part of the kingdom of Poland, and during which time my lady of Suffolk had given birth to her last child, a son christened Peregrine. The Berties knew of the Hertford marriage plan. Richard Bertie had been shown the letter drafted by Adrian Stokes, and Lady Catherine may very well have appealed to Duchess Catherine for help; but after Lady Frances's death Edward Seymour seems to have lost heart or got cold feet or both. At any rate he told Adrian Stokes that he meant to meddle no more in the matter, and the unhappy Catherine was left to mope about the court, beset by rumours of foreign kidnappers lying in wait round every corner and apparently doomed to a life of spinsterhood serving a mistress she both dreaded and disdained.

Elizabeth had reacted to Thomas Challoner's warnings about

Spanish interest in Catherine with a ferocious display of amiability, and in January 1560 Bishop Alvaro de Quadra, the new Spanish envoy in London, was telling his predecessor that 'the Queen calls Lady Catherine her daughter, although the feeling between them can hardly be that of mother and child, but the Queen has thought best to put her in her chamber [that is, restore her entrée to the privy chamber] and makes much of her in order to keep her quiet. She even talks of formally adopting her.' All this probably frightened Lady Catherine more than any amount of coldness and perhaps it is not surprising that neither she nor Edward Seymour appear at any time to have contemplated making a direct appeal to their terrifyingly unpredictable sovereign.

Throughout the spring and summer of 1560, while public attention was riveted on the Queen's unfolding 'romance' with her Master of the Horse, Lord Robert Dudley, and the scandal of the mysterious death of Lord Robert's wife Amy, Lady Catherine's affairs remained at a standstill. There were conjectures that the queen meant to bestow her on the Earl of Arran, son of the Scottish heir presumptive, and rumours that the Earl of Pembroke wanted her back for his son. The Earl of Hertford was beginning to show signs of taking an interest in another, quite inferior young lady and the whole boy and girl attachment would most likely have died a natural death had not Lady Jane Seymour decided to take a hand. Lady Jane, naturally forceful and ambitious and now consumed by the febrile, euphoric energy of tuberculosis, was determined that her much-loved brother should not lose the chance of making a royal marriage. She had already helped the lovers to enjoy occasional unchaperoned meetings at Hanworth and in convenient corners of the various royal residences. Now she brought them together again and arranged a reconciliation, and it was almost certainly she who put the disastrous idea of a secret marriage into their heads. The three of them met in Lady Jane's private closet which opened off the Maidens' Chamber at Westminster some time in October 1560, and there Catherine Grey and Edward Seymour solemnly plighted their troth. Nearly half a century had passed since Mary Tudor, Queen of France, had exchanged similar secret promises with Charles Brandon, Duke of Suffolk, and it was in a similar spirit of optimism and bravado that her granddaughter now embarked on the one course of action most exactly calculated to bring about her ruin.

It was agreed that the wedding should take place at Hertford's house in Cannon Row 'the next time that the Queen's Highness should take any journey'. Lady Jane undertook to have a clergyman standing by and Hertford had a ring made for the occasion. This was what was known as a 'posy ring', a plain gold band with a concealed spring opening five links on which were engraved a little verse composed by himself.

> *As circles five by art compact show but one ring*
> *in sight,*
> *So trust uniteth faithful minds with knot of*
> *secret might,*
> *Whose force to break (but greedy Death) no wight*
> *possesseth power,*
> *As time and sequels well shall prove; my ring can*
> *say no more.*

Between All Saints' Day and Christmas, probably early in December, the Queen decided to go out to Eltham for a few days' hunting, and Catherine and Jane were ready with their excuses. Catherine pleaded toothache and Jane Seymour was well known to be always ailing. As soon as Elizabeth was safely out of the way, at about eight o'clock in the morning, the two girls slipped out of the palace by the stairs in the orchard and hurried together along the sands by the river to Cannon Row. Hertford was waiting rather nervously to meet them 'at his chamber door', but the minister had not yet appeared and the bridal couple had to wait for a tense quarter of an hour while the dauntless Lady Jane went to fetch him – a shortish, middle-aged man with a ruddy complexion and auburn beard, they were later to remember, wearing a plain black gown with a falling collar, 'such as the ministers used when they came out of Germany'. Nobody asked his name – it was not an occasion for asking, or answering, any unnecessary questions – and he performed the ceremony then and there in Lord Hertford's bedroom, reading the marriage service 'in that order as it is set forth in the book of Common Prayer'.

As soon as this was done, the priest went hurriedly on his way, Lady Jane seeing him off the premises and giving him his fee of ten pounds out of the regular pocket-money which her brother gave her 'for her apparel and other expenses'. Still in her self-appointed role of stage-manager cum hostess, Jane Seymour then came back and offered Catherine some refreshment from the wine, beer and sweetmeats which had been laid out on the cupboard in the bedroom, but seeing her brother's impatience soon tactfully withdrew.

Left alone, the lovers wasted no time in undressing and going to their 'naked bed' where, as Hertford was to relate baldly, they had carnal copulation. They had little enough time together, for it would certainly attract unwelcome notice if Lady Catherine failed to be present at midday dinner with the Comptroller of the Household, and after about an hour and a half they had to start scrambling back into their clothes. This in itself was later enough to rouse grave suspicion in the official mind, which could not visualize two such gently nurtured young people performing the admittedly complicated feat of getting dressed unaided. For this reason if no other it was felt they must have had assistance – and accomplices. Nevertheless, according to Lord Hertford, his wife successfully 'trimmed and tired' herself within half a quarter of an hour and he then escorted her down to the water gate, kissed her and bade her farewell, and saw her and Lady Jane into a wherry – the tide having risen by this time – for their return journey to Whitehall.

9

A Sorrowful Woman for the Queen's Displeasure

I never came to her, but I found her either weeping or else saw by her face she had wept.

Catherine might have achieved her immediate ambition and her heart's desire, but although, as she was to confess, she used herself with the earl as his wife in her own heart, the marriage had made no practical difference to her circumstances. The couple were still obliged to be content with occasional furtive meetings, a few odd hours snatched whenever they could manage it without arousing suspicion. According to Hertford, they lay together several times in the Queen's houses in Westminster and Greenwich, but were never able to spend a night together. Jane Seymour would help them to have 'secret company' when she could, and Catherine's maids, who must have had a very good idea of what was going on, would discreetly make themselves scarce when they saw their mistress and her lover whispering together.

Just how long the young people expected this peculiar state of affairs to last is impossible to say. Neither of them appear at any time to have given any serious consideration to the problem of how they were going to break the news. But, of course, it wasn't long before events began to catch up with them. Jane Seymour died in March 1561 and without her assistance it grew increasingly difficult for them to meet – especially as the only other person in the secret, one of Catherine's maids, had become frightened by her unwanted involvement. This woman, a Mrs Leigh, asked permission to go home on a visit and never returned. Then the Queen decided to send the Earl of Hertford abroad as a companion to William Cecil's son Thomas, who was going on a European tour to finish his education. This presented an unexpected complication, to be closely followed by another, not so unexpected.

Catherine had first 'mistrusted' herself to be with child early in March, and when she told her husband and sister-in-law they had both agreed that there would now be nothing for it but to 'make it known how the matter stood' and trust to the Queen's mercy. But whether the inexperienced Catherine was genuinely uncertain, or whether she simply could not bring herself to face the consequences of pregnancy, she continued to do nothing. When her husband questioned her again about her condition, Catherine would only answer that 'she could not tell'. She was still refusing to say one way or the other when Hertford went off to France in April, probably conscious of a rather guilty sense of relief at the prospect of escaping, albeit temporarily, from a situation he was powerless to control. He did, however, promise to return if and when Catherine let him know definitely that she was with child. About a week before his departure he took steps to fulfil another of his husbandly obligations by giving his wife 'a writing' in his own hand, duly signed and sealed, by which he made over to her as much of his lands and possessions (more of these having now been restored to him) as would ensure her an income of a thousand pounds a year in the event of his death.

This formal recognition of their highly irregular relationship may have been a slight consolation, but with her mother and Lady Jane Seymour both in their graves and her husband overseas, Catherine was very much alone as she waited for the rapidly approaching day of reckoning. She had already received some ominous, if rather belated warnings from Secretary of State William Cecil, from the Marchioness of Northampton and Lady Clinton 'to beware of too great familiarity with the Earl of Hertford' but went on stubbornly denying that there was any such thing. There was, though, no longer any denying the fact of her pregnancy, which was becoming all too visible.

By midsummer Catherine seems at last to have begun to realize something of the enormity of her conduct. She wrote frantically to Hertford, begging him to come home and support her, but she had no means of knowing whether her letters were reaching him. In fact, their correspondence was being delayed and no doubt opened and read by the courier, a man named Glyn, who was almost certainly a government informer.

In July Lady Catherine, in her capacity as lady-in-waiting, was obliged to accompany the court on its annual summer progress, which that year took the royal road show to East Anglia. It was at Ipswich early in August that she was finally driven to disclose to

Mistress Saintlow of the privy chamber that she was married to the Earl of Hertford, who was the father of her child. It was natural enough in the circumstances that Catherine Grey or, more properly, Catherine Seymour, should have turned in her extremity to Elizabeth Saintlow, later Countess of Shrewsbury and better known as Bess of Hardwick. Lady Saintlow, as she then was, was an old family friend who had probably held some paid position in the Dorset household after the early death of her first husband, for her second marriage to William Cavendish had taken place at Bradgate and Lady Catherine had later stood godmother to one of the numerous Cavendish offspring. But old friend or not, Bess, a hardbitten and dedicated social climber now on her third marriage to the rich West Country landowner Sir William Saintlow, had not attained her present degree of success by getting mixed up in other people's troubles. Her immediate instinctive reaction was to distance herself from Catherine's by bursting into floods of tears and angry reproaches.

The unfortunate Catherine's second choice of confidant proved hardly more sympathetic. According to her own account, 'the Sunday following (which was 9 August) at night, I went to the Lord Robert Dudley's lodgings and declared the same to him at his bedside, requiring him to be a means to the Queen's Highness for me'. It's true that Lord Robert Dudley was also an old acquaintance. They had, after all, once briefly been brother and sister-in-law. At the same time, it does not require any great effort of the imagination to guess what Lord Robert must have felt on receiving an unannounced nocturnal visit from a distraught, heavily pregnant young woman. The surviving Dudleys still bore the stigmata of their late father's unpopularity but, on becoming the Queen's acknowledged favourite and 'best friend', Robert had acquired an active and tenacious circle of enemies all his own. It was not yet a year since the shocking business of his wife's fatal fall 'from a pair of stairs' at Cumnor Hall near Oxford and, although a coroner's inquest had returned a verdict of death by misadventure on Amy Dudley, née Robsart, the world at large remained unconvinced, leaving the widower in an understandably touchy frame of mind.

Dudley got rid of Catherine with more speed than finesse and first thing next morning went straight to the Queen with the whole story. Writing to the Earl of Sussex a few days later, William Cecil remarked laconically that at Ipswich was 'a great mishap' discovered. 'The Lady Catherine is certainly known to be big with child, as she saith by the Earl of Hertford, who is in France. She is committed to the Tower. He is sent for. She saith that she was married to him secretly before Christmas last. Thus is God displeased with us.'

But God's displeasure was of less immediate concern to the young Hertfords than the Queen's. It was unlucky, yet somehow all too typical of Lady Catherine's story, that her secret should have come to light at a moment when Elizabeth was least likely to feel indulgent over her cousin's misdemeanours. Just how close she herself had come to losing her heart to Robert Dudley the previous autumn remains a matter for conjecture, but a number of people at the time, with good opportunities for observing the situation at first hand, had been seriously afraid that she was having an affair with him and meant to marry him against all the odds. William Cecil certainly did – or said he did. At the Spanish embassy Bishop de Quadra was not so sure but, as he told the Duchess of Parma, 'with these people it is always wisest to think the worst'. In France they had not only been thinking the worst, they had been unashamedly hoping for it and the Queen of Scots is reputed to have exclaimed, 'So the Queen of England is to marry her horsekeeper, who has killed his wife to make room for her!' – a remark which pretty well summed up opinion in the courts of Europe. Elizabeth's own representatives abroad had been beside themselves with anxiety and annoyance at the salacious rumours being spread about the Queen's private life. Nicholas Throckmorton in Paris had followed up a series of doomful despatches by sending his secretary, young Mr Jones, to convey an urgent personal warning on the disastrous consequences to English prestige which would inevitably follow a Dudley marriage.

But Elizabeth had known that it would not do. Not even for the sake of a longed-for male heir would the country have tolerated the spectacle of an upstart, wife-murdering Dudley wearing the crown matrimonial. As Caspar von Breuner, an emissary of the Hapsburg family in London to press the suit of Archduke Charles, had put it, if the Queen married my Lord Robert she would incur so much enmity that she would be in danger of going to bed one night as Queen of England and rising next morning to find herself plain Madam Elizabeth.

We are never likely to know with any certainty how compelling had been the temptation to consider the world well lost for love, but it is not unreasonable to postulate that the late summer and autumn of 1560 may have seen the one really painful struggle between Elizabeth Tudor's sense of royal responsibility and her natural biological urges. By the following summer the crisis was over, but it had left her irritable, out of sorts and suffering from an apparent revulsion of feeling on the subject of men in general and marriage in particular. She told the Archbishop of Canterbury that she wished she had never appointed any married clergy, and in a burst of petu-

lance went on to speak with such bitterness of the holy estate of mat-
rimony that good Dr Parker was 'in a horror to hear her'. When she
heard that her heir presumptive had blithely entered the same holy
estate which she had so recently renounced for herself, without so much
as a by-your-leave, the Queen's fury was not unnaturally exacerbated.

She had never liked Catherine, but considered she had always
treated her fairly, keeping her and Mary Grey at court and allowing
them all the privileges due to their rank, only to have her generosity
repaid with insolence, ingratitude, deceit and perhaps worse. Anything which touched on the succession touched Elizabeth on her
most sensitive spot. She was never to forget her own experiences as 'a
second person' or of the poisonous atmosphere of intrigue which
automatically gathered around the heir to the throne, and in the
activities of the present heir she had caught a sulphurous whiff of
treason. A directive was therefore sent to Edward Warner, Lieutenant of the Tower, ordering him to 'examine the Lady Catherine very
straitly how many hath been privy to the love betwixt the Earl of
Hertford and her from the beginning; and let her certainly understand that she shall have no manner of favour, except she will show
the truth, not only what ladies or gentlewomen of this court were
thereto privy, but also what lords and gentlemen. For it doth now
appear that sundry personages have dealt herein. . . '. Amongst
those whom the Queen suspected was Lady Saintlow, and Warner
was instructed to send for her 'and so deal with her that she may confess to you all her knowledge in the same matters. It is certain that
there hath been great practices and purposes; and since the death of
the Lady Jane (Seymour), she hath been most privy'.

Apart from the social crime of getting married without asking the
Queen's permission, Catherine's choice of husband had been especially tactless. The Seymours had a reputation for being politically
ambitious – something else which Elizabeth had good reason to
remember – and their connections with the royal house were already
uncomfortably close. The Earl of Hertford, who had been hauled
back from the Continent to give an account of himself, was deposited
in the Tower on 5 September and, over the next few weeks, he and his
wife, his brother Henry, their servants and Bess Saintlow were inter-
rogated in depth by a Privy Council committee which solemnly
probed every last detail of that rather pathetic hole-and-corner wedding at the house in Cannon Row. How long was the priest or minister at the solemnization of the marriage? Did they stand or kneel during the service? How long did the priest tarry in the Earl's chamber
after the marriage? Were they served with any banqueting dishes or
drink, and if so who served them?

Catherine was asked if any man or woman had seen her arrive at the Earl's house, and what 'communication' she and Hertford had had while they waited for the priest to arrive. She could not remember exactly what they had said, but their talk 'was only such as passeth between folks that intended as we did'. Which of them had been first in bed, 'and who first rose out of the bed?' Hertford thought they had gone both together, 'but I somewhat afore her, as I remember'. He had lain sometimes on one side of the bed and sometimes on the other, and 'we rose nigh about the same time' but 'no person did help us either to undress or make ourselves ready after we rose'.

The investigation was still in progress when, on 21 September, Catherine was brought to bed and delivered of a healthy son. This infant, whose inopportune arrival would, of course, complicate the dynastic situation even further, was baptised four days later and given the name of Edward within the precincts of the Tower – in close proximity to the headless remains of his grandfather, his aunt Jane Grey and two great-uncles, not to mention a Dudley uncle and great-uncle-in-law.

Meanwhile his parents continued to insist that no one – apart from the strong-minded Jane Seymour – had ever 'advised, counselled or exhorted them to marry' and the most exhaustive enquiries had failed to reveal any evidence of conspiracy, although the Queen was still not entirely convinced. William Cecil, however, who evidently felt Her Majesty was over-reacting, told Nicholas Throckmorton that for his part he did not believe anyone had been privy to the marriage 'but maids or women going for maidens'. The question therefore now arose of what was to be done with the culprits. Since the wholesale repeal of Henry VIII's treason acts by Mary in 1553 it was no longer a treasonable offence *per se* for a member of the royal family to get married without the consent of the sovereign, so the sovereign was obliged to resort to attacking the validity of the marriage itself.

The Church had always recognized the binding nature of private spousals and, while they were generally frowned on by society, there was nothing in canon law to forbid secret or clandestine marriages – that is, those where the banns had not previously been published on three successive Sundays or holy days. A religious ceremony performed by an ordained priest and witnessed by a minimum of two other persons was, however, insisted upon. In the Hertfords' case the officiating cleric had vanished without trace, the only witness was dead and Lady Catherine was, predictably, unable to produce the deed of jointure given her by her husband before his departure for France. This document, she tearfully informed her interrogators, had been put safely away, but 'with moving from place to place at progress time, it is lost and she cannot tell where it is become'. The couple might, as one of Nicholas Throckmorton's correspondents wrote that September, 'agree upon the time, place and company of their marriage' but could not between them bring a scrap of evidence to prove that it had ever taken place. So, remarked John Somers, 'they must either find out the minister, or determine what the law will say, if it be a marriage or no. The matter', he added, 'lies chiefly, notwithstanding all determination, in the Queen's mercy.' And the Queen, presented with this gift-wrapped opportunity to discredit her tiresome and potentially dangerous cousin, was showing no signs of inclining towards mercy. At the beginning of 1562 she put the whole matter in the hands of the ecclesiastical authorities and on 10 May the Archbishop of Canterbury gave judgement that there had been no marriage between the Earl of Hertford and Lady Catherine Grey. He censured them both for having committed fornication and recommended a heavy fine and imprisonment during the Queen's pleasure.

The domestic misfortunes of Lady Catherine Grey were, of course, having their repercussions on the wider political front, especially with regard to Mary Queen of Scots, whose own fortunes had fluctuated wildly during the past two years. In July 1559, when the death of her father-in-law had brought her to the French throne, a queen twice over at sixteen-and-a-half, she had seemed to be standing on the threshold of a career of unexampled brilliance. But by December 1560 her husband, too, was dead, leaving her a childless widow a few days before her eighteenth birthday, 'dispossessed of the Crown of France, with little hope of recovering that of Scotland', where an aggressively Calvinistic regime, unlikely to welcome the return of a Roman Catholic Queen, was now in power. Mary, however, had proceeded to display an unexpected degree of political maturity, her 'great judgement in the wise handling of herself and her matters', her 'kingly modesty' and willingness 'to be ruled by good counsel' coming as a considerable and not entirely pleasant surprise in some quarters. But the Scots, reassured by reports of her conciliatory attitude towards 'the Religion', got ready to give her an honourable reception and when she landed at Leith on 19 August 1561 everyone – with the notable exception of John Knox – was prepared to be captivated by the beauty, the out-going warmth of manner, the gaiety and shining personal charisma which all combined to create that legendary 'inchantment whareby men ar bewitched'.

Fairly or unfairly, it has been said of Mary Stewart that she looked

on her homeland as no more than a convenient stop-over between
the France of her youthful triumphs and England which would, she
hoped, be the scene of a yet more glorious future. Certainly she
wasted no time in opening her long campaign to try to persuade
Elizabeth formally to recognize her claim to be regarded as heir presumptive. (Since the Protestant take-over and French retreat from
Scotland during the spring and summer of 1560, France had conceded Elizabeth's right to occupy her own throne and Mary had
abandoned her provocative use of the English royal arms.) Now she
and the Scottish nobility were hoping, not unreasonably, to profit
from the disgrace of her chief rival, Lady Catherine Grey, and in September 1561 William Maitland of Lethington, ablest of the Edinburgh Council, came south to discuss matters of mutual interest with
the Queen of England.

Elizabeth had tried and failed to prevent Mary's return home –
she trusted her Scottish cousin no further than she did her English
one, which was no further than she could see either of them.
Nevertheless, she gave Maitland a friendly welcome and in the
course of several audiences talked with unusual freedom about her
attitude towards Mary and the whole tangled issue of the succession.
She was ready to acknowledge that the Queen of Scots was 'of the
blood of England' and her nearest kinswoman, whom she was bound
by nature to love. But she refused to meddle in the rights and wrongs
of the succession to the Crown. It was like the sacrament of the altar.
Some thought one thing, some another and 'whose judgement is
best, God knows'. If Mary's right was good, Elizabeth would do
nothing to prejudice it. 'I for my part', she told Maitland, 'know
none better, nor that myself would prefer to her.' Nor indeed could
she think of any serious competitor. 'You know them all', she
remarked, 'what power or force has any of them, poor souls!'
Although, the Queen added sourly, it was true that one of them had
recently demonstrated her worthiness by broadcasting to the world
that she at least was not barren. Elizabeth then proceeded to touch
briefly 'upon my lady Catherine's fact', making it clear that she considered both the Grey sisters to be disqualified by their father's
treason. But, try as he would, Maitland could not prevail upon her to
give the Queen of Scots' claim any public recognition. She did not
agree that this would bring them closer together. On the contrary.
'Think you that I could love my own winding sheet?' enquired
Elizabeth Tudor brutally.

And there was another, even more compelling factor to be taken
into account. 'I know the inconstancy of the people of England'

observed their Queen, 'how they ever mislike the present government and have their eyes fixed upon the person that is next to succeed, and naturally men be so disposed.' She went on:

> I have good experience of myself in my sister's time, how desirous
> men were that I should be in (her) place and earnest to set me up. And
> if I would have consented, I know what enterprises would have been
> attempted to bring it to pass. . . . No princes' revenues be so great that
> they are able to satisfy the insatiable cupidity of men. And if we . . .
> should miscontent any (of) our subjects, it is to be feared that if they
> knew a certain successor of our crown they would have recourse
> thither. . . . I deal plainly with you, albeit my subjects I think love me
> as becomes them, yet is nowhere so great perfection that all are con-
> tent.

Fear of intrigue and double-dealing surrounding Catherine Grey's
marriage was very much on the Queen's mind just then, for, as Maitland reported, she referred to it again 'with no obscure signification
that she thought there was more hidden matter in it than was uttered
to the world, and that some of her nobility were partners in the making of that match'.

'So long as I live I shall be Queen of England, when I am dead they
shall succeed that have most right.' Thus Elizabeth succinctly stated
her personal position on the succession in conversation with Maitland of Lethington, and she never budged an inch from it. Apart
from her almost superstitious aversion to having a named heir, she
never saw any reason to modify her strongly held conviction that to
attempt to 'solve' the problem would encourage rather than disarm
faction and controversy. Her instinct was to do nothing, to go on
gambling on her own survival until, as she had told the Speaker of
the Commons back in 1559, such time as Almighty God saw fit to
make 'good provision . . . whereby the realm shall not remain destitute of an heir that may be a fit governor'.

Time was to prove her instinct right, but the risks inherent in this
laissez faire policy were dramatically high-lighted in the autumn of
1562 when the Queen, who was then in residence at Hampton Court,
fell victim to a virulent strain of smallpox which had already
attacked several of her ladies. Her fever mounted and she was soon
gravely ill. William Cecil, summoned from London at midnight,
reached the palace in the small hours of 16 October and, as Elizabeth
lay unconscious, perhaps dying, the Council went into emergency
session in an adjoining room to discuss the horrifying crisis now facing them.

According to the Spanish ambassador, out of the fifteen or sixteen members present, 'there were nearly as many different opinions about the succession to the Crown'. In fact, the Council seems to have been split more or less down the middle. One group, almost certainly headed by Cecil, wanted to follow Henry VIII's will and nominate Catherine Grey. Others, 'who found flaws in the will', pressed the claims of Henry Hastings, Earl of Huntingdon, who was known to be reliably Protestant. The Earls of Bedford and Pembroke supported Huntingdon and so, although they were not then Council members, did Thomas Howard, the influential young Duke of Norfolk and Lord Robert Dudley. Huntingdon, of course, was married to Catherine Dudley and Bishop de Quadra believed Lord Robert would have been prepared to back his brother-in-law by force of arms if necessary. A third, small group, led by that professional survivor, the Marquess of Winchester, urged against too much haste and suggested referring the matter to a committee of jurists who could examine the titles of the various claimants and advise the Council accordingly. No one, it appears, within the precincts of Hampton Court at any rate, had mentioned the name of the Queen of Scots and de Quadra reported that the Catholics, too, were divided, some favouring Mary, others her aunt Margaret, the Countess of Lennox, who had been born on the right side of the Border and was considered to be 'devout and sensible'.

Only one fact emerged with any real clarity out of the terror and confusion of that dreadful day: if Elizabeth had died – and she was 'all but gone' – she would have left a political vacuum which would rapidly have filled with political anarchy, with bitter faction fighting and, most probably, sectarian civil war after the contemporary French pattern. To everyone's unspeakable relief, she recovered. She even escaped the disfigurement of the pox, and within a remarkably short space of time she was up and about again and once more in full command. But the nation had had a bad fright, and pressure on the Queen to put an end to the uncertainty about her successor would now no longer be coming from Scotland alone. Before the end of the year de Quadra heard that groups of gentlemen were meeting privately, on the excuse of dining together, in order to discuss the matter further. One such gathering, held at the Earl of Arundel's house and attended by his former son-in-law, the Duke of Norfolk, went on until two o'clock in the morning and was believed to have come down in favour of Catherine Grey. When Elizabeth heard about this, she was furious. 'They say she wept with rage', wrote de Quadra. The succession, like her marriage, was something which she regarded as being entirely her own business and over which she would tolerate no interference from any quarter. She summoned Arundel to her presence and they appear to have had a first-class row, the Earl telling her that if she wanted to govern the country by passion he could assure her that the nobility would not allow it. The succession was an issue which affected them all vitally and they had every right to be concerned and consulted.

Catherine Grey, all this time, was still in the Tower and so was the Earl of Hertford, but there were some compensations. The Lieutenant, Edward Warner, was a kindly man. He let Catherine have the company of her pet monkeys and dogs, in spite of the damage which these quite unhouse-trained creatures were doing to government property. He also, on occasion, let her have the company of her husband, turning a discreetly blind eye to unlocked doors. He was later to justify himself, somewhat ingenuously, by saying that having once been over-persuaded, he thought there was no point in continuing to strive to keep the couple apart. Thus, during the summer of 1562, while public attention was focussed on the developing relationship between the Queens of England and Scotland, the Lady Catherine enjoyed the nearest approach to a normal married life she was ever to know.

Even this was precarious enough, as indicated by a note, probably one of many, scribbled to her 'dear lord' some time that year. 'No small joy,' she wrote, 'is it to me the comfortable understanding of your maintained health.' She herself had not been so well lately, but was better now and longing 'to be merry with you as you do to be with me. She went on, in a possible reference to some private joke,

> I say no more but be you merry as I was heavy when you the third time came to the door and it was locked. Do you think I forget old, fore-past matters? No, surely I cannot, but bear in memory far more than you think for. I have good leisure so to do when I call to mind what a husband I have of you, and my great hard fate to miss the viewing of so good a one. Thus mostly humbly thanking you, my sweet lord, for your sending both to see how I do and also for your money, I most lovingly bid you farewell.

For a brief, comparatively halcyon period it seemed almost as if the lovers had been forgotten behind their prison walls. But then came the scare over the Queen's illness and in February 1563, just as Elizabeth was engaged in fending off the increasingly importunate demands of both Houses of Parliament that she get married or name her successor or both, Lady Catherine, with her usual disastrous sense of timing, made another declaration to the world that she was not barren. 'The Earl of Hertford', wrote the veteran diplomat and Council member Sir John Mason in some exasperation to Thomas

Challoner, 'the Earl of Hertford having by corruption of his keepers had secret access by night to the Lady Catherine, she by his company hath brought a boy child into the world. He has therefore been called before the council in the Star Chamber and hath for that offence a fine set on his head of fifteen thousand pounds.'

This stupendous fine – it was later reduced to £3,000 – was for having first deflowered a virgin of the blood royal under the Queen's own roof, for breaking prison by visiting Catherine in the Tower and for having then ravished her a second time. The Earl, although never exactly a heroic figure, nevertheless defended himself before the Star Chamber with a certain forlorn dignity. He considered that he and the Lady Catherine were lawfully married and would not deny that he had passed through the doors of their prison, left standing open, to comfort his wife in her loneliness and pay his conjugal duty, for which he would not apologise.

But the Queen was now really angry. Apart from all the extra problems their witless behaviour was causing her, she found it especially hard to forgive the Hertfords' apparently cynical contempt for the authority and prestige of the Crown; for the fact that her cousin and putative heiress, instead of showing contrition or even any proper understanding of the enormity of her offence, had deliberately gone and done it again. To one of Elizabeth Tudor's disciplined intelligence and finely-tuned political awareness, the notion that Catherine could have acted out of sheer thoughtlessness and inability to grasp the realities of her position, rather than pre-meditated malice or ambition naturally seemed incredible.

The Queen's temper and the Hertfords' prospects were not improved by the existence of widespread public sympathy for the plight of the young couple, who were held to have been 'sharply handled' by the government. Their romantic story had appealed to the imagination of the Londoners, and their failure to prove the existence of their marriage was felt to be more their misfortune than their fault. According to John Mason, some 'very broad speeches of the case of the Earl of Hertford' were circulating in the city and other parts of the country too, ignorant folk 'not letting to say they be man and wife, and why should man and wife be let from coming together'. Mason himself did not share this view of the case of the Earl of Hertford. He thought the Earl a thoroughly spoilt and conceited youth who needed to be taught a sharp lesson. 'If a good part of his living might answer some part of his offence, and the imprisonment therewithal continue, it would make him to know what it is to have so arrogantly and contemptuously offended his Prince.'

Neither Hertford nor Catherine were to be left in any doubt in future about what it meant to have offended their prince. Nor was Edward Warner, who had been summarily sacked from his post and temporarily incarcerated in his own prison. Catherine's second son was christened Thomas, with two of the Tower warders acting as godfathers, but there were to be no more stolen meetings between his parents: no one cared to contemplate the probable royal reaction to news of a third illicit Seymour pregnancy.

The plague was bad in London that summer – it even invaded the Spanish embassy at Durham House and carried off Bishop de Quadra – and by August more than a thousand deaths a week were being reported. Nobody who could avoid it stayed in town at such times, and the Queen agreed that the Hertfords should be moved. In fact, the epidemic provided an excellent excuse for separating the little family still more completely. While the Earl and his elder son were sent to live under house arrest with his mother at Hanworth, Lady Catherine and the baby Thomas departed in the opposite direction, to her uncle Lord John Grey at Pirgo in Essex, with strict instructions that she was to be kept 'as in custody' and not allowed any uncensured contact with the outside world. His lordship was to make quite sure she understood that, although she might no longer be in the Tower, she remained very much a prisoner and any hope of remission would depend entirely on her good behaviour. John Grey hastened to assure William Cecil that his erring niece was indeed 'a penitent and a sorrowful woman for the Queen's displeasure', and Catherine herself wrote to the Secretary from Pirgo on 3 September, beseeching his help 'for the obtaining of the Queen's Majesty's most gracious pardon and favour towards me, which with upstretched hands and down bent knees, from the bottom of my heart, most humbly I crave'.

This was rather more like it. But, although there could now be no question as to the sincerity of Catherine's repentance, no immediate signs of pardon or favour were forthcoming and towards the end of the month John Grey ventured to remind Cecil of his 'offered friendship and great good will'. Lady Catherine, it seemed, was pining away for want of the Queen's mercy. She was eating hardly anything and spent most of her time dissolved in tears. Lord John may not have cared for his niece, but the sight of her constant misery was distressing to any Christian man – 'I never came to her, but I found her weeping or else saw by her face she had wept' – and he implored Cecil, 'for the love wherewith God hath loved us', to find some means of persuading the Queen to relent. He was also beginning to be seriously worried about the state of his charge's health, for 'she is so fraughted with phlegm by reason of thought, weeping and sitting still that many times she is like to be overcome therewith; so as if she had not painful (painstaking) women about her, I tell you truly cousin Cecil, I could not sleep in quiet'. Catherine, too, wrote again about this time, saying that if her disgrace were to last much longer, she would rather be dead and buried in the fear and favour of God than live in this 'continual agony'. 'I must confess', she went on, 'I never felt what the want of my prince's favour was before now', and if it were once restored, it would not be lost again through her default, 'so mindful, God willing, shall I be not to offend her Highness'.

But these and all other cries for help, addressed both to William Cecil and Lord Robert Dudley, fell on stony ground. The wretched Catherine's troubles were yet further aggravated by the fact that she appears to have been virtually destitute. When she was first committed to the Tower, some household stuff – that is, carpets, curtains, bedding and a few small items of upholstered furniture – had been allocated to her out of the royal stores. But, according to Edward Warner, this was old and well used even before her monkeys and dogs had been let loose on it. By the time she came to Pirgo, she had no money, no plate and was so 'poorly furnished' that John Grey was positively ashamed to let Cecil have an inventory of her possessions. Lord John had reluctantly supplied the most glaring deficiencies, but he baulked at paying for his prisoner's keep, and the Queen was soon complaining about his expenses. His lordship retaliated by sending in a detailed account to William Cecil. The weekly rate for 'my lady of Hertford's board, her child and her folks' amounted to less than seven pounds. As this included eight servants and five shillings for the widow employed to wash the baby's clothes, it hardly seems extravagant. But Elizabeth, who was never averse to having things both ways, decided that henceforward the Earl of Hertford should be made responsible for Catherine's maintenance, and he was ordered to pay a sum of over a hundred pounds to the Greys.

Hertford seized this opportunity of making another appeal for clemency on behalf of his wife and himself, writing to Robert Dudley in March 1564 craving his Lordship's especial means to Her Majesty:

> that we may be unburdened of her intolerable displeasure, the great weight whereof hath sufficiently taught us never again to offend so merciful a princess. . . . My trust is God will bless your lordship's travails . . . and by your means, wherein, next Him, we only depend, turn the sorrowful mourning of us, her majesty's poor captives, into a countershine of comfort, for the which I rest in continual prayer.

But whatever chances Her Majesty's 'poor captives' might have had of gaining some relief from the burden of her displeasure were about to be effectively destroyed by the machinations of one John Hales, Clerk of the Hanaper (a senior appointment in the Court of Chancery) and extreme left-wing MP which, in the Elizabethan context, meant militant Protestant activist. Hales, nicknamed 'Hales the hottest', was violently opposed to any idea of settling the succession on the Catholic Queen of Scots. He was not alone in this, the strength of the opposition to Mary's claims in the House of Commons having been made very clear during the last Parliamentary session. But he had unwisely taken it upon himself deliberately to promote the cause of Catherine Grey – or rather of the Protestant succession, he had no personal interest in Catherine herself – and in pursuit of this objective had prepared a paper setting out the superior claims of the Suffolk line. This 'book' – the *Declaration or Discourse on the Succession of the Crown Imperial of this Realm* – was apparently written while the 1563 Parliament was sitting and had since been circulating in manuscript form among the author's friends. When it came to the Queen's notice, however, in the spring of 1564, it created a reverberating explosion of royal wrath. 'Here is fallen out a troublesome, fond matter' wrote William Cecil crossly at the end of April.

Hales' crime did not merely consist of meddling in matters which were none of his business, or even of his outspoken support of the Suffolk claim. More to the point was the fact that he had involved other people and had taken active steps to try to establish the legality of the Grey/Seymour family alliance, consulting European jurists and procuring from them 'sentences and counsels . . . maintaining the lawfulness of the Earl of Hertford's marriage'. This was the most serious aspect of the affair as far as Elizabeth was concerned. With the vital exception of the Queen herself, Lady Catherine Grey, an Englishwoman born and bred and boasting an impeccable Protestant pedigree, had always been first choice of heir presumptive among the influential Protestant Establishment. If a viable case were now to be made out for the validity of her marrige, then, as the mother of two sons, her claim and that of the Suffolk line generally to be given precedence over the Stewarts would be immensely strengthened. It was not to be supposed that the Queen of Scots and *her* party would let this pass without protest, and the whole delicate equilibrium of Anglo-Scottish relations – not to mention England's relations with France and Spain – would be endangered at a time when international tension caused by the growing ideological Catholic versus Protestant conflict was being steadily heightened. Vexed beyond measure, Elizabeth clapped the officious Mr Hales into prison and ordered a full enquiry.

The Seymours, of course, had a strong interest in proving the legitimacy of the Earl of Hertford's sons. Francis Newdigate, the Earl's stepfather and another natural busybody who had helped to finance the foreign trips made by Hales' representative Robert Beale, was among those taken in for questioning. So was Lord John Grey, also in trouble for having discussed family matters with John Hales. Hales' official chief, Nicholas Bacon, the Lord Chancellor or Lord Keeper, was another public figure under something of a cloud and William Cecil himself was not entirely immune from suspicion. He had close connections with several of those involved and had always been noted as 'a favourer of my Lady Catherine's title'. 'But my truth therein is tried', he wrote rather complacently to his friend Thomas Smith in November, 'and so I rest quiet, for surely I am and always have been circumspect to do nothing to make offence.' Not that there had ever been any question of disloyalty. Hales swore in considerable agitation that he 'refuseth the merits of Christ's passion if there were any change meant or thought by him thereupon'. His sole motive had been to urge the case for a Protestant succession and, so far from wishing to put Catherine Grey in Elizabeth's place, he had always said he thought it a mercy that she should be such a poor and friendless creature, unable to harm the Queen's Majesty or the state.

Although the Queen's Majesty was still not entirely appeased, the commotion caused by the *tempestas Halisiana* was now beginning to subside. John Grey died during the autumn, as a result of all the worry he had been through according to his friends, but Cecil thought his gout alone was enough to kill him. Catherine, meanwhile, had been transferred to the custody of Sir William Petre at Ingatestone, her prospects of being reunited with her 'dear lord and husband' looking more remote than ever. 'The Queen's displeasure continueth still towards my lord of Hertford and the lady Catherine' Cecil noted on the last day of the year. A letter addressed to him by his old friend, the Duchess of Somerset, complaining about the way in which the young couple were being left to 'thus wax old in prison' – surely it was time the Queen relented and, in any case, better all round 'for them to be abroad and learn to serve' – seems to have gone unanswered, as did another appeal from the Duchess on her son's behalf written in Holy Week, hopefully 'a charitable time of forgiveness'. After the Hales affair, the circumspect Mr Secretary was taking absolutely no unnecessary chances.

All the same, in that spring and early summer of 1565 Elizabeth's freely expressed annoyance over the Queen of Scots' impulsive marriage to their mutual kinsman, Henry Stuart, Lord Darnley, elder son of Margaret, Countess of Lennox, led to speculation in some quarters that she might now be moved to rehabilitate Lady Catherine. Philip of Spain, in particular, was worried lest she should decide to nominate Catherine as her successor after all. But, unlike her father, Elizabeth never regarded the Crown Imperial of the realm as a piece of real estate to be bequeathed according to whim, or considerations of political or religious expediency. Always a strict legitimist, she had meant exactly what she said to Maitland of Lethington: that she took the Queen of Scots to be her nearest kins-woman and next and lawful heir. Certainly no arguments, whether constitutional, political or just plain nationalistic, could ever per-suade the Queen even to discuss the dynastic claims of the Suffolk line.

In August 1565 an element of black comedy entered the Suffolk saga. 'Here is an unhappy chance and monstrous' wrote William Cecil to Thomas Smith. 'The sergeant-porter, being the biggest gentleman in this court, hath married secretly the Lady Mary Grey, the least of all the court. They are committed to several (separate) prisons. The offence is very great.' The current Spanish ambassador, Guzman de Silva, passing on the news to King Philip on 20 August, explained that the Queen had had in her house a sister of Jane and Catherine Grey. 'She is little, crook-backed and very ugly, and it came out yesterday that she had married a gentleman named Keys, sergeant-porter at the palace. They say', he added ominously, 'the Queen is very much annoyed and grieved thereat.'

Little enough is known about the background to this bizarre romance of the dwarfish, nineteen-year-old Mary Grey and the enormous gate-keeper, a middle-aged widower with several chil-dren. As a child, Mary had been briefly betrothed to her kinsman, Arthur Grey of Wilton, but no other attempt had ever been made to arrange a marriage for her and, since Catherine's disgrace, it was obvious that none ever would be. Mary, who appears to have shared some at least of her sister Jane's intellectual proclivities as well as her stubborn independence of spirit, had therefore decided to make her own arrangements, seemingly undeterred by the example of Catherine's unfortunate experience. Her attachment to Thomas Keys (whose surname most probably derived from his office) is said to have begun about a year before their marriage which, as with those of the widowed Duchesses of Suffolk and Somerset, was not quite so unequal as might at first appear – Keys being related to the highly respectable and royally connected Knollys family.

The actual wedding took place at nine o'clock at night on either 10 or 12 August in the porter's rooms over the Watergate at Westmins-ter. As in the case of Catherine and Edward Seymour, the officiating priest, described as an old man, short and very fat, neglected to leave his name and address. There were, however, a sufficient number of witnesses present – the groom's brother Edward, Martin Cawsley, a friend from Cambridge, an anonymous manservant, and a Mrs Goldwell who supported the bride – to testify that the ceremony had taken place. Ironically, this turned out to have been rather a mistake, for a year later, when Keys offered formally to renounce the marriage in return for his release from prison, the Bishop of London rejected the suggestion as 'not available in law'. If the contract were to be dissolved it would have to be done judicially in the ecclesiastical courts. This never seems to have happened. At any rate the ex-sergeant porter remained in the Fleet gaol, where he passed the time by shooting sparrows with a stone-bow (a form of catapault) and complaining about the conditions of his confinement which were particularly trying for one of his 'bulk of body'. He certainly appears to have suffered from harsh treatment – probably because he lacked the means to fee his gaolers adequately – and there's a gruesome story about his being fed some meat laced with poison intended to destroy a dog with mange!

Lady Mary, meanwhile, had been removed to a safe distance. The authorities were not risking a repeat of Lady Catherine's performance, and in September 1565 a warrant was issued to William Hawtrey Esquire, of the county of Buckingham, ordering him to repair forthwith to the court to 'take into his charge and custody the Lady Mary Grey, and convey her to his house, the Chequers, without permitting her to hold conference with anyone, or to have liberty to go abroad, suffering only one waiting woman to have access to her. For Mr Hawtrey's charges and expenses concerning the said Lady Mary', the warrant continued, 'the Queen's majesty will see him satisfied in reason.'

Mary Grey languished at Chequers for the next two years, during which time she wrote a number of tear-stained appeals for mercy addressed, of course, to Mr Secretary Cecil and following the accepted pattern:

> I trust you conceive what a grief the Queen's displeasure is to me, which makes me to wish death rather than be in this great misery . . . therefore I am forced to crave your help and goodness to be a continual mean for me to her majesty, to get me her majesty's favour again. . . . I assure you I do as much repent as ever did any for that I have incurred the queen's displeasure, which is the greatest grief to me. . . . I most woeful wretch . . . desiring rather death than to be any longer without so great a jewel as her majesty's favour should be to me. . . .

In August 1567 Mary was transferred to the guardianship of her step-grandmother, Catherine, Duchess of Suffolk. The Duchess of Somerset had apparently been Cecil's or the Queen's first choice, but there was a sudden change of plan and my lady of Suffolk found herself landed with Mary at a moment's notice, and a very inconvenient moment at that, since she had been on the point of leaving London for Grimsthorpe when her new charge was delivered to her at the house where she was staying in the Minories – the lease of which, by a curious quirk of fate, had formerly been granted to Henry Grey, Duke of Suffolk.

This was especially ironical as, according to the Duchess, Lady Mary was even less well equipped with household goods than her sister had been. Catherine Bertie was, she declared, quite unable to help out. She was in the habit of borrowing what she needed from friends on the rare occasions when she came to town, and she and her husband had lost so much as a result of their enforced sojourn abroad that they had barely enough for themselves in their Lincolnshire houses. They had meant to buy some new but, what with her son's recent illness and other domestic problems, there had really been no opportunity. 'The special cause', though, was lack of money, and in what she frankly described as a 'begging letter' to that all-purpose recipient of appeals, confidences and complaints, Mr Secretary Cecil, my lady of Suffolk explained that she had been obliged to tell Mr Hawtrey how matters stood and ask that Lady Mary's 'furniture' should be sent on ahead of her. But, 'would God you had seen what stuff it is!' – an old feather-bed without either bolster or counterpane, two old pillows, one longer than the other, a silk quilt so ragged that all the stuffing was coming out and two 'little pieces of old, old hangings, both of them not seven yards broad'.

Lady Mary had been given two little rings and a gold chain by her husband; she owned a Geneva bible and the two volume edition of *Foxe's Book of Martyrs* but otherwise, it seemed, possessed 'nothing in the world', not so much as a basin and ewer. At Chequers the rich and hospitable Mr Hawtrey had supplied her needs, but now her grandmother, quite possibly with an eye to the chance of getting her own cupboards replenished from the royal wardrobe, entreated William Cecil to arrange for the Queen's cousin to have at least the furniture of one chamber for herself and her maid (her manservant could make shift with the old bed); also, if it were not too much to ask, 'some old silver pots to fetch her drink in and two little cups to drink in, one for beer another for wine'.

The Duchess went on:

I trust she will do well hereafter for notwithstanding that I am sure she is very glad to be with me, yet, I assure you, she is otherwise, not only in countenance but in very deed, so sad and ashamed of her fault so that I cannot yet, since she came, get her to eat: in all that she has eaten now these two days not so much as a chicken's leg. She makes me even afraid for her; and therefore I write the gladlier, for that I think a little comfort would do well.

It was a pitiful situation, but there was to be no comfort in the end for either Mary or Catherine Grey. Indeed, their predicament offers a graphic and frightening illustration of just how much power the Sovereign was able to exert over the lives of those who threatened, or seemed even indirectly to threaten, the security of the state. When John Somers had written of Catherine Grey's marriage that 'the matter lies chiefly, notwithstanding all determination, in the Queen's mercy', he had been speaking no more than the literal truth. As under any modern totalitarian regime, so in sixteenth-century England the civil rights of the Grey sisters and their respective husbands could be and were unhesitatingly sacrificed to political expediency. All four remained in prison without trial during the Queen's pleasure – Catherine Grey and Thomas Keys would be released only by death – while Elizabeth had no compunction whatever in putting asunder those whom God had joined together.

10

There is No More Left of Them

. . . of so noble a stock they were, there is no more left of them.

The autumn of 1566 saw the most serious confrontation yet between Queen and Parliament over the still unresolved problems of her marriage and the succession, with the House of Commons, in a belligerent mood, determined not to be put off with any more evasions or 'answers answerless', the Queen equally determined to defend her prerogative against all-comers but, at the same time, in the embarrassing position of having to ask for money in time of peace. It was a situation which seemed to contain all the makings of a battle royal and the Spanish ambassador, who was taking a keen and well-informed interest in the progress of events at Westminster, reported that the political pundits were forecasting that if the Queen persisted in refusing either to get married or to name her successor, the Commons would refuse to vote her any supplies. Although Elizabeth had recently taken the initiative in re-opening negotiations with her long-standing (and long-suffering) suitor, the Hapsburg Archduke Charles, Guzman de Silva privately very much doubted her sincerity; nor did he believe she would ever consent to settle the succession, 'as she understands very well that it will not be to her advantage'. The majority of the heretics, he informed King Philip, were still furiously in favour of Catherine Grey, and added ominously that their party was very powerful in the Lower Chamber.

The Lords, too, were showing signs of restiveness. De Silva heard that the Duke of Norfolk – England's premier nobleman and only surviving duke – would support Catherine's cause in the matter of the succession, while Robert Dudley, now elevated to the dignity of Earl of Leicester, favoured the claims of the Queen of Scotland. The ambassador was of the opinion that William Cecil had influenced the Duke, 'with whom he is very friendly', offering the inducement of a marriage between one of Norfolk's daughters to Catherine's son. This story had been going round at the time of the last Parliamentary session, and de Silva thought it quite possible that the idea might now be formally proposed in order to put pressure on the Queen to agree to hasten her own marriage. 'There are communications going on amongst the aristocracy here which threaten a storm', he wrote, 'but they do not declare themselves and I think . . . that they will not dare to make any open movement.'

In fact, when Parliament re-assembled at the end of September, everyone seemed reluctant to make the first move. At a Council meeting on 12 October the Duke of Norfolk made a rather forlorn attempt to persuade the Queen to soften her attitude, reminding her as tactfully as he could of the petitions presented by the Lords and Commons back in 1563 urging her to name both her husband and her heir presumptive. So far, no further action had been taken because they still awaited her final answer, but now, in the name of the rest of the nobility and all those who had the best interests of the country at heart, he begged her to agree to let Parliament debate these two vital matters of public concern.

Elizabeth was unimpressed. No one had any reason to complain about how she had governed the country to date. The succession was her business and she wanted no advice from anyone on how to handle it. She had no intention of allowing herself to be buried alive as her sister had been. She remembered only too vividly the way people had flocked to pay court to her at Hatfield during those last months of Mary's reign and wanted to see no such journeyings during *her* lifetime. As for her marriage, they knew quite well that it was not far off. As for Parliament, she bade the members to do their duty.

This did not sound very promising and when, a week later, the presentation of the subsidy bill could no longer be postponed, the storm finally broke. The House of Commons, or rather a well-organized aggressive pressure group within the Commons, now had a weapon with which to coerce the Crown and proceeded to make it clear that there would be no supplies until the far more important matter of the succession had been disposed of. Government efforts to cool the situation met with no success and the reply to one councillor who urged a little more patience was uncompromising, 'We have express charge to grant nothing before the Queen gives a firm answer to our demands. Go to the Queen and let her know our intention, which we have in command from all the towns and people of this Kingdom, whose deputies we are.' After a bad-tempered debate, which went on for two days and during which, according to the Spanish ambassador, the members even came to blows, it was decided to make another approach to the Lords with a view to renewing their combined pressure on the Queen. 'These heretics', commented de Silva, 'neither fear God nor obey their betters.'

Elizabeth was angry and possibly rather taken aback by so much open insubordination. De Silva reported again on 26 October:

> The discussion about the succession still goes on in Parliament and the Queen is extremely annoyed, as she fears that if the matter is carried further they will adopt Catherine. . . . I have always pointed out to the Queen the grave difficulties which might result from such a nomination, and the peril in which she and her affairs would be if Catherine were appointed her successor. . . . She quite understands it, and three days ago told me that on no account would she allow this nomination to be discussed.

Elizabeth had always got on well with Guzman de Silva, the only one of Philip's ambassadors to make a genuine effort to understand the English point of view and to work towards improving Anglo-Spanish relations. The Queen liked him as a person, trusted him and confided in him to a sometimes surprising degree. She told him now that the Commons had offered to vote her £250,000 if she would agree to allow the nomination of Catherine Grey as heir presumptive to be debated, but that she had refused, saying she would not accept any conditions. The money she was asking for was for the common good, to strengthen the navy and for the defence of Ireland, and should therefore be given freely and graciously. 'She is quite determined to concede nothing in this matter of the succession', de Silva continued, 'although she wishes to dissemble and let them talk, in order that she may know what are their opinions and discover the lady of each one's choice, by which she alludes to the Queen of Scotland and Catherine.'

There was certainly plenty of talk going on, if not much else. After nearly a month virtually no government business had been transacted, as a solemn deputation from the Upper House, headed by the venerable old Marquess of Winchester, pointed out to Her Majesty. One by one the peers reminded her yet again of the urgent need to provide for the future, and one by one they begged her to declare her will in the matter of the succession – either that, or else dissolve Parliament and let everyone go home. Elizabeth's reply offered no hint of compromise. The Commons, she declared, were no better than rebels. They would never have dared to behave in such a way in her father's time. As for the Lords, they could do as they pleased, and so would she. The succession was far too serious a question to be left to such a light-witted assembly and she was thinking to taking advice from the best legal brains in the country.

Three days later, when the Lords and Commons agreed to make another joint onslaught on the palace, the Queen felt herself cornered and reacted accordingly. De Silva heard that in the course of a blazing row with some of her most senior councillors, she had called the Duke of Norfolk a traitor, 'or something very like it'. The Earl of Pembroke had also felt the rough edge of her tongue, and she told the Marquess of Northampton that he had better remember the arguments which got him married again while he had a wife living, instead of mincing words with her. Nor was the Earl of Leicester immune. Elizabeth said she had thought that if all the world abandoned her, he would not, and when Robert Dudley hastily protested his willingness to die at her feet, she retorted crossly that that had nothing to do with the matter. Then, having ordered them all to get out of her sight and stay out of it, she flounced off to pour her troubles into the sympathetic ear of the Spanish ambassador.

On 27 October William Cecil noted that the Earls of Pembroke and Leicester were still banned from the Presence Chamber for pressing for a succession debate in Parliament against the Queen's wishes; several behind-the-scenes attempts to reach a settlement had failed and tension at Westminster was mounting. By 4 November both Houses were ready to present the Queen with what amounted to an ultimatum. But they under-estimated their sovereign lady, who proceeded to get in first by commanding a delegation of thirty members from both Houses to appear before her on the afternoon of the fifth. The Speaker of the Commons was expressly excluded from the invitation. On this occasion Elizabeth intended to do all the speaking herself.

After some scathing remarks about unbridled persons in the Commons whose mouths had never been snaffled by a rider, and certain noble lords who might have been expected to know better, the Queen turned to the matter in hand. She had already said that she would marry, and would never break the word of a prince 'for her honour's sake'. She could only repeat now that she meant to get married as soon as she conveniently could, adding 'and I hope to have children, otherwise I would never marry'.

As for the limitation of the succession, she again referred to her experiences during Mary's reign, when she had 'tasted of the practices' against her sister and had stood in danger of her life as a result. There were those now sitting in the House of Commons who knew exactly what she was talking about and whom she could have named had she chosen. But none of them knew what it was like to be 'a second person', or had any notion of what it would mean for her as Queen to have an impatient heir presumptive breathing down her neck. It was not convenient to settle the succession, 'nor never shall be without some peril unto you and certain danger unto me'. If a suitable opportunity to name an heir ever did arise then she would take it, but it would be her decision and hers alone made without prompting or request, for it was monstrous that the feet of the body politic should attempt to direct the head. Indeed, one thing Elizabeth made abundantly clear. 'Though I be a woman, yet I have as good a courage, answerable to my place, as ever my father had. I am your anointed Queen. I will never be by violence constrained to do anything.'

This was certainly one of those occasions when she left no doubt in anyone's mind as to 'whose daughter she was', and it is an indication of the strength of feeling roused by the subject that the House of Commons was still defiantly prepared to go ahead with its controversial 'suit for the limitation of the succession'. The Queen reacted by prohibiting any further discussion of the matter, bidding the members to 'satisfy themselves with her Highness's promise of marriage'. This led to another revolt, Paul Wentworth, a leader of the militants, going so far as to challenge the Crown's authority to curtail the 'accustomed lawful liberties' of the Commons.

Guzman de Silva reported that 'the insolence of these heretics' was infuriating the Queen. 'It appears', he wrote on 13 November, 'that they claim the right to proceed in the appointment of a successor to the crown, and in this case, although the Scotch Queen has a large party in the House of Lords, it is thought that Catherine would have nearly all of the members of the Lower Chamber on her side.'

By this time, however, the main issue at stake was no longer the Queen's marriage or even the succession, but royal violation of Parliamentary privilege, and it was beginning to look as if a serious constitutional crisis might be looming. Elizabeth had allowed temper and something very like panic to ride her, and consequently had got herself into an untenable position. Faced now with a choice between dissolving Parliament, doing without her much needed supplies and admitting a damaging defeat at the hands of the radical Protestants or giving way, she wisely gave way. On 25 November she lifted her embargo on freedom of debate, a concession 'most joyfully taken' by all concerned. She also, reluctantly, remitted a third of the taxation she had been asking for and, in return, the succession debate was dropped and the subsidy bill got its first reading.

The Queen may thus be said to have won on points, but the

episode had provided a salutory reminder not merely of the growing organizational power of Parliamentary pressure groups, but also of the continuing and implacable hostility towards the Queen of Scots among an influential and articulate section of the community. Nor had agitation been confined to the precincts of the Houses of Parliament. Broadsheets and handbills had been widely circulated through the city – some had even appeared in the Queen's own private apartments – while the law students of Lincoln's Inn had held a disputation which found that 'by all the laws and customs of England' Mary Queen of Scots, as a foreigner born outside the realm, could never succeed to the Crown, 'even if she were the nearest in birth and the ablest'.

As it happened, even those who supported Mary's claim were about to have their loyalty severely tested when, the following February, the whole of Europe was electrified by the news coming out of Scotland. It was, of course, already widely known that the Queen's marriage was on the rocks, for Lord Darnley, the 'fair jolly young man' who had so fatally captivated Her Majesty two years earlier, had quickly revealed himself to be a bully, a drunkard and a coward. It was also an open secret that the King of Scotland had been a marked man ever since his betrayal of the murderers of David Riccio the previous spring. No one, therefore, was unbearably surprised when he came to his messy and melodramatic end at the old provost's lodging at Kirk o'Field in the early hours of 10 February 1567. Nor, in the circumstances, would anyone have been disposed to blame the Queen of Scots unduly for conniving at this drastic solution to her matrimonial problems – not, that is, if she had played the game according to the rules. But, even in sixteenth-century Scotland, certain rules, certain decencies, had to be observed. When, therefore, so far from showing any interest in bringing her husband's killers to justice, Mary continued to be seen regularly in the company of the Earl of Bothwell, cast by popular consent in the role of first murderer, the waves of shock horror reaction gathered irresistible force. Suspicion that she had been a party to the outrage at Kirk o'Field was being voiced in Edinburgh within days of the event, and rumours had reached London before the end of the month.

When Queen Elizabeth first discussed the tragedy with Guzman de Silva on 22 February she spoke of it with much apparent sorrow, he reported, saying she thought it very extraordinary but could not bring herself to believe that the Queen of Scotland could be guilty of so dreadful a crime, 'notwithstanding the murmurs of the people'. De Silva agreed that the whole thing seemed incredible. All the same, he advised Elizabeth 'to be on the alert to prevent undue ela-

tion of the opposite party who were strong and might cause trouble'
– meaning, of course, the partisans of Catherine Grey, although he
was careful not to mention names. Elizabeth replied that she had
already thought of this and taken the necessary precautions.

But none of the remarkable goings on of the past few months,
either in London or Edinburgh, could any longer affect Catherine's
prospects. In February 1567 she was living at Gosfield Hall, near
Halstead in Essex, in the charge of Sir John Wentworth, and in September was moved again, to Cockfield Hall, home of Sir Owen Hopton and his wife, in the remote Suffolk village of Yoxford. She was by
this time a very sick woman, in the final stages of tuberculosis, and
soon after her arrival Sir Owen was obliged to send for one of the
royal physicians to visit her. Catherine was writing no more letters
and giving no sign of interest in the outside world. She had, it
seemed, long since abandoned all hope of release, much less of ever
seeing her husband again. Perhaps even the memory of the boy who
had once courted her at Hanworth, with whom she had made hurried nervous love in the house in Cannon Row and shared those
strange dreamlike months in the Tower of London was itself fading
into shadow, insubstantial as a dream. There was nothing left for
Catherine now but to die as becomingly, if less dramatically, as once
her sister Jane had done. And in January 1568 Owen Hopton wrote
to inform William Cecil that the end was not far off.

It came on the morning of the twenty-seventh. His charge had
spent the night in prayer, reported Sir Owen, 'saying of psalms and
hearing them read of others . . . divers times she would rehearse the
prayers appointed for the Visitation of the Sick, and five or six times
the same night she said the prayers appointed to be said at the hours
of death'. When those watching with her through those long dark
hours made well-meaning efforts to divert her mind, saying 'Madam
be of good comfort, with God's help you shall live and do well many
years', she would only answer, 'No, no life in this world . . . for here
is nothing but care and misery and there is life everlasting.' From
time to time she lapsed into semi-consciousness. The women at the
bedside chafed her cold hands and feet and heard her whisper,
'Father of Heaven, for thy son Christ's sake, have mercy upon me.'
When Lady Hopton, too, tried to rally the dying woman, telling her
to be of good comfort, 'for with God his favour you shall live and
escape this', and reminding her that she had been as gravely ill
before and recovered, Catherine replied, 'No, no my lady, my time is
come and it is not God's will that I should live any longer, and his
will be done, not mine.' Looking round her, she added, 'As I am, so
shall you be; behold the picture of yourselves.'

Between six and seven o'clock she roused herself to ask that Sir Owen should be sent for. When he came in she prayed him 'and the rest that be about me to bear witness with me that I die a true Christian, and that I believe to be saved by the death of Christ, and that I am one that he hath shed his most precious blood for; and I ask God and all the world forgiveness, and I forgive all the world'. Then she begged Owen Hopton to promise her that he would himself ask the Queen, 'even from the mouth of a dead woman', that she would at last 'forgive her displeasure towards me, as my hope is she hath done. I must needs confess I have greatly offended her in that I made my choice without her knowledge, otherwise I take God to witness I had never the heart to think any evil against her majesty.'

Catherine went on to plead that Elizabeth would be good to her children 'and not impute my fault unto them, whom I give wholly unto her majesty; for in my life they have had few friends, and fewer shall they have when I am dead, except her majesty be gracious unto them; and I desire her majesty to be good unto my lord, for I know this my death will be heavy news unto him'.

Finally there were 'certain commendations and tokens' which she asked Sir Owen to deliver to Lord Hertford. She handed him a ring with a pointed diamond which her lord had given her when they plighted their troth in Jane Seymour's closet in the Maidens' Chamber at Westminster, and that other ring with the five links of gold which he had put on her finger on their wedding day seven years before. The knot of secret might, already effectively broken by the Queen, was now about to be severed permanently. Catherine adjured her husband, via Owen Hopton, that, as she had been a true and faithful wife, he would be a loving and natural father to their children, and she sent her little sons her blessing – the same which God had given Abraham, Isaac and Jacob.

There was one thing more, a ring engraved with a death's head and the motto 'While I live yours' which would be 'the last token unto my lord that ever I shall send him; it is the picture of myself'. Catching sight of her hands, she saw the finger nails had turned purple and exclaimed 'as it were with a joyful countenance, "Welcome death!"' Sir Owen Hopton, 'perceiving her to draw towards her end', gave orders for the passing bell to be rung and Catherine Seymour, Countess of Hertford, born Lady Catherine Grey, 'yielded unto God her meek spirit at nine of the clock in the morning' having given, at any rate according to the official account of the matter, the eloquent, smoothly polished performance expected of persons of breeding and education as they stood on the brink of eternity. Catherine was twenty-seven years old. She had spent the past six and a half years in prison or house arrest and the whole of her life under the doom of her royal blood.

Her death, coming at a time when attention was still largely centred on Scottish affairs, caused little stir. A pawn had been removed from the political chessboard. The players adjusted their dispositions slightly and went on with the game. Queen Elizabeth expressed sorrow over her cousin's death to Guzman de Silva, but, he wrote, 'it is not believed that she feels it, as she was afraid of her'. Nevertheless, Elizabeth knew what was due to the dead woman and she gave Lady Catherine an elaborate and expensive funeral, costing over a thousand pounds, in Yoxford parish church.

The Queen has often been criticized for her implacable attitude towards Catherine Grey and, with the benefit of hindsight, this is natural enough. But while there may well have been an element of personal rancour involved, to Elizabeth, engaged as she was in an unremitting struggle to keep the monarchy strong and secure, and England free from internal dissension and foreign interference, private happiness, her own and other people's, inevitably became something of secondary importance. Neither, of course, was it an age which placed over-much importance on individual earthly happiness. The Queen may not have been actively afraid of her cousin, not at least for her qualities as a person, but Catherine still represented a threat to national security simply by her existence as a possible figurehead or stalking horse for the extreme Protestant left wing, or Puritans as they were beginning to be known – a faction which Elizabeth always loathed and which she feared more than she did the Catholics. It is therefore unlikely that she mourned the loss of Lady Catherine.

As for the Earl of Hertford, his wife's death held out new hope of release and rehabilitation. He was then living comfortably enough in the custody of Sir John Spencer of Althorp, but he had to wait for another two years before his freedom of movement was finally fully restored and he was able to come to court and receive the Queen's pardon. Arguments about the payment of the fine imposed on him by the Star Chamber, though, dragged on until the end of the 1570s.

By then Lord Hertford was actively contemplating remarriage, but again he had to wait. It was not until 1586 that he and Frances Howard, daughter of William, first Baron Howard of Effingham, became man and wife. The marriage seems to have been a success but Frances, who died in 1598, gave her husband no more children and he never abandoned the fight to get his first marriage recognized and his sons legitimated. In 1591 his pertinacity in pursuing the matter through the Church courts irritated Elizabeth sufficiently to earn him another brief spell in the Tower. At last, in 1606, three years after the old Queen's death, perseverance was rewarded when, it appears, the clergyman who had performed the ceremony in the Earl's bedroom at Cannon Row that December morning nearly half a century before was suddenly and miraculously resurrected, and 'other circumstances agreeing, a jury at common law found it a good marriage'.

The two boys born in the Tower of London were brought up by their Somerset grandmother, writing stiff little notes in Latin and French to their father and sending him copies of arithmetic exercises to illustrate their progress at their lessons. Occasional, not very convincing attempts were made to canvas their claims to the succession and in October 1572, when the Queen was ill with a rash and a high fever, a Spanish correspondent in London heard that 'the earl of Leicester, the Treasurer [William Cecil], and the earl of Bedford were closeted together several times to arrange, in case the Queen died, to proclaim as king one of the two sons of the earl of Hertford by Lady Catherine'. Again, in the winter of 1574, when Elizabeth was temporarily indisposed, the Spanish merchant-banker Antonio de Guaras reported that if the Queen were to die the Catholic party would proclaim the Queen of Scots – now, of course, a state prisoner in England – while the heretics would take up arms against her and proclaim the elder son of the Earl of Hertford. But as time passed and the Queen of Scots' son James grew to sober Protestant maturity, the problem of the succession, which had overshadowed English politics for so long, gradually faded away and Elizabeth's confidence that with God's help good provision would be made in convenient time 'whereby the realm shall not remain destitute of an heir that may be a fit governor' turned out to have been justified after all.

Thomas Seymour, the younger of Hertford's sons by Lady Catherine, died in 1600 and the elder, Edward Viscount Beauchamp, also pre-deceased his father. In 1582 Lord Beauchamp married considerably beneath his station to Honora Rogers, daughter of a Dorset country squire. His father was furious and did his utmost to prevent and afterwards break up the match. Indeed, so strained did relations become that, at one point, young Beauchamp was driven to appeal for help to the Secretary of State Francis Walsingham, threatening to kill himself if he were forced to return to his father's house.

The Earl of Hertford was to survive until January 1621, having lived to see his grandson, William Seymour, re-enact his own story with almost uncanny precision by making a secret marriage with another junior member of the royal house, the tragic Arbella Stuart.

This William Seymour, restored to favour in the reign of Charles I, became an energetic supporter of the royalist cause in the Civil War and in 1660, at the end of his life, was also restored to the Somerset dukedom of his great-grandfather, the Lord Protector. It was he who erected a pompous monument over his grandfather's tomb in Salisbury Cathedral, sacred to the memory of Edward, Earl of Hertford and his most dear and beloved consort Catherine Grey. She is eulogized as 'a woman distinguished as an example of uprightness, piety, beauty and faith', he as 'the most perfect pattern of nobility . . . endowed with eloquence, wisdom, innocence and gravity'. This 'incomparable pair' it is proclaimed, after having experienced 'alternative changes of fortune', at length rest together 'in the same concord in which they lived', so presumably Catherine's grandson had brought her remains from Yoxford to this more fitting resting place. But the line of the incomparable pair, with its romantic tincture of Tudor blood, died out in the mid-eighteenth century. The present dukes of Somerset come from the Seymours of Berry Pomeroy, descendants of the Protector and his first wife, Catherine Fillol.

Lady Mary Grey, or rather Mary Keys – for her improbable marriage, although officially ignored, never seems to have been officially challenged – was still with Duchess Catherine at Grimsthorpe when her sister died. But in June 1569 she was transferred to the care of the financier Sir Thomas Gresham and his wife, who complained bitterly and often about the burden thus placed upon them. The custom of billeting political detainees on selected members of the aristocracy and gentry had certain obvious advantages from the Crown's point of view and, according to the status of the prisoner, sometimes conferred a certain cachet, being regarded as a sign of the monarch's especial trust and favour. Poor little Mary Grey, though, possessed neither political, financial nor social standing to compensate her unwilling hosts for the inconvenience her presence caused them. As Thomas Gresham pointed out pathetically, it meant that his wife could not even go and visit her old mother, who was 'a very weak woman, not like to live long'.

In October 1570 he wrote to tell William Cecil that because of a case of plague in his household at Osterley Park, he was proposing to take his family down to his other country house at Mayfield in Sussex. He wanted to know what he was to do with Mary Grey, 'trusting that now her Majesty would be so good unto me as to remove her from me, considering that she hath now been with me these sixteen months'. Her Majesty, however, remained unresponsive and presumably Lady Mary travelled to Sussex with the Greshams.

A year later, on 8 September 1571, Sir Thomas was again writing to Cecil to report:

that one Mr Doctor Smythe (my Lady Mary Grey's physician) has this day at twelve of the clock at noon, brought me word that Mr Keyes, late Sergeant Porter, is departed; which I have broken unto my Lady Mary – whose death she grievously taketh. Who hath requested me to write unto you, to be a mean to the Queen's Majesty to be good unto her, and that she may have her Majesty's leave for to keep and bring up his children. As likewise, I desire to know her Majesty's pleasure, whether I shall suffer her to wear any black mourning apparel or not.

Gresham's hopes of being 'despatched' of his unwelcome charge were now revived and Lady Mary herself wrote to Cecil, recently elevated to the peerage as Baron Burghley, begging once more to be restored to the life-giving sunshine of the Queen's favour, 'seeing that God had taken away the occasion of her majesty's justly conceived displeasure' in the person of the unfortunate Sergeant Porter. Gresham kept up the pressure, writing on 5 October that 'it may please you to see me have an end of my suit for the removing of my Lady Mary Grey, for the quietness of my poor wife'. Still nothing happened and the following spring Sir Thomas continued to importune the lords Leicester and Burghley. A letter dated from Mayfield on 5 March 1572 sounds a faint note of optimism and thanks Burghley 'for the good remembrance that you will have of my wife's suit for the removing of my Lady Mary Grey; wherein your lordship shall do her no small pleasure, considering what bondage and heart sorrow she hath had for these three years'. It sounds as if Lady Gresham was reaching the end of her tether.

The chief problem seems to have been finding a suitable refuge for Mary Grey once she had been set free. She herself had previously suggested that she should join forces with her step-father Adrian Stokes, now re-married, who was the principal life beneficiary of her mother's will. For some reason this idea had been rejected by Lord Burghley, but Lady Mary said she knew of no one else who would offer her a home, and as she pointed out, 'my living is no way so great whereby I may help myself that way into any place'.

In fact, her financial position had been succinctly outlined by Thomas Gresham in one of his numerous letters to Burghley, 'It may like your lordship to understand that the Queen's majesty doth give my Lady Mary yearly eighty pounds and she hath in land twenty pounds by year; and this is all that she hath in possession. And in reversion of the Duchess of Suffolk (that is, Lady Frances) five hundred marks (£333.6.8d) and five hundred marks of her father-in-law (Adrian Stokes).' Lady Mary put it even more succinctly, 'Of my own I have but twenty pounds and as your lordship knoweth, there is nobody will board me for so little. As for my father-in-law, I know he will give me nothing now; for before his marriage I had little; and now I look for less.'

All the same Mary Grey had been released before the end of 1572 and early in 1573 wrote a letter to her former brother-in-law, the Earl of Hertford, in which she says, 'Now that I have become a house-keeper I would willingly meet with some trusty servant to whom I might give credit to do my business truly. I hear that Harry Parker, who was in my sister's service and is true and honest, is still in yours. Please let me have him for my sister's sake. My house. 21 February.' Where this house was situated is not recorded, but in her will she describes herself as Lady Mary Keys, of the parish of St Botolph's without Aldersgate, which puts her close enough to the Barbican to make it seem at least possible that the Bertie family had found her somewhere to live. Certainly what little property she did possess was bequeathed to the Berties, 'To my very good Lady and Grand-mother, the Duchess of Suffolk, one pair of hand bracelets of gold, with a jacint stone in each bracelet, which bracelets were my Lady Grace my mother's, or else my jewel of unicorn's horn.' Whichever of these trinkets Her Grace refused was to go to Susan Bertie, now Countess of Kent, and to Peregrine Bertie and his wife Mary, the Earl of Oxford's daughter, were left 'my best gilt cup and the best silver and gilt salt cellar'.

Mary Grey died in poverty and obscurity some time between 20 April 1578, the date of her will, and 1 June, the date on an inventory of her library – which contained, among other similar titles, a volume of Bishop Latimer's sermons, *Doctor Fulkes his answer to the popish demands . . . touching Purgatorie, Mr. Knox his answer to the adversary of God's predestination* and *The second course of the hunter at the Romishe fox.* The Lady Mary would have been thirty-two years old and with her death vanished one of the last remnants of the once proud House of Suffolk. But outcast though she had become, under the terms of her great-uncle Henry's will, Mary Keys, widow, of the parish of St Botolph's without Aldersgate, died heiress presumptive to the throne of England – that deadly legacy which had poisoned the lives of the descendants, of Mary Brandon, born Mary Tudor.

The lives and deaths of Catherine and Mary Grey made no impact on the history of their times; both were in many ways irresponsible, obstinate and foolish young women and neither qualify as heroines of high tragedy or romance. Nevertheless, their tenacious attempts to lay claim to a measure of personal happiness and independence in the face of well-nigh impossible odds have a certain touching gallan-try and surely deserve a mention, however brief, in the record of struggling, suffering humanity.

Duchess Catherine, Mrs Richard Bertie, outlived the last of her Grey step-granddaughters by just over two years, dying in September 1580 at the age of sixty-one. A great lady, a great character and 'a valiant spirit', her influence, patronage and tireless devotion to the cause of the gospel had made an important contribution to the early growth and development of English Protestantism. Although no trained scholar herself, her piety and her forceful personality combined to give her a place among the leaders of those zealously evangelical, fearsomely erudite ladies who were such a vital feature of that period of social and intellectual ferment. My Lady of Suffolk was buried in the church at Spilsby in her native Lincolnshire, not far from her ancestral manor of Eresby. There, eighteen months later, her husband came to lie beside her. Their son Peregrine, who assumed the title of Lord Willoughby on his mother's death, would have nothing to do with the court or a courtier's life, saying 'he was none of the Reptilia'. He became a professional soldier instead – unassuming, loyal and efficient, and consequently highly thought of by the Queen. 'My good Peregrine', she wrote to him in 1589 when he was commanding an expeditionary force in France, 'I bless God that your old prosperous success followeth your valiant acts, and joy not a little that safety accompanieth your luck.'

The only surviving representative of the junior branch of the Suffolk line – Eleanor Brandon's daughter Margaret who had married Lord Derby's heir – became Countess of Derby and Queen in Man when her husband succeeded to the title in 1572. Lady Margaret's life, blighted by ill-health and family quarrels, was not a happy one but did at least avoid the calamities which befell her cousins Catherine and Mary Grey. In spite of chronic rheumatism and toothache, her husband's infidelity and extravagance and their acrimonious financial disputes, the Countess of Derby raised a family of four sons and one daughter and lived on into the mid-1590s. She, too, was a silly woman in many ways. The contemporary historian William Camden said of her that 'through an idle mixture of curiosity and ambition, supported by sanguine hopes and a credulous fancy, she much used the conversations of necromancers and figure flingers'. An interest in the occult, although widespread among Elizabethans, could be a dangerous hobby; an interest in any form of fortune-telling especially so for one in Lady Margaret's position on the periphery of the succession dispute, and for a time it earned her Queen Elizabeth's serious displeasure.

Margaret's eldest son, Ferdinando Lord Strange, courtier, man of letters, friend and patron of poets and poet in a small way himself, stood out as a colourful and slightly sinister figure on the Elizabethan scene. He is best remembered for his interest in the theatre – Lord Strange's Men were among the foremost acting companies in the profession. When he succeeded his father, one of the richest peers in the country, in 1593, he became briefly the target of a more than usually optimistic Catholic plot which sought to exploit his 'propinquity of blood' to the royal house. But although well known for their Catholic sympathies, the earls of Derby had always remained conspicuously loyal and Ferdinando wasted no time in informing the government of the approaches being made to him.

He died the following year at the early age of thirty-four in circumstances which gave rise to some suspicion of foul play, and the Derby earldom passed to his brother William who married Elizabeth de Vere, old Lord Burghley's granddaughter. This wedding, which took place at Greenwich in January 1595, was the social event of the season. In a sense it may be said to have marked the final flicker of the Tudor–Brandon connection; rather suitably, too, if the beginning of that connection is marked by another wedding at Greenwich back in May 1515, when cloth of frieze was publicly matched with cloth of gold, and it is remembered that weddings, public and otherwise, had formed such a recurring theme in the saga of the House of Suffolk.

Actually, of course, the Tudor–Brandon connection dated back some thirty years earlier, to 1485. By lucky (or unlucky) chance it had all begun at Bosworth Field under the banner of the red dragon on that long ago August day of blood, battle and destiny. Chance had played a part, too, in the bringing together of two boys of similar physical aptitudes and enthusiasms just at the time when they were most likely to form a lasting friendship. And there had been an element of chance in the fact that a favourable opportunity for physical attraction to ripen between a virile, sexually experienced man and a sensual, passionate young woman widely separated by social caste had presented itself at a time when such opportunities were rare.

In those early innocent days, before the canker of fear and greed, ambition and suspicion crept in to destroy it, there had been something positive and valuable in the association between the two families – a good and loving relationship between husband and wife, friend and friend. Charles Brandon, it is said, was the only man Henry VIII ever really loved, while his young sister was probably the only woman for whom he ever felt a genuine human warmth.

As always in the story of sixteenth-century England, so much comes back to the fatal Tudor inability to get sons. If only Henry's first wife had been able to give him a male heir. . . . If only he had never become infatuated by the fascinating, dark-eyed Anne

Boleyn. . . . If only Edward had survived to perpetuate his line. . . . So many 'if onlys': if only Catherine Willoughby's clever, promising sons had lived. . . . But most poignant of all must surely be: if only Jane Grey could have lived. How would she have developed, how might her life have influenced the history of her times?

It was indeed 'great pity of their death . . . of so noble a stock they were, there is no more left of them'.

A Note on Sources

The story of the House of Suffolk wreathes its way through the histories and chronicles of the time, the calendars of state papers, collections of correspondence and ambassadors' despatches, and there are modern biographies of most of the individual members of the family. These notes mention only those printed sources which I found most useful in writing this book and are not intended to be more than a general guide to further exploration. For fuller details the interested reader is referred, in the first instance, to the *Bibliography of British History, Tudor Period*, ed. Conyers Read, Oxford, 1959.

For the general political background *The Earlier Tudors*, J.D. Mackie, Oxford, 1952; *The Reign of Elizabeth*, J.B. Black, Oxford, 1959; and *England Under the Tudors*, G.R. Elton, 1962 are all standard. *Tudor England*, S.T. Bindoff, Volume 5 of the Pelican History of England, 1950 is a classic short survey and *Elizabeth I and the Unity of England*, Joel Hurstfield, 1960 is another.

For the religious background, so fundamental to any understanding of Jane Grey and her contemporaries, *The English Reformation to 1558*, T.M. Parker, Oxford, 1966; *The Reformation*, Owen Chadwick, Volume 3 of the Pelican History of the Church, 1964; and *The English Reformation*, A.G. Dickens, 1967 all provide good and lucid introductions.

Chapter One

There is no full-length biography of Charles Brandon, Duke of Suffolk; only an unpublished sketch, *An History of the Illustrious House of Brandon*, Mark Noble, 1807, in the Bodleian Library, Oxford and, of course, the entry in the Dictionary of National Biography. Contemporary references to the family can be found in *The Paston Letters*, ed. J. Gairdner, 1904 and see also *The Pastons and Their England*, H.S. Bennett, Cambridge, 1932. The story of Brandon's pursuit of Margaret of Austria can be followed in *The Chronicle of Calais*, ed. J.G. Nichols, Camden Society, Vol. XXXV, 1846, *Chronicle of the Union of the Two Noble Families of Lancaster and York*, Edward Hall, standard edition, H. Ellis, 1809 and in Volume 1 of the monumental *Letters and Papers, Foreign and Domestic of Henry VIII*, ed. Brewer, Gairdner and Brodie, 21 volumes, 1862–1932, and hereinafter referred to as L. & P. See also the Calendar of State Papers, Venetian, ed. R. Brown, 1864. Volume 2 covers the period 1509–1519.

There are several studies of Mary Tudor, Queen of France and Duchess of Suffolk, starting with Volume 5 of Mary Everett Green's *Lives of the Princesses of England*, 1849 and Agnes Strickland's *Lives of the Tudor Princesses*, 1868. Although naturally dated in style and approach, these are well worth reading and useful for the letters and documents they transcribe. Modern lives include *Mary Tudor, Queen of France*, Mary Croom Brown, 1911, *The Sisters of Henry VIII*, Hester Chapman, 1969 and, best, most recent and most scholarly, *Mary Tudor, the White Queen*, W.C. Richardson, 1970. Primary sources for the story of Mary's marriage to Louis XII and its immediate aftermath are L. & P. Hall's *Chronicle* and the C.S.P. Venetian.

Chapter Two

For the Suffolks' return to England and their public marriage at Greenwich, see L. & P., Hall, and the C.S.P. Venetian. Mary's life as Duchess of Suffolk is naturally not so fully documented, but references to her various social activities, court appearances and so on are scattered through L. & P. and the Calendars of State Papers Venetian and Spanish. For her and Brandon's attitude towards Henry's divorce see L. & P. Volume 5, the C.S.P. Venetian Volume 4, C.S.P. Spanish, Volume 5 and also George Cavendish's *Life of Cardinal Wolsey*, ed. Sylvester and Harding, New Haven, 1962. For the Suffolks' own dealings with the Vatican with reference to Dame Margaret Mortimer, see L. & P. Volume 4, Part iii.

Chapter Three

There are two biographies of Catherine Willoughby – *A Woman of the Tudor Age*, Cecilie Goff, 1930 and *Catherine Duchess of Suffolk*, Evelyn Read, 1962. For Suffolk's mission to Buckden, see C.S.P. Spanish, Volume 4, Part ii and L. & P. Volume 6. For Charles Brandon's last years and death, see references in L. & P. For a modern study of Henry VIII's last years and a discussion of the much discussed last will and testament see *Henry VIII the Mask of Royalty*, Lacey Baldwin Smith, 1971.

The growth of the Protestant movement can be followed in John Strype's *Ecclesiastical Memorials*, Oxford, 1820, three volumes which print many original documents and take the story up to 1558; see also

A Chronicle of England, Charles Wriothesley, Camden Society, New Series, Vols XI and XX, 1875, 1877, and *Acts and Monuments*, John Foxe, ed. Cattley & Townsend, 8 vols. 1837 (commonly known as the Book of Martyrs). For Catherine Parr, see Agnes Strickland's *Lives of the Queens of England*, 1840, and for a modern view of Anne Askew and her contemporaries, *A Tudor Tapestry*, Derek Wilson, 1972.

Chapter Four

For a definitive modern study of the politics and personalities of Edward's reign, see W.K. Jordan's two volumes – *Edward VI: The Young King* and *The Threshold of Power*, 1970, but also *The Last Tudor King*, Hester Chapman, 1958. *The Literary Remains of King Edward VI* J.G. Nichols, 2 vols. Roxburghe Club, 1857 contains Edward's Journal and other writings and *England Under the Reigns of Edward VI and Mary*, P.F. Tytler, 1839, prints much valuable source material in full.

Of the several older lives of Lady Jane Grey, *The Nine Days Queen, Lady Jane Grey and her Times*, R.P.B. Davey, 1909 is considered to be the best; see also Agnes Strickland, *Lives of the Tudor Princesses* and *Lady Jane Grey and Her Times*, George Howard (F.C. Laird) 1822 – this last chiefly for its curiosity value. The only full length modern biography is Hester Chapman's *Lady Jane Grey*, 1962.

The letters, interrogations and depositions concerning Thomas Seymour's pursuit of the Princess Elizabeth and his attempt to profit by his wardship of Jane Grey are mostly printed in the *Collection of State Papers . . . left by William Cecil, Lord Burghley*, ed Samuel Haynes, 1740, and some are also in Tytler.

The Literary Remains of Lady Jane Grey with a Memoir by N.H. Nicolas, 1825, contains her surviving letters to Bullinger, but for the rest of the correspondence see *Original Letters Relative to the English Reformation* (also known as the Zurich Letters) ed. H. Robinson, Parker Society, 1846. John Strype's *Life of John Aylmer*, Oxford, 1821, is the biography of Lady Jane's tutor who later became Bishop of London.

For the lives and deaths of the Brandon boys see Goff, *A Woman of the Tudor Age* and *Five Generations of a Loyal House*, Georgina Bertie, 1845.

Chapter Five

The battle of the Princess Mary's Mass is chronicled in the despatches of the Imperial ambassador printed in C.S.P. Spanish, Vol.11. The best biography is *Mary Tudor*, H.F.M. Prescott, 1952 and *Privy Purse Expenses of the Princess Mary*, F. Madden, 1831 gives details of her gifts to her Grey cousins.

Edward's Device for the Succession is printed in Nichols' *Literary Remains* and Jane's account of the events which followed his death is contained in her letter to Mary, printed in an Appendix to J.M. Stone's *History of Mary I, Queen of England*, 1901. The description of Jane's arrival at the Tower by Baptista Spinola appears in Davey's *Nine Days Queen*.

Chapter Six

The *Annals* of John Stow, 1601 edition, the *Chronicle of the Greyfriars*, ed. J.G. Nichols, Camden Society, 1852, and the *Diary* of Henry Machyn, J.G. Nichols, Camden Society, 1848 are all primary sources for the events of 1553–4, but first in importance is the *Chronicle of Queen Jane and Two Years of Queen Mary*, written most probably by an official of the Royal Mint resident in the Tower of London, ed. J.G. Nichols, Camden Society, 1850 and which also prints a number of documents relevant to the Wyatt Rebellion and the Spanish marriage. See also especially the C.S.P. Spanish, Volume 12.

Chapter Seven

Rival Ambassadors at the Court of Queen Mary, E.H. Harbison, 1940, is the best guide to the Franco–Spanish diplomatic battle. Otherwise sources as for Chapter Six. Jane's encounter with Feckenham is printed in Foxe and the description of her execution can be found in the *Chronicle of Queen Jane*. See the *Chronicle of Queen Jane* also for her father's end. The description of Catherine Suffolk's escape is printed in Foxe and see also *Five Generations of a Loyal House*.

Chapter Eight

Simon Renard's despatches, a prime source for Mary's reign, are to be found in the C.S.P. Spanish, Volumes 12 and 13, and see the C.S.P. Venetian, Volume 6.

There is a biography of Catherine Grey in Strickland, *Lives of the Tudor Princesses*, and for a modern study, see *Two Tudor Portraits*, Hester Chapman, 1960.

The classic life of Elizabeth is still *Queen Elizabeth I*, J.E. Neale, 1934. Of the more recent biographies Paul Johnson's *Elizabeth I – A Study in Power and Intellect*, 1974 is probably the best. The early years of the reign are covered in detail by Wallace T. MacCaffrey in *The Shaping of the Elizabethan Regime*, Princeton, 1968, and for the despatches of de Feria and de Quadra, see the C.S.P. Spanish Elizabeth, Volume 1. Other material is printed in the Calendar of State Papers, Foreign, Elizabeth.

Chapter Nine

For Throckmorton's despatches see the C.S.P. Foreign and for a survey of the succession problem, *The Early Elizabethan Succession Question*, 1558–68, Mortimer Levine, Stanford, 1966. An account of Elizabeth's talks with Maitland of Lethington in 1561 is printed in *A Letter from Mary Queen of Scots to the Duke of Guise*, J.H. Pollen, Scottish Historical Society, 1904. Other material appears in Haynes' *Burghley Papers*, in *Queen Elizabeth and her Times*, ed. Thomas Wright, 2 volumes, 1838 and in *Original Letters Illustrative of English History*, ed. H. Ellis 2 series Vol. 2 1827.

Chapter Ten

For the Parliament of 1566 – and all Elizabeth's other Parliaments – the definitive work is J.E. Neale's *Queen Elizabeth I and Her Parliaments*, 2 volumes, 1953. For de Silva's despatches, C.S.P. Spanish, Elizabeth, Vol. 1. The description of Catherine Grey's deathbed is printed in Ellis, *Original Letters*.

For Mary Grey, see Strickland, *Lives of the Tudor Princesses* and *The Life and Times of Sir Thomas Gresham*, J.W. Burgon, 1839. See also Report on the Longleat MSS, Volume 4, Seymour Papers in the Historical Manuscripts Commission Series, H.M.S.O., 1968. For Margaret Clifford, see Strickland.

Anglo-Hapsburg Connection

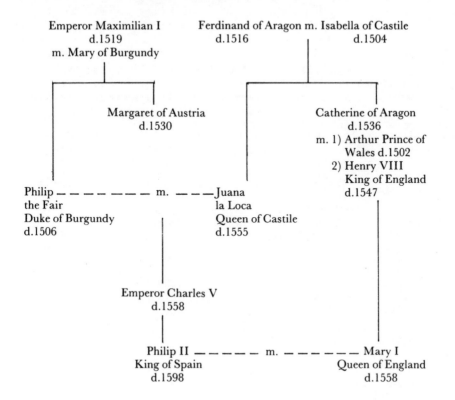

Emperor Maximilian I
d.1519
m. Mary of Burgundy

Ferdinand of Aragon m. Isabella of Castile
d.1516   d.1504

Margaret of Austria
d.1530

Catherine of Aragon
d.1536
m. 1) Arthur Prince of
       Wales d.1502
    2) Henry VIII
       King of England
       d.1547

Philip — — — — — — — m. — — —Juana
the Fair   la Loca
Duke of Burgundy   Queen of Castile
d.1506   d.1555

Emperor Charles V
d.1558

Philip II — — — — — m. — — — — — Mary I
King of Spain   Queen of England
d.1598   d.1558

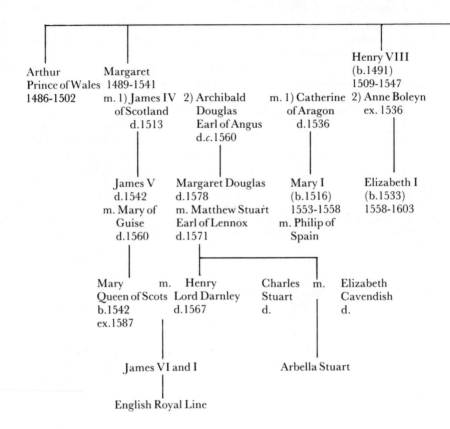

Henry VII m. Elizabeth of York
d.1509   d.1503

Arthur
Prince of Wales
1486-1502

Margaret
1489-1541
m. 1) James IV
of Scotland
d.1513

2) Archibald
Douglas
Earl of Angus
d.c.1560

m. 1) Catherine
of Aragon
d.1536

Henry VIII
(b.1491)
1509-1547
2) Anne Boleyn
ex. 1536

James V
d.1542
m. Mary of
Guise
d.1560

Margaret Douglas
d.1578
m. Matthew Stuart
Earl of Lennox
d.1571

Mary I
(b.1516)
1553-1558
m. Philip of
Spain

Elizabeth I
(b.1533)
1558-1603

Mary   m.
Queen of Scots
b.1542
ex.1587

Henry
Lord Darnley
d.1567

Charles   m.
Stuart
d.

Elizabeth
Cavendish
d.

James VI and I

Arbella Stuart

English Royal Line

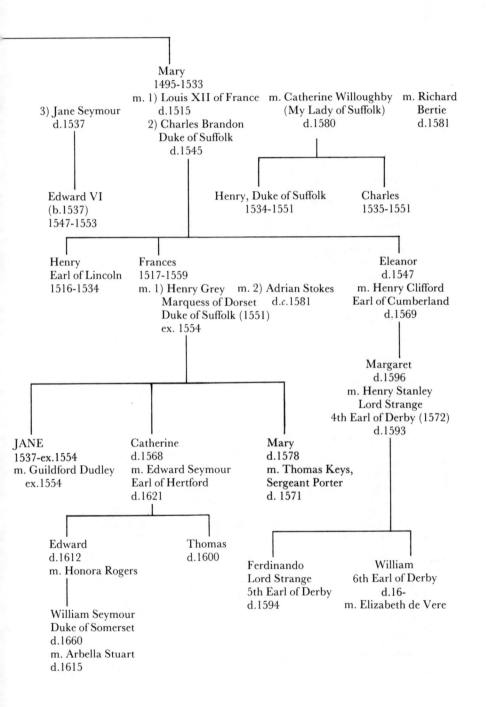

Mary
1495-1533
m. 1) Louis XII of France   m. Catherine Willoughby   m. Richard
     d.1515   (My Lady of Suffolk)   Bertie
2) Charles Brandon   d.1580   d.1581
Duke of Suffolk
d.1545

3) Jane Seymour
d.1537

Edward VI
(b.1537)
1547-1553

Henry, Duke of Suffolk   Charles
1534-1551   1535-1551

Henry
Earl of Lincoln
1516-1534

Frances
1517-1559
m. 1) Henry Grey   m. 2) Adrian Stokes
Marquess of Dorset   d.*c.*1581
Duke of Suffolk (1551)
ex. 1554

Eleanor
d.1547
m. Henry Clifford
Earl of Cumberland
d.1569

Margaret
d.1596
m. Henry Stanley
Lord Strange
4th Earl of Derby (1572)
d.1593

JANE
1537-ex.1554
m. Guildford Dudley
ex.1554

Catherine
d.1568
m. Edward Seymour
Earl of Hertford
d.1621

Mary
d.1578
m. Thomas Keys,
Sergeant Porter
d. 1571

Edward
d.1612
m. Honora Rogers

Thomas
d.1600

William Seymour
Duke of Somerset
d.1660
m. Arbella Stuart
d.1615

Ferdinando
Lord Strange
5th Earl of Derby
d.1594

William
6th Earl of Derby
d.16-
m. Elizabeth de Vere

Index

Abbeville, 13, 14
Amory, Stephen, 94
Arthur, Prince of Wales (d. 1502), 3, 29, 32
Arundel, Earl of, *see* Fitzalan, Henry
Ascham, Roger, 69, 70, 127, 143
Ashley, Catherine, 64
Askew, Anne, 48, 49, 51
de l'Aubespine, Claude, 87
Aylmer, John, 69, 70, 71, 80, 127

Bacon, Nicholas, 145, 147
Badoer, Andrea, 8
Badoer, Federigo, 88
Battle of the Spurs, 6, 11
Beale, Robert, 167
Beaufort, Lady Margaret, 54
Bedford, Earls of, *see* Russell
Bertie, family of, 129, 184
Bertie, Lady Mary, 184
Bertie, Peregrine (Lord Willoughby), 148, 184, 185
Bertie, Richard, 129, 130, 131, 132, 133, 148
Bertie, Susan, 130, 132, 184
Blackfriars, 30, 32
Blount, Elizabeth, 30
Boleyn, family of, 29, 35
Boleyn, Anne, Queen of England, 28, 29, 31, 33, 34, 35, 39, 40, 50, 126, 138, 146, 187
Boleyn, Mary, 29
Bonner, Edmund, Bishop of London, 45, 47
Bonnivet, Guillaume, Lord Admiral of France, 27, 28
Bosworth, Battle of, 1, 3, 44, 186
Bothwell, Earl of, *see* Hepburn, James
Boulogne, 13, 43
Bradgate, Leicestershire, 42, 52, 64, 69, 70, 71, 72, 110, 126, 154
Brandon, family of, 1, 2, 9
Brandon, Anne, 8, 27; marries Lord Powis, 34
Brandon, Catherine (née Willoughby) Duchess of Suffolk, later Bertie; marries Charles Brandon, 38–39; 41; character of,

46–7; 48, 49, 55, 56, 65, 66, 73, 74, 75, 76, 81; marries Richard Bertie 129; 130, 131; escapes to Flanders 132–3; 136, 148, 170, 182, 184; death of 185; 187
Brandon, Charles, Viscount Lisle, 1513; Duke of Suffolk 1514 (d. 1545); birth of, 3; education and early career, 4; marriages, 5; created Viscount Lisle, 6; courts Margaret of Austria, 7; created Duke of Suffolk, 8–9; 10, 11, 14; mission to France, 16–18; marries Mary Tudor, 19; 20, 21, 22, 23, 24, 25, 26, 27, 30; attack on Wolsey, 32; attitude to the Divorce, 33–34; 35, 36; marries Catherine Willoughby, 38–9; 40; godfather to Prince Edward, 42; last years and death, 43, 44, 46, 49, 67, 68, 130, 131, 139, 149, 186
Brandon, Lord Charles (d. 1551); birth of, 41; 49, 73, 74; death of, 75, 76
Brandon, Eleanor, *see* Clifford, Eleanor
Brandon, Frances, *see* Grey, Frances
Brandon, Henry, Earl of Lincoln (d. 1534); birth and christening of 26; created Earl of Lincoln, 30; 32, 36; death of, 39, 51
Brandon, Henry, Duke of Suffolk (d. 1551); birth of, 39; 49, 73, 74; death of, 75, 76
Brandon, Mary, 27; marries Lord Monteagle 34
Brandon, Robert, 2
Brandon, Sir Thomas (d. 1510), 2, 3, 4, 5
Brandon, Sir William (d. 1491), 2, 3
Brandon, William (d. 1485), 1, 2, 3
Brett, Alexander, 119
von Breuner, Caspar, 155
Browne, family of, 6
Browne, Anne, 5, 6
Browne, Sir Anthony, 5
Brussels, 86, 97, 131, 145, 147
Bruyn, Sir Henry, of South Ockendon, 2
Brydges, Sir John, 125, 126
Brydges, Thomas, 126
Buckden, 40, 75, 76
Buckingham, Dukes of, *see* Stafford

Bullinger, Henry, 71, 72, 73, 81, 82
Burghley, Lord, *see* Cecil, William
Bury St Edmunds, 34, 35, 36, 37, 101
Butley Priory, 34, 42

Caister Castle, 2
Calais, 7, 13, 23, 28, 100, 145
Cambridge, 35, 47, 53, 73, 74, 75, 88, 99, 103
Camden, William, 185
Campeggio, Cardinal, 32
Carew, Sir John, 5
Carew, Sir Peter, 118, 119
Carlos, Don, 147
Carne, Sir Edward, 145
Catherine of Aragon, Queen of England
    (d. 1536), 3, 19, 24, 25, 26, 27, 28, 29, 30,
    31, 32, 33, 38, 40, 47, 53, 75, 112, 115, 138,
    146
Cavendish, George, 32
Cavendish, William, 154
Cecil, Sir William, Lord Burghley, 65, 66, 73,
    75, 86, 90, 103, 132, 152, 153, 154, 155,
    157, 160, 161, 164, 165, 166, 167, 168, 169,
    170, 173, 175, 178, 181, 182, 183, 186
Cecil, Thomas, 152
Challoner, Sir Thomas, 147, 148, 163
Chapuys, Eustace, Imperial ambassador, 33,
    35, 36, 38
Charles I, King of England, 182
Charles V, Holy Roman Emperor, 6, 7, 10,
    17, 28, 78, 80, 84, 86, 87, 94, 95, 97, 98, 101,
    106, 115, 117, 131, 139
Charles (von Hapsburg) Archduke, 144, 145,
    155, 172
Cheke, Sir John, 47, 60, 111
Chelsea, 53, 54, 55, 58, 59, 64, 69, 91
Cheyne, Sir Thomas, 101
Claude, Queen of France, 28, 29
Clifford, Eleanor (née Brandon), Countess of
    Cumberland; birth of, 27; marriage, 35;
    39, 50, 51, 85, 140, 185
Clifford, Henry, 2nd Earl of Cumberland, 35
Clifford, Margaret, *see* Stanley
Clinton, Lord, 95
Clinton, Lady, 153
Cluny, Palace of, 15, 16, 19, 21, 126
Cobham, Lord, 97, 98, 102, 145
Cockfield Hall, 178
Colet, John, 53
Courtenay, family of, 24
Courtenay, Catherine, 26, 105
Courtenay, Edward, Earl of Devon, 105, 115,
    116, 117, 118, 119, 120, 140
Coverdale, Miles, 63
Cranmer, Thomas, Archbishop of
    Canterbury, 42, 78, 79, 89, 90, 111, 112,
    113, 136

Cranwell, Robert, 132, 133
Crofts, Sir James, 119
Cromwell, Thomas, 39, 41, 42
Culpepper, Thomas, 43

de la Pole, family of, 8
Denny, Sir Anthony, 61
Denny, Joan, 46, 48, 61
Derby, Earls of, *see* Stanley
Derby, Countess of, *see* Stanley
Devon, Earl of, *see* Courtenay, Edward
Dormer, Jane, 61
Dorset, Lord *see* Grey, Henry
Dorset, Lady, *see* Grey, Frances
Douglas, Archibald, Earl of Angus, 26
Douglas, Lady Margaret, *see* Stuart, Mar-
    garet
Dover, 13, 23, 28, 131, 135
Dover Castle, 13
Dudley, family of, 67, 77, 86, 90, 91, 99, 104,
    111, 113, 126, 154
Dudley, Lord Ambrose, 112
Dudley, Amy (née Robsart), 73, 149, 154
Dudley, Andrew, 104, 107
Dudley, Catherine, 86, 87, 161
Dudley, Edmund, 67
Dudley, Lord Guildford, 85, 86, 87, 90, 91,
    92, 93, 97, 98, 103, 105, 106, 112, 122, 124;
    executed, 125; 127, 141
Dudley, Henry, 100
Dudley, Lord Henry, 112
Dudley, Jane, Duchess of Northumberland,
    46, 90, 93, 96, 104, 124
Dudley, Lady Jane, see Grey, Lady Jane
Dudley, John, Viscount Lisle, Earl of
    Warwick, Duke of Northumberland,
    executed 1554; 44, 58, 64, 65, 66, 67, 68, 73,
    77, 78, 79, 80, 84, 85, 86, 87, 88, 89, 91, 94,
    95, 96, 97, 98, 99, 100, 101, 102, 104, 105,
    106, 107, 108, 112, 115, 121, 123
Dudley, John, Earl of Warwick, 73
Dudley, Robert, Earl of Leicester; 73, 96,
    149, 154, 155, 161, 165, 172, 173, 175,
    181, 183
Durham House, 87, 90, 92, 99, 101, 164

East Anglia, 1, 3, 25, 27, 28, 29, 34, 42, 66, 95,
    99, 153
Edinburgh, 177, 178
Edward III, 8
Edward IV (d. 1483), 2, 26, 34, 115
Edward VI (d. 1553); birth of, 41;
    christening, 42; 44, 47, 49, 50, 51, 54, 58,
    59, 60, 63, 65, 67, 68, 73, 77, 78, 79, 80, 83,
    84, 85, 87; Device for the Succession, 88–9;
    death of, 90; 91, 95, 96, 97, 105, 111, 121,
    187

Elizabeth I, Queen of England; birth of, 39;
47, 50, 54, 58, 59, 60, 61, 63, 64, 69, 74, 77,
80, 85, 88, 89, 114, 117, 118, 119, 126, 127,
128, 137, 138, 139; accession, 142, 143,
144, 145, 146, 147, 148, 149, 150, 152, 153,
154, 155, 156, 157, 158, 159, 160, 161, 162,
163, 164, 165, 166, 167, 168, 169, 170, and
1566 Parliament, 172–6; 177, 178, 179,
180, 181, 182, 183, 185, 186
Elizabeth of York, Queen of England, 10
Ellen, Mrs, 52, 109, 125, 126
England, 3, 5, 9, 15, 18, 20, 21, 24, 29, 38, 43,
47, 52, 53, 58, 59, 60, 67, 71, 75, 85, 86, 87,
94, 95, 97, 98, 117, 134, 135, 136, 137, 145,
148, 159, 180, 181, 184, 187
Essex, county of, 2, 34, 132, 178

Fastolf, Sir John, 2
Feckenham, John, 122, 123, 125, 127
Ferdinand, King of Aragon, 9, 28
Ferdinand (von Hapsburg) Archduke, 144
de Figueroa, Don Gomez Suarez, Count de
Feria, Spanish Ambassador, 147
Fitzalan, Henry, Earl of Arundel, 91, 93, 100,
102, 103, 104, 121, 128, 161
Fitzroy, Henry, Duke of Richmond, 30, 51
Flanders, 7, 8, 13, 17, 21, 133
Flodden, Battle of, 8
Fotheringay Castle, 128
Fowler, John, 64
Foxe, John, 49, 70, 110, 123, 127, 130, 131, 132
Framlingham Castle, 101, 103
France, 6, 9, 14, 16, 17, 21, 22, 24, 25, 26, 28,
29, 30, 31, 34, 35, 43, 77, 87, 117, 119, 145,
146, 153, 154, 155, 157, 158, 159
François I, King of France, 15, 16, 17, 18, 20,
23, 24, 27, 28, 36
Francois II, King of France, 88, 98, 138, 139,
145

Gardiner, Stephen, Bishop of Winchester,
45, 46, 47, 48, 49, 105, 116, 119, 130, 131,
132, 133, 134, 136, 142
Garnish, Sir Christopher, 13
Gates, Henry, 107
Gates, Sir John, 107
Greenwich, 11, 24, 26, 27, 31, 33, 84, 95, 186
Gresham, Sir Thomas, 182, 183
Gresham, Lady, 183
Grey, family of, 34–5, 77, 114, 127
Grey, Lady Anne, 81
Grey of Wilton, Lord Arthur, 101, 168
Grey, Lady Catherine (d. 1568); 52;
betrothal to Lord Herbert, 86–7, 114, 124,
134, 140, 141, 146, 147, 148, 149; marries
Earl of Hertford, 150–1; 152, 153; sent to
the Tower, 154; 155, 156, 157, 158, 159,
160, 161, 162, 163, 164, 165; and the
Succession, 166; 168, 169, 171, 172, 173,
174, 176; death of, 178–80; 181, 182, 184, 185
Grey, Elizabeth, Viscountess Lisle, 5, 6, 21,
24, 38, 68
Grey, Elizabeth, mother of John Dudley, 68
Grey, Frances (née Brandon), Marchioness
of Dorset, Duchess of Suffolk (d. 1559);
birth of, 27; marriage to Henry Grey, 34–5;
36, 39, 41, 50, 51, 52, 55, 62, 63, 77, 80, 85,
86, 88, 90, 91, 96, 104, 114; remarries, 129;
134, 135, 139, 140, 146, 147; death of, 148;
183, 184
Grey, Henry, 3rd Marquess of Dorset, Duke
of Suffolk (1551), executed 1554; 34, 52,
59, 62, 63, 64, 69, 71, 77, 81, 85, 86, 93, 98,
103, 104, 114, 119, 121, 124, 127; executed
128; 170
Grey, Lady Jane (Dudley), executed 1554; 19,
birth of, 41; 42, 51; early education, 52;
with Catherine Parr, 54–6; projected
marriage to King Edward, 59; relations
with Elizabeth, 61; 62, 63, 64, 68, 69;
relations with parents, 70; correspondence
with Bullinger, 71–2; 73, 77, 80, 81, 82, 83;
betrothal to Guildford Dudley, 85–6;
marriage 87; 88, 90, 91; arrives at Tower,
92; proclaimed Queen 93; 94, 96, 97, 98,
99, 100, 102, 103, 104; writes to Mary, 105;
106, 107, 108, 109, 110, 111; trial of 112,
113, 114, 121; disputation with Feckenham,
122–3; execution, 124–6; 127, 139, 140, 146,
157, 168, 178, 187
Grey, Lord John, 81, 121, 128, 148, 164, 165,
167
Grey, Lady Mary (d. 1578), 52, 92, 114, 134,
146, 156; marries Thomas Keys 168; 169,
170, 171, 182, 183, death of 184; 185
Grey, Thomas, 2nd Marquess of Dorset, 14,
30, 35, 52
Grey, Lord Thomas, 81, 128
Grimsthorpe, 41, 43, 65, 75, 130, 132, 170,
182
Grindal, William, 47
Grocyn, William, 53
de Guaras, Antonio, 181
Guildford, Sir Edward, 67, 68

Haddon, James, 70, 71, 81
Hales, John, 166, 167
Hall, Edward, 7, 25
Hamilton, James, Earl of Arran, 149
Hampton Court Palace, 41, 42, 43, 67, 77,
136, 160, 161
Hanworth, Middlesex, 59, 69, 140, 141, 149,
164, 178

Hapsburg, family of, 6, 10, 12, 28, 135, 137, 155

Harding, Dr, 52, 110, 111

Harington, John, 59, 64

Hastings, Francis, 2nd Earl of Huntingdon (d. 1560), 86, 91, 121, 128

Hastings, Henry, 3rd Earl of Huntingdon (d. 1595), 86, 87, 161

Hatfield, Palace of, 27, 63, 64, 173

Hawtrey, William, 169, 170

Heath, Nicholas, Archbishop of York, 142

Hepburn, James, Earl of Bothwell, 177

Henri II, King of France, 87, 89, 100, 117, 139, 145, 146, 148

Henry VII, (d. 1509), 2, 3, 4, 10, 67, 75

Henry VIII (d. 1547), 3, 4, 5, 6, 7, 8, 9, 10, 11, 13, 14, 15, 16, 17, 18, 19, 20, 21, 22, 23, 24, 25, 26, 27, 28, 29, 31, 32, 33, 34, 35, 36, 39, 40, 42, 43, 44, 45; death of, 49; will of, 50–1, 54, 55, 56, 57, 59, 61, 66, 67, 68, 85, 88, 89, 97, 98, 103, 112, 126, 129, 130, 134, 136, 138, 139, 142, 157, 161, 184, 186, 187

Herbert, Lord Henry, 86, 187, 149

Herbert, William, Earl of Pembroke, 86, 91, 93, 100, 101, 102, 114, 120, 121, 149, 161, 175

Hertford, Earls of, *see* Seymour

Hoby, Sir Philip, 97

Hoddesdon, 95

Hoggins, Robert, 147

Holland, 8

Hooper, John, 136

Hopton, Sir Owen, 178, 179

Hopton, Lady, 178

Howard, family of, 44, 95

Howard, Catherine, Queen of England, 43, 46, 126

Howard, Frances, 180

Howard, Henry, Earl of Surrey, 49

Howard, Thomas, 2nd Duke of Norfolk, 8, 9, 21

Howard, Thomas, 3rd Duke of Norfolk, 30, 33, 42, 49, 105, 119

Howard, Thomas, 4th Duke of Norfolk, 161, 172, 173, 174

Howard, Lord William, 120, 180

Hunsdon, Herts., 95

Huntingdon, Earls of, *see* Hastings

Ireland, 30, 100, 174

Italy, 5, 26, 53, 128

Jacob, Mrs, 109

James I, 181

James IV, King of Scotland, 12, 50

James V, King of Scotland, 39, 50

Kenninghall, Norfolk, 95, 96, 101

Kent, county of, 118, 119

Keys, Thomas, 168, 169, 183

Kirk o'Field, 177

Knollys, family of, 168

Knox, John 158

Latimer, Hugh, Bishop of Worcester, 41, 46, 111, 130, 136, 184

Lea, Rowland, 108, 109

Leicester, Earl of, *see* Dudley, Robert

Leicestershire, 52, 53, 68, 71, 121, 127, 128

Lily, William, 53

Linacre, Thomas, 53

Lincolnshire, 38, 41, 43, 48, 50, 64, 94, 130, 132, 185

London, 8, 11, 12, 20, 24, 27, 31, 35, 36, 42, 43, 52, 53, 57, 59, 63, 66, 67, 76, 84, 87, 96, 102, 104, 118, 119, 120, 127, 130, 132, 135, 136, 137, 142, 146, 149, 155, 160, 164, 170, 178, 181

Louis d'Orléans, Duc de Longueville, 11

Louis XII, King of France (d. 1515), 9, 10, 11, 12, 13; death of, 14; 15, 20, 22, 23, 24, 29, 139

Louise of Savoy, 15

Machyn, Henry, 76

Maitland, William, Laird of Lethington, 159, 160, 168

Margaret of Austria, Duchess of Savoy, Regent of the Netherlands, 6, 7, 8, 9, 21

Margaret Tudor, Queen of Scotland, 12, 26, 50, 51, 139

Marguerite of Navarre, 15, 28

Mary of Guise, 77, 80

Mary Stewart, Queen of Scots, 50, 51, 77, 88, 98, 138, 139, 145, 146, 147, 148, 155, 158, 159, 161, 166, 167, 173, 174, 176, 177, 181

Mary Tudor, Queen of France, Duchess of Suffolk (d. 1533); 6, 9; birth of, 10; betrothal to Louis XII, 11; 12; crosses Channel, 13; marries King of France, 14; widowed, 15; 16, 17, 18; marries Charles Brandon, 19; 20, 21, 22; returns to England 23; 24, 25; birth of children 26–7; 28; and Anne Boleyn, 29; 30; ill-health, 31; 32; attitude to Divorce 33–4; last years and death, 35–7; 38, 39, 42, 130, 139, 146, 149, 184

Mary Tudor, Queen of England (d. 1558); birth and christening of, 26; betrothal to Dauphin, 27; 40, 47, 50, 53, 61, 77, 78, 79, 82, 84, 85, 88, 89, 94, 95, 96, 97, 98, 101; proclaimed in London 102; 103, 104, 105, 106, 107, 108, 112, 114, 115, 116, 117, 118, 119, 120, 121, 122, 124, 128, 129, 130;

marries Philip of Spain 134; 135, 136, 137, 138, 139, 140; death of, 141; 142, 143, 145, 146, 157, 173, 175
Mason, Sir John, 97, 98, 100, 102, 162, 163
Maximilian I, Holy Roman Emperor, 6, 7, 9, 28
Michiel, Giovanni, 139, 140, 142, 143
Montague, Sir Edward, 89, 111
More, Margaret, 53
More, Sir Thomas, 40, 53
Morgan, Richard, 112
Mortimer, Margaret (née Neville), 5, 21, 32
Mowbray, family of, 2
Mowbray, John, Duke of Norfolk (d. 1476), 2

Neville, Lucy, 5
Newdigate, Francis, 140, 167
Newhall Boreham, Essex, 82, 105
de Noailles, Antoine, French ambassador, 97, 98, 103, 115, 116, 118
Norfolk, county of, 1, 2, 34, 66, 95
Norfolk, Dukes of, see Howard, Thomas and Mowbray, John
Northumberland, Duchess of, see Dudley, Jane
Northumberland, Duke of, see Dudley, John
Norwich, 101

Paget, William, Secretary of State, 43, 58, 102, 103
Palmer, Thomas, 107
Paris, 18, 21, 32, 25, 35, 155
Parker, Matthew, Archbishop of Canterbury, 156, 158
Parma, Duchess of, 155
Parr, Catherine, Queen of England, 46, 47, 48, 49, 50, 53, 54, 55, 56, 58, 59, 60, 61, 62, 63, 64, 65, 66, 69, 86, 91, 140
Parr, William, Marquess of Northampton, 65, 91, 95, 107, 175
Parry, William, 64
Partridge, Master, Gentleman Gaoler, 108, 109, 125
Pasqualigo, Lorenzo, 9, 12, 13
Paston, family of, 1, 2
Paston, John, 2
Paulet, William, Marquess of Winchester, 92, 95, 100, 102, 103, 121, 161, 174
Percy, Henry, 5th Earl of Northumberland, 29
Percy, Henry, 6th Earl of Northumberland, 29
Petre, William, 100, 167
Philibert, Emmanuel, Duke of Savoy
Philip I, King of Spain, 115, 116, 118, 119, 131, 134, 135, 137, 138, 144, 146, 147, 148, 168, 172, 174
Picardy, 6
Pirgo, Essex, 164, 165

Pole, Cardinal, 135
Pope, Sir Thomas, 138
Potter, Gilbert, 94, 95
Pratt, James, 94

de Quadra, Bishop Alvaro, Spanish ambassador, 149, 155, 160, 161

Radcliffe, Thomas, Earl of Sussex, 154
Renard, Simon, Imperial ambassador, 97, 98, 101, 102, 104, 106, 107, 112, 113, 114, 115, 116, 127, 128, 136, 137, 138
Riccio, David, 177
Rich, Sir Richard, Solicitor General, 48
Richard III (d. 1485), 1, 2, 3
Ridley, Nicholas, Bishop of London, 46, 96, 130, 136
Rochester, 119
Rogers, Honora, 181
Rome, 25, 31, 32, 33, 145
Rosso, Raviglio, 85, 87
Russell, John, 1st Earl of Bedford, 63, 100, 102, 161
Russell, Francis, 2nd Earl of Bedford, 181

Saintlow, Elizabeth (Bess of Hardwick), 154, 156
Saintlow, Sir William, 154
de Salinas, Maria (Lady Willoughby), 38
Scotland, 44, 77, 87, 139, 145, 158, 159, 161, 177
de Scheyfve, Jehan, Imperial ambassador, 84, 85, 87, 95, 106
Seymour, family of, 140, 141, 166, 182
Seymour, Lady Anne, 73
Seymour, Anne (née Stanhope), Countess of Hertford, Duchess of Somerset, 46, 48, 60, 87, 140, 141, 164, 167, 170, 181
Seymour, Edward, Earl of Hertford, Duke of Somerset (Lord Protector), executed 1552; 44, 49, 50, 55, 57, 58, 60, 62, 63, 64, 65, 66, 67, 73, 78, 86, 87, 107, 140, 141, 182
Seymour, Edward, Earl of Hertford (d. 1621), 86, 106, 140, 141, 147, 148, 149, 150, 151, 152, 153, 154, 155, 156, 157, 158, 162, 163, 164, 165, 166, 167, 168, 178, 179, 180, 181, 182, 184
Seymour, Edward, Viscount Beauchamp, 157, 181
Seymour, Jane, Queen of England, 41, 42, 49
Seymour, Lady Jane, 140, 149, 150, 151, 153, 156, 157, 179
Seymour, Mary, 61, 65, 66
Seymour, Thomas, Baron Seymour of Sudeley, Lord Admiral, executed 1549; 55, 58, 59, 60, 61, 62, 63, 64, 65, 66, 68
Seymour, Thomas (d. 1600), 164, 165, 181

Seymour, William, 181, 182
Shaxton, Nicholas, 46
Sheen, 90, 103, 104, 119, 147
Shelley, Richard, 97
Sherington, William, 63, 64
Shrewsbury, Earl of, *see* Talbot, Francis
Sidney, Henry, 90
Sidney, Mary, 91
de Silva, Guzman, 168, 172, 173, 174, 175, 176, 177, 178, 180
Smith, Thomas, 167, 168
Somerset, Charles, Earl of Worcester, 12
Somerset, Duke of, *see* Seymour, Edward
Southampton, 134
Spain, 14, 21, 117, 137, 139, 145, 146, 147
Spencer, Sir John, of Althorp, 180
Spinola, Baptista, 92
Stafford, Edward, 3rd Duke of Buckingham, executed 1521, 8
Stafford, Henry, 2nd Duke of Buckingham, executed 1483, 2
Stanley, Ferdinando, Lord Strange, Earl of Derby, 186
Stanley, Margaret (née Clifford), Lady Strange, Countess of Derby and Queen in Man (d. 1596), 51, 85, 140, 185, 186
Stanley, William, 186
Stokes, Adrian, 129, 147, 148, 183, 184
Stow, John, 27
Strasbourg, 70, 131, 143
Stuart, Arbella, 182
Stuart, Henry, Lord Darnley, 51, 167, 177
Stuart, Margaret (née Douglas), Countess of Lennox, 26, 50, 51, 161, 167
Sturm, John, 70, 143
Suffolk, county of, 1, 2, 34, 36, 38, 178
Suffolk, Dukes of, *see* Brandon, Charles Brandon, Henry Grey, Henry
Switzerland, 131
Syon House, 43, 91, 92, 93

Talbot, Francis, 5th Earl of Shrewsbury, 95, 100, 102
Tattersall Castle, 41, 42, 44
Therouanne, 6
Throckmorton, Lady, 103
Throckmorton, Nicholas, 95, 155
Tournai, 6, 7, 20, 22, 27
Tower of London, 41, 43, 48, 67, 92, 93, 94, 95, 96, 97, 101, 102, 103, 104, 105, 108, 111, 112, 114, 115, 116, 118, 120, 124, 125, 126, 127, 128, 142, 154, 156, 157, 162, 163, 164, 165, 178, 181

Troughton, Richard, 94, 95
Tylney, Elizabeth, 109, 125, 126
Tyrwhit, Sir Robert, 64

Udall, Nicholas, 47
Ulmer, John, 71, 73, 81

Van der Delft, François, Imperial ambassador, 54
Vaudey Abbey, 41, 43
de Vere, Elizabeth, 186
Vives, Juan Luis, 53, 55

Walpole, Horace, 37
Walsingham, Sir Francis, 181
Wanstead, 5, 10
Warner, Sir Edward, 156, 162, 164, 165
Wentworth, Sir John, 178
Wentworth, Paul, 176
West, Dr Nicholas, 17
Westhorpe Hall, Suffolk, 34, 35, 36
Westminster, 33, 54, 79, 83, 84, 90, 92, 112, 149, 168, 172, 175, 179
Wharton, Anne, 82
Willoughby, Sir Henry, 81
Willoughby d'Eresby, Lord William, 38
Willoughbys of Woollaton, family of, 81
Wilson, Thomas, 74, 75
Winchester, 129, 134, 135
Winchester, Bishop of, *see* Gardiner, Stephen
Winchester, Marquess of, *see* Paulet, William
Windsor, 44, 49, 67, 84, 135
Wingfield, family of, 2
Wingfield, Sir Richard, 8, 17
Wolsey, Thomas, Cardinal Archbishop of York (d. 1530), 8, 9, 10, 12, 15, 16, 18, 20, 21, 22, 24, 25, 26, 27, 28, 29, 31, 32, 33, 39
Woodstock, 129
Woodville, Elizabeth, 34, 35
Wotton, Nicholas, 117, 146
Wriothesley, Thomas, Lord Chancellor, 48, 49, 129
Wyatt, Sir Thomas, 34
Wyatt, Sir Thomas, executed 1554, 118, 119, 120, 121

Yarmouth, 101
Yorkshire, 41
York, 43
Yoxford, Suffolk, 178, 180, 182

Zurich, 71, 81, 131